Catherine Weate

CLASSIC VOICE

Working with Actors on Vocal Style

OBERON BOOKS
LONDON

First published in 2009 by Oberon Books Ltd
521 Caledonian Road, London N7 9RH
Tel: 020 7607 3637 / Fax: 020 7607 3629
e-mail: info@oberonbooks.com
www.oberonbooks.com

A catalogue record for this book is available from the British Library.

ISBN: 978-1-84002-827-0

Cover photograph: Teatro Olimpico, Vicenza by Patrizia Viggi

Printed by CPI Antony Rowe, Chippenham, Wiltshire

For

Francesco
(who likes to talk)

and

Massimiliano
(who loves sound)

ACKNOWLEDGEMENTS

Heartfelt thanks to Francesco and Max for their patience and understanding. I couldn't have completed this book without their love and support.

Thanks too to Les Cartwright, who started me off on a journey of discovery about the voice, and, Dorothea Cerutty, no longer here, who gave me a life-long passion for literature. I'll never forget those intense and inspirational discussions with her about the power of the spoken word.

Credit must also go to my two main readers: David Shirley and Mia Ball. Their unfailing support and incisive comments kept me focused throughout the writing process. Thanks also to Jan Haydn Rowles and Ailsa Gudgeon who encouraged me throughout and provided comment on my initial attempts with the first few chapters.

All the voice teachers and voice coaches I've worked with over the years need special thanks as well. Their work has continued to inspire me. Likewise, all the student and professional actors I've come into contact with need acknowledgement. It is their work that has deepened my understanding of how the human voice can be lifted off the written page and brought to life for an audience.

Lastly, I'd like to thank the team at Oberon Books for their support, help and humour. Special thanks must go to James Hogan, who has continued to believe in me and champion my work. And I couldn't have completed the job without my editors Stephen Watson and Daisy Bowie-Sell, who cast meticulous eyes over my writing.

Thanks to you all.

CONTENTS

PREFACE

About this book

Classical texts require actors to grapple with character and story in heightened language, using complex images and, more often than not, text that is written in verse form. Add the performance demands of audience and space and no wonder it becomes difficult to maintain free, open, energised and agile voices.

So those of us who are lucky enough to work with actors need plenty of ideas up our sleeves. As a teacher, trainer, coach or director you'll require practical information and detailed plans for exploring the vocal demands of classical text within your classes, workshops or rehearsals. Individual actors react differently to the same exercises, so range and variety are key. This book doesn't rely on one particular methodology and draws ideas from many different sources in order to provide you with the breadth of inspiration that you'll need.

The term 'actor' is used throughout the book but encompasses students from secondary schools, performing arts courses, universities and drama schools, as well as the amateur performer, the untrained professional and the trained professional. The exploratory exercises and activities listed in *Classic Voice* are appropriate for all these actors and have been tested out in each context although occasionally there may be different requirements depending on training and experience. Any adjustments that need to be made for different skill levels are explained along the way.

Part One of *Classic Voice* focuses on how to prepare actors for working on classical texts. Chapter 1 explores *warming up* in order to ensure that voices are open and flexible enough to deal with the demands of the text to come. Chapters 2, 3 and 4 provide information on the nuts and bolts of text work: *sound, word* and *rhythm*. A practical understanding of these elements is the core foundation of any text work.

The remainder of *Classic Voice* focuses on the specific demands of different types of classical text: Part Two deals with vocal style in Greek Tragedy, Part Three with Jacobethan (Elizabethan and Jacobean) Drama and Part Four with Restoration Comedy. Three significant periods in western theatre history when actors were challenged by the vocal demands within their texts.

Each of these sections includes an initial overview, samples of text and a series of workshop plans. The workshops are offered as a starting point for dealing with the text as a whole and, therefore, can be used as an initial vocal exploration prior to embarking on a full scale project or rehearsal. However, they shouldn't replace in-depth one-to-one exploration of text in preparation for performance.

None of the workshops are constructed within a particular time-frame (given the variations in timetabling between schools, colleges, training academies, conservatoires and universities) and range from half an hour to full day explorations, which can be broken up into smaller units if necessary. They provide an insight into how to structure a session, what to focus on in the vocal warm up and exercises/information on how to deal with the vocal demands of the sample text.

The sample texts have been included to provide a starting point for exploration and there is no need to feel limited by them (particularly if the gender breakdown doesn't work for your group). The workshop exercises and activities can be applied just as easily to other texts from the same period.

What is classical text? What is vocal style?

The notion of what constitutes *classical text* or *classical drama* has changed over time. Nowadays, literary scholars will point to texts from antiquity, such as those produced by the Romans and Greeks; however, for the contemporary actor, *classical drama* can span a period from antiquity through to the twenty-first century. This is primarily to do with the nature of the text and not necessarily the period. The use of heightened language, complex images and adherence to a particular form or structure indicates drama of a classical nature. Many of our modern playwrights grapple with classical constructs within contemporary plots to great effect, such as the English playwright Sarah Kane.

Equally confusing is the concept of *literary style*. It's a difficult term to pin down and there are numerous definitions to be found in dictionaries, literary books and the internet. This is because every piece of written text has its own distinctive identity (or style) but is often placed within a particular category or genre for ease of reference by the creative artist, academic scholar, literary critic or marketing director of a publishing house.

In drama, some categories are defined by the style of a particular playwright: for example, Harold Pinter. He uses language sparsely in his plays, creates verbal games between characters and places pauses and silences to form specific rhythmical patterns. This style of writing is often referred to as Pinteresque.

There are other styles that are defined by a specific period in time: for example, Revenge Tragedies, which appeared in England during the late sixteenth and early seventeenth centuries and captured the essence and energy of the age. *The White Devil* by John Webster and *The Changeling* by Middleton and Rowley are good examples.

Style can also be defined by genre: for example, Comedy of Manners, where the social manners and attitudes of a particular class of people are explored in witty comedies. The Restoration playwrights in the seventeenth century, Oscar Wilde in the nineteenth century and Noël Coward in the twentieth century are the most famous proponents of this style of play.

These stylistic categories (grouped together by playwright, period or genre) can also be defined by: ***the way in which thoughts are expressed by the playwright*** (through choices made about sound, word or syntax) and ***the way in which thoughts are structured by the playwright*** (through the arrangement of words on the page). For example, the sonnet form used by Shakespeare with fourteen lines of rhyming metrical rhythm creates a specific framework for the individual sounds and words he has chosen to use. In turn, this helps to define meaning and emotion for the reader, speaker or audience.

Therefore, the style of a text can provide actors with important clues about its performance demands in order to move it from page to stage. Of course the actor must understand, inhabit and convey the emotional truth of a character in a realistic way and create a believable world around that character for a modern audience; however, realism in drama is a relatively modern phenomenon and the particular stylistic demands of classical drama outside this tradition need to be explored by the actor if the play and its characters are to be brought to life.

The voice is an incredibly important tool in this process through which sound can be formed, shaped and driven to meet the demands of the text. Sometimes the world of the play and a characters' inner motivation can't be fully realised without a focus on *vocal style*. For example, the witty verbal repartee present in a Comedy of Manners play is not only a driving force behind the comedy but also provides us with the mindset of a particular class of people in a particular period in time.

This means that the *vocal style* of a text may also include *period voice*, depending on the vocal attributes of the period in which the play is set. Most of these attributes will be determined by accent, which this book discusses at various points but doesn't cover in technical detail because it's such a lengthy area of study in itself. However, it's important to note that accents evolve over time, for example, the variation of Standard British Speech or Received Pronunciation that's spoken today is not the same version that was spoken during the time when Oscar Wilde was writing his plays or even the same version in a Noël Coward play. Obviously, the further back we go in time the less likely we are to know about *period voice*, given that vocal recordings aren't available. I know some people who will always want their Shakespeare spoken in Received Pronunciation but, of course, Received Pronunciation didn't exist at the time Shakespeare was writing, being only a relatively recent development in the nineteenth century. However, nowadays, a wider range of accents can be heard in Shakespearean performances and accent choice is more likely to be based on a character's class and context.

How do you teach it?

So if actors are to successfully realise the *vocal style* within a piece of classical drama they must understand the intrinsic performance demands of text, character and period that affect vocal delivery. You will need to set up a variety of exercises and activities so your actors can explore this in detail as part of their rehearsal process. Of course there will be times when information about a particular style, period or text should be directly provided but, in the majority of cases, you will need to lead them through a *practical process* to their own discoveries. This is the way in which actors can make the work their own in performance.

It isn't enough for an actor to mentally analyse the stylistic demands of a text and hope that in some way this will translate physically into the voice. A dancer would never just analyse movement or think through the steps in their head and expect this would be enough to execute and communicate their performance. Likewise, actors shouldn't spend their entire time sitting around a table in rehearsal focusing internally on the text. Vocalising words and thoughts is a physical and muscular activity, like dancing, and needs a practical approach. Vice-versa, it isn't enough for the actor to practise technical voice exercises in the hope that this will inform their work. Vocal exercises do not necessarily translate into delivery unless they are linked to an understanding of sound and word and, ultimately, the work will be empty without some sort of textual analysis.

Working practically with actors requires careful management and coaching them through an exercise from the sidelines needs sensitivity. Know when to be silent so they have the time and space to think through (internally) what you've asked them to do and in order for them to explore the full potential of the exercise. However, don't leave them in silence for too long, otherwise the impetus and energy of the exercise will lose its momentum and they may start to question the work in a negative way. Finding the appropriate timing will only happen if you try some of the exercises yourself, away from the classroom and/or rehearsal space, so you can explore for yourself what works and what doesn't work.

Be aware that the level of your own vocal energy will feed into the success of an exercise. If you over-energise or push your voice at the group then this will be unconsciously imitated by them within the exercise. Likewise, under-energising your voice may mean that they lose vocal energy. You will learn from experience the most appropriate vocal level at which to pitch the work. In the meantime, experiment with different levels of vocal energy and, mentally, file away the response for future work.

Many exercises that require actors to think through a process internally may need a follow-up debrief. This will help them to articulate what worked or didn't work for them and what they discovered about their voice and/or the text during the exercise. In this way they will understand in greater detail the process they've just been through and provide you with important information on where the work needs to go next. There are a couple of ways in which this can be handled, depending on the type of exercise. If you've asked the group to work on some simple vocal exercises, try getting each person to articulate one word that describes how they feel. Debriefing in this way will maintain the flow of the class or rehearsal and you can quickly move onto other work. If you've asked them to try something more text-based and there is a natural break point in the work then you could ask them to sit and discuss the process more thoroughly.

You may need some technical information at hand to inform the work. I've thought long and hard about whether to include detailed terminology in this book because, ultimately, does it matter whether an actor knows the difference between a *metaphor* and *simile* in order to bring a character to life for an audience? I know those who would say 'yes – absolutely'. I don't think so, although actors do need to know about how writers use sound, juxtapose meaning and play with rhythm, as ultimately we are on a journey to discover how to re-create the energy and drive of human speech. The actual words we use to describe how writers do this aren't important. The only reason I've included them is for your own background knowledge.

So, in summary, keep your classes, workshops and rehearsals practical but underpin this work with a strong technical base. This means that you must bring knowledge about the voice and the text to the classroom or rehearsal room floor and use that knowledge in practical ways to help your actors bring the drama to life.

PART ONE: PREPARATION

CHAPTER I

WARMING UP

Actors need to warm up their voices prior to working on text, which will help them to explore the words much more openly, freely and flexibly.

There is a very real difference between a voice class, session or workout and a voice warm up. In essence, voice classes, sessions or workouts are exploratory in nature, focusing on a specific learning experience and/or objective. Warm ups are about preparing voices for the work to come, whether that be within a class, workshop or rehearsal, or for performance.

There are those of us who spend our lives ensuring actors are vocally prepared and whole books are devoted to the subject. This chapter doesn't set out to train you as a voice coach but it will explain ways in which you can work, with some knowledge and sensitivity, around the vocal needs of your actors.

I know you may be short of time and will want to spend as much time as possible on the text itself but, without a warm up, you may not achieve your aims and objectives as your actors won't be ready for the work. Essentially, you might be preventing them from reaching their true potential in the session and the time could be wasted. Conducting a vocal warm up will help you to achieve more.

Vocal warm ups vary in length: some directors and companies prefer a good hour in the morning before the start of rehearsals but most tend to allocate thirty minutes. If this sounds daunting, particularly if your session is a short class or workshop, then think about combining exercises so that a number of vocal objectives are covered in the one go. By vocal objectives I mean what needs to be achieved in the warm up (please refer to the end of this chapter for summarised details).

The exercises in this chapter are presented as group warm ups although most of them can be adapted for warming up individual actors as well. Of course you may need to modify the exercises to suit your own needs but be aware that the overall structure is important: each section feeds into the next (don't even think about working on resonance without securing a strong, supported breath first). For easy reference, I've boiled it down into five categories: *releasing, breathing, resonating, stretching range* and *articulating*.

Releasing

Our voices come from our bodies so you must help your actors achieve the best possible physical state for vocalisation. They will bring all sorts of physical tensions to the classroom or rehearsal room floor on which you will need to spend some time focusing during the course of the warm up. Perhaps they had a difficult journey getting to rehearsal, maybe there's a personal problem bothering them at the moment or possibly they're nervous about the work to come. These stresses will manifest themselves in physical tensions that will put their voices under pressure. Add in performance anxiety and their voices may become strained.

You certainly won't be able to (and shouldn't try to) solve any of the problems that your actors bring to the classroom or rehearsal room floor but you can help them to relieve a little of the tension that they're carrying with them. So the objective is to release unnecessary tension whilst retaining or building physical energy for the work to come.

Some voice coaches use the word 'relaxation' rather than 'release' but 'relaxation' implies a totally floppy, sleepy body without control or energy. We tense the body simply by standing up so 'release' implies 'letting go' of *unnecessary* tension: in other words, finding the balance between relaxation and tension.

Everybody holds tension in the body differently however, if there's unnecessary tension in one area then usually it will connect into another. For example, excess shoulder tension will create excess neck and jaw tension. This means it's better to work up the body, releasing different areas as you go. So be aware that the order of exercises is important.

I'm not going to include a full physical warm up here, just a series of interlinked exercises that you can start off with at the beginning of a warm up. If you have the time to do a full physical warm up prior to a vocal one then by all means do so but very few classes or rehearsals have the space and time for this experience. I've only included physical exercises that directly affect vocalisation.

Working with the breath during these exercises is an important part of the process as well so please read the section on *breathing* before you start.

Release Exercises (some ideas)

- **Semi-supine.*** Ask your actors to lie down on their backs with their knees bent and their feet flat on the floor. They may wish to use a small book under their head for comfort and spinal alignment. Get them to experiment with the placement of their feet (perhaps closer towards their buttocks) so that they feel more of their back touching the floor (without pushing down). Now coach them to give in to gravity and release their weight into the floor, particularly around the lower back. Help them to think their way up the spine, lengthening along the floor as they do so. When they reach the neck, ask them to move their head, gently, from side to side to release tension and then bring it back to centre. This is the point at which you might like to introduce some breathing exercises (please refer to the section entitled *Breathing*).

- **Prayer Stretch.** From semi-supine, ask your actors to roll onto their side and rest for a few seconds. Then ask them to come onto their knees with their forehead on the floor and their arms stretched out in front of them. If they're flexible enough, they should be able to sit back onto their feet without lifting their forehead off the floor. Don't worry if they can't do this on the first go. Ask them to feel a stretch from the fingertips right

---

* A word of caution: working in semi-supine can place actors in a very relaxed state so I try to avoid it unless there is the time and space for them to recover fully or it's part of a whole teaching process about the voice. I wouldn't use it in a pre-show warm up. However, it's a useful tool for you to know about, particularly if there are some seriously stressed voices during the rehearsal process. Otherwise, you can start the warm up from either the *prayer stretch,* the *spinal roll* or *stretching and yawning*.

through to the lower back and manufacture a yawn (either silent or vocalised, it doesn't matter at this point). Again, introduce some breathing exercises (please refer to the section entitled *Breathing*).

- **Spinal Roll**. From the prayer stretch, ask your actors to come up into a crouch position with their heads still dropped (another good point for breathing exercises). Then into a standing position but with their weight balanced slightly forward, their knees bent and their upper body flopped over from the lower back. Coach them into rolling up the spine into an upright standing position, keeping their head dropped all the way up. The final movement should be the head slowly floating up.

- **Stretching and Yawning.** Once they're up, allow them to take a few seconds to adjust, then ask them to try three different types of stretches, yawning at the same time (either silent or vocalised).

- **Grounding, Centring, Aligning.**
  - Ask your actors to do some firm stomping into the ground with their feet.
  - Then get them to balance their weight between both feet and balance their weight between their toes and their heels.
  - They now need to release their weight down through their feet, letting go into the floor.
  - Centre their pelvis by asking them to bend their knees, place one hand on their lower stomach and one hand on their lower back. Coach them to tilt the pelvis forward and then back (in both cases taking them away from their centre of gravity). Allow them to centre the pelvis again and slowly bring their knees up, feeling the tail-bone dropped.
  - Check that they haven't locked their knees back into place (getting them to wobble their knees backwards and forwards can help).
  - Ask them to touch a point at the crown of the head (they may wish to pull on a small piece of hair there) and feel the body lift and lengthen up towards this point (without losing a sense of their feet placed firmly on the floor). Make sure that they focus on a point just below the horizon so that the back of the neck is lengthened.

- **Shoulder Release.** Ask your actors to lift their shoulders up towards their ears for a moment before letting them go with an out-breath. As the shoulders drop, the head should lengthen upwards. Now ask them to hold their shoulders back for a moment before releasing them with an out-breath. Finally, ask them to move their shoulders forward for a moment before releasing them with an out-breath. Try all three actions a few times through, varying the order.

- **Neck Release.** Avoid warming up with full head rolls as it could put your actors' spines out. Instead, ask your actors to do gentle half head rolls from shoulder to shoulder. Finish with a gentle head nod, again from shoulder to shoulder and back again. Always treat the neck with care.

- **Jaw Release.** Ask your actors to smooth down the jaw line with their hands a few times. Then ask them to let their mouths hang open so that their lower jaw just hangs off the skull, giving in to the weight of gravity. Make sure they don't collapse their spine in the process. If their mouth gets dry then encourage them to swallow before coming back to the exercise. When you feel that they've given in sufficiently to gravity then get them to take their lower jaw in both hands and slowly move it up and down (never side to side or around in circles as it could click the lower jaw out of alignment). Make sure that the movement comes from their hands and not the lower jaw. This could be a difficult exercise for those actors who've been tensing their jaws for some time: if they can't do it then just move on (after all it's a warm up not a class). Finally, ask your actors to gently shake their jaws out by clasping their hands together and shaking them up and down, letting their jaw go at the same time. Sound can be added to the shake-out, which helps the release process.

- **Pharyngeal Release.** The pharynx is the upper throat, which extends from the mouth down to the larynx. Tension here is connected to jaw and neck tension so it's important to release these areas first. The basis of all release exercises for the pharynx is yawning. Get your actors into the habit of doing open mouthed, vocalised yawns whenever they feel like it in classes and rehearsals. As part of a warm up ask them to yawn and speak at the same time, for example, yawning whilst counting aloud. This automatically opens up the upper throat. Immediately afterwards, ask them to speak in their natural voice and they should be able to feel the difference: their voices will be much more open, wide and free.

Breathing

We breathe to live and we breathe to speak: in-and-out, in-and-out, simple.

Breathing in

When we decide to speak, air flows in through the mouth and the lungs fill and expand. Three sets of muscles help this process along: the diaphragm (the dome-shaped muscle attached to the lower edges of the rib cage, the bottom of the sternum and the back vertebrae), the intercostals (the muscles between the ribs), and the abdominal muscles. A message from the brain is sent directly to the diaphragm, which flattens out and becomes less dome-shaped. Because the diaphragm is attached to the lower edges of the rib cage, its movement pulls the rib cage outwards, stretching the intercostal muscles and creating extra space for the incoming breath and expanding lungs. The abdominal muscles release to make space for the descending diaphragm.

Breathing out

The muscles now move back into their original positions, supporting the release of the outgoing breath: the diaphragm returns to its dome shape (assisted by the abdominal and pelvic floor muscles), causing the rib cage and intercostals to move back into place. The lungs then compress and air flows out of our bodies.

Sometimes we don't use these muscles to their fullest potential (maybe our body is holding onto unnecessary tension or flexibility has been lost over time) which means that we speak without muscular support. Release and breathing exercises can help wake these muscles up. Of course this process must be an unconscious one for the actor (they can't be thinking about their breathing process in performance) so it's important that the warm up allows some time for these muscles to be stretched, strengthened and motivated.

Our breath is acutely linked to our feelings: the depth and rhythm of our breathing changes according to our emotional response to a situation, for example, when we panic, our breath shortens and becomes shallower, thereby increasing our panic. This means that we can also be emotionally strengthened by a deep, supported breath, using those muscles low in the body that calm our nervous system. This, of course, is perfect for actors. Not only does it create a strong, secure breath stream for resonant vocalisation but it also calms the nervous system so they're energised without excessive performance fear taking over.

It's always a surprise to learn how fraught the process of working with the breath can be for voice coaches: I've seen vicious debates at conferences and outright war waged in one drama school over a particular way of teaching. Then, of course, there are all the arguments between singing voice coaches and speaking voice coaches. One of the reasons for this fracas is that the way in which we teach breathing has changed over time and new fashions and trends have emerged.

Some voice coaches prefer their actors to breathe in through the nose when working on breathing exercises. However, when we speak we naturally take a quick breath in through the mouth, which is why I prefer actors to breathe in through the mouth during exercise so that the process of using muscular support with mouth breathing becomes an unconscious one. I tend to use the phrase 'drop the breath in'. If they find their mouths drying out then encourage them to swallow and create some saliva before starting the exercise again. Of course when we aren't speaking and are simply breathing in air to survive (and haven't got a cold or nose blockage) then we breathe air in through the nose. Try speaking a few phrases with in-breaths via the nose, you'll find that it's awkward and time-consuming.

Another exercise that seems to keep turning up in rehearsal rooms is breathing in on a slow internal count. I think breathing exercises should encourage a gentle but rapid intake of air through the mouth so that actors can get used to breathing in, quickly and cleanly, with muscular support. Also, try to avoid old exercises that encourage 'holding' of the muscles in any one position for a period of time. This 'holding' will mean that your actors will, more than likely, end up holding and tensing in the larynx at the same time, which may become habitual.

So to summarise, there are two objectives to pursue with the breath in a vocal warm up: (1) To free up the flow of breath through the body; and (2) To strengthen muscular support for vocalisation.

Breathing Exercises (some ideas)

- **Semi-supine Breathing (waking up the diaphragm and abdominal muscles).** When your actors have spent some time in semi-supine releasing into the floor (please refer to the section entitled *Release Exercises*), ask them to place their hands on their lower abdomen and allow their shoulders to ease out across the floor. They should now be taking the air in and out gently through the mouth, and, slowly deepening their intake so that they can feel the muscles move beneath their hands (the lower the better). Coach them to start releasing their breath on a long fffff sound, right to the end of their breath stream so they feel the muscles contract, ready for the next intake of breath. After a series of these breaths, move them onto a long sssss sound, followed by a vvvvv sound, then a zzzzz sound. Keep coaching them to 'pour' the sound out of their body. If the sound seems tense in any way encourage them to wobble their head from side to side during the next vocalisation to ensure that there isn't any holding around the neck or throat.

- **Side Breathing (waking up the intercostal muscles).** From semi-supine, allow your actors to roll over onto their right side and ask them to place a hand on the side of their rib cage that is closest to the ceiling. It doesn't matter which hand they use as long as they're in a relatively comfortable position. Now ask them to repeat the previous exercises (fffff, sssss, vvvvv, zzzzz) but get them to focus on feeling the rise and fall of the rib cage towards the ceiling. Repeat on the other side.

- **Prayer Stretch Breathing (waking up the lower back muscles).** Now ask them to come onto their knees with their forehead on the floor and their arms stretched out in front of them (please refer to the section entitled *Release Exercises*). Get them to feel a stretch from the fingertips right through to the lower back and manufacture a yawn (either silent or vocal-

---

* Again, a word of caution: working on the floor can place actors in a very relaxed state so I try to avoid it unless there is the time and space for them to recover fully or it's part of a whole teaching process about the voice. I wouldn't use it in a pre-show warm up. However, it's a useful tool for you to know about, particularly if there are some seriously stressed voices during the rehearsal process. Otherwise, you can start the warm up from either *prayer stretch breathing, spinal roll breathing* or *intercostal stretches.*

ised, it doesn't matter at this point). Again, coach them to start deepening and lengthening their breath stream on fffff, sssss, vvvvv, then zzzzz, but this time feeling the muscular movement in the lower back.

- **Crouching Breathing (waking up the lower back muscles).** From the prayer stretch, ask your actors to come up into a crouch position (on their toes with their palms flat on the floor). They should try and bring their head up slightly so that their spine is semi-aligned. Again, coach them into the fffff, sssss, vvvvv then zzzzz sounds, feeling the muscular movement in the lower back. This exercise can also be done in pairs with one person placing a hand on their partner's lower back so that they have a focal point for the breath.

- **Spinal Roll Breathing (freeing breath through the body).** Now ask them to come up onto their feet but with their weight balanced slightly forward, their knees bent and their upper body flopped over from the lower back. Coach them into rolling up the spine into an upright standing position, keeping their head dropped all the way up, releasing on one of the fffff, sssss, vvvvv or zzzzz sounds. The final movement should be the head slowly floating up. You can ask them to try the other sounds as well, rolling up and down the spine, matching each roll to one full breath release of sound.

- **Upper Body Stretches (waking up the intercostals muscles).** Ask your actors to raise one arm above them, feeling the stretch from the fingertips right down that side of the body. They should then place their other hand on the front of the rib cage they're stretching and move through the fffff, sssss, vvvvv and zzzzz sounds, focusing on the breath moving into that side of the body. When they allow their arm to flop down, one side of their body may feel more open. Get them to repeat the exercise on the other side.

- **Panting (waking up the diaphragm).** Now ask them to place their hands in the hollow just below their sternum. A little bit of panting will help them to feel the action of the diaphragm and wake it up. I wouldn't try this for too long, though, as it can quickly move into panic breathing.

- **Swings (freeing the breath).** Ask your actors to swing one of their arms, bending their knees on the downward movement. Allow them time and space to find a natural rhythm for this. Now ask them to open their mouth and let the breath travel in and out with the natural rhythm of the movement. Once they've found the rhythm then get them to add the word 'whoooosh' to each out-breath. This exercise also helps to release shoulder tension and afterwards one side of the body may look and feel different to the other side. Repeat the exercise with the other arm.

- **Focus Points (focusing the breath).** Waking up muscles and releasing breath freely is all very well but eventually your actors will need to focus their breath to a specific point or task in preparation for text and character work. Coach your actors to ground, centre and align their body (please refer to the boxed section entitled *Release Exercises*). Make sure that they focus on a point (like a mark on a wall) just under their horizon so that the back of their neck is aligned. They may like to place their hands on their lower abdomen so they can feel the breath low in the body as they work. They should let the breath 'drop in' to their body, quickly and easily, and release on the fffff sound to their point. Add in the other sounds when you feel they are working from that low muscle base.

- **Focus Walks (moving the breath).** Actors need to be able to move and breathe at the same time. This sounds easy, but many people start holding their breath whenever they have to perform some sort of action, which, of course, restricts vocalisation. This exercise should help your actors' bodies remember that they can move and breathe at the same time. Link this exercise to the previous exercise on breathing to a point. Ask your actors to walk to the point they've been focusing on (watching out, with their peripheral vision, for other people moving in the room). Ask them to turn, find a new point and walk to that. Coach them to find the most direct route there. After a few different walks, ask them to turn, find a new point, breathe in and release a sound all the way to their point. You can start with fffff, sssss, vvvvv and zzzzz and then move it onto other sounds, followed by words. Using text, especially verse text with particularly long breath thoughts, will help them to find their breath to the end of the line, easily and naturally.

Resonating

When the breath moves up the trachea and into the larynx, it motivates the vocal folds into movement, creating a small sound. The breath carries this sound onward and upward into different spaces or cavities, where the sound bounces around and vibrates into something much more audible.

Actors need to intensify these vibrations in a warm up so that their voices are much more open and resonant: the vibrations from a resonant voice will travel through space automatically and easily. As we've already learnt, actors need to release tensions so that their voices aren't restricted and strengthen muscular support so that sound is securely carried by the breath stream; however, the face also needs to be warmed up ready for work on placing the sound forward. Your actors should be 'buzzing' after these exercises and feel as though they want to use their voices. It's a good sign if the noise and energy in the room increases.

Resonating Exercises (some ideas)

FACIAL WARM UP

- **Patting.** Ask your actors to gently pat their face and scalp so they become a little bit tingly. If you need to build some energy at this point (especially if you've included some floor work earlier on in the warm up) then get them to pat all over their bodies. They can ask a partner to pat down their back for them.

- **Massaging.** Now ask them to massage the face with their fingertips. If it's a morning warm up then it's important that they spend some time around the sinuses, which may help to shift any excess mucus that has built up over night. Excess mucus will block the vibrations around the nasal cavities and seriously affect vocal resonance. Humming on an 'ng' sound (like the final sound in 'sing') will also help. Have some tissues handy as they might need to blow their noses! (If any of your actors have a cold then this exercise isn't helpful.)

- **Chewing.** Get your actors to chew with their mouths open, using as much of the face as possible. Make sure they include chewing into the upper lip.

- **Sneering.** Try getting them to sneer: this means lifting what I call the two 'sneer muscles' on the upper lip. Try a few lifts and drops. Then ask them to try a one-sided sneer, using only one of the sneer muscles. Most people will have a strong side and a weak side. See if they can use their weaker side and swap between the two.

- **Blowing Through the Lips.** Blowing through the lips is one of those magical exercises that just about every voice coach I know uses at some point in their work. There has to be a strong supported breath for the exercise to work (breath strength will motivate the lip movement) so it automatically helps actors connect back to their breath *and* brings resonant vibration forward onto the face. Basically, the out-going breath needs to be strong enough to motivate the lips into a movement and sound not unlike a horse blowing through their lips. See if your actors can add vocalised sound to it. There may be someone in the group who has trouble with this (usually because of a weak breath stream). If so just ask them to try it in short spurts or blips. If this is still too difficult then ask them to reconnect back to their breath on an fffff sound. Those that can make it work may find their faces feel 'itchy' afterwards, which is perfect.

FORWARD PLACEMENT

- **Humming.** Ask your actors to place their lips gently together, drop the back of the tongue and hum on any pitch (whatever comes to them naturally). They should try to think the sound forward onto their lips, concentrating on building the vibration there.

- **Hum on the Run.** Now ask them to take that hum for a heavy jog around the room. Coach them to use the whole of their feet (they shouldn't be running on their toes) and ask them to drop their arms. Let them bounce around with the sound for a few minutes. When they come to a stop ask them to flop over from the waist so their breath centres. Then they can come up through a spinal roll to standing. Make sure they reconnect to their breath with an fffffff sound before trying the hum again. They should feel the sound is much easier to produce as the vibration has automatically bounced forward.

- **Placing the Hum.** Repeat the humming exercise on the lips and then move on to the cheekbones, bridge of the nose, temples, top of the head and the chest. Ask them to place their hands on each of these points in turn so that they can really think (and feel) the vibrations coming off their body. Make sure their spines stay aligned and their hands come up to meet their faces rather than their faces sinking down to meet their hands. Some of these resonating centres will have stronger vibrations than others and, because this is a warm up and not a voice class, there is no need to linger over an area with weaker vibrations. Repeat the exercise but this time ask your actors to see if they can still feel the vibrations when they move their hand a centimetre or two away from the body, ie feeling the vibrations moving off into space.

- **Placing Vowels.** Now ask them to gently glide the hum into some open vowel sounds: mmmOO, mmmOH, mmmAW, mmmAH, mmmAY, mmmEE. See if they can still feel vibration coming off their body into the space. It helps if their arm travels in an arc away from their face as they release into the vowel, gently easing the sound into the space.

Stretching range

An actors' pitch range needs to be flexible enough to communicate the subtleties within the character and text on which they're working. Therefore, the objective in a warm up is to wake up your actors' full pitch range, easily and safely. If you introduce exercises that try to push them outside of their natural range then you'll end up straining their voices. For this reason, I tend to avoid pitch exercises that use counting or words in a warm up situation. Try to focus on a free and easy vocalisation of sound, particularly at the upper and lower notes of their range, which might not have much use and, therefore, are more prone to strain.

Because these exercises involve humming and blowing through the lips, you can always integrate them with the exercises listed under

Resonating. Encourage your actors to really play with sound, whether they be students or professionals.

<table>
<tr><td>Stretching Range Exercises (some ideas)</td></tr>
</table>

- **Top to Bottom.** Follow the guidelines for teaching the 'blowing through the lips' exercise in the *Resonating Exercises* section. Then, ask your actors to start at the top of the range, gliding through to the bottom and then back up to the top on the vocalised sound version. It's useful if they start with their finger high up in the air and bring it down to the floor so that they end up in a crouch position, as they make the sound (and vice versa going up the range). Movement will help free up their vocalisation.

- **Imaginary Writing.** Ask your actors to ground, centre and align themselves, as explained in the *Release Exercises* section. Try a few gentle fffff releases to ensure there is muscular support for their breath and then follow the guidelines for teaching 'humming' in the *Resonating Exercises* section. Now get them to draw their names in the air, slowly. The pitch of their voice should follow the movement of their finger, which means they should be moving all over their range. Once they've finished, get them to rub their writing out with their hand(s), again using the humming sound. This exercise can be done with 'blowing through the lips' as well.

- **Imaginary Drawing.** Following on from 'imaginary writing', using either 'humming' or 'blowing through the lips', ask your actors to draw an imaginary square picture frame in front of them, again allowing the vocalised sound to follow the movement of their finger. Then, they need to draw an imaginary beach scene within the frame, using sound (sand, sun, sea, palm trees, etc). When they've finished, ask them to take a good look at their imaginary scene so that they don't forget it, then they can rub it out with their hand(s), not forgetting the sound.

- **Imaginary Drawing in 3D.** 'Imaginary drawing' was the test picture. Now ask them to re-create that imaginary beach picture in 3D using the entire room, again not forgetting to use the sound. When they've finished, you can either get them to draw a beach towel and lie down in semi-supine to re-centre their breath, or, if you wish to maintain the energy, allow them the time to drop in a couple of fffff sounds, before they rub the entire beach out (again, with sound).

Articulating

The next chapter on *Sound* provides more detailed information on the formation of vowels and consonants; however, prior to this work, you will need to warm up the speech organs associated with articulating these sounds.

The speech organs include: the lower jaw, the lips, the tongue, the soft palate (which are all movable); and the teeth, the tooth-ridge and the hard palate (which are all fixed). Your objective in a warm up is to ensure that the movable speech organs are muscularly free and flexible.

The lower jaw is attached to the facial bones by hinge joints and its movements alter the size and shape of the mouth. Because you will have already completed work on the lower jaw in *Release Exercises* we will need to focus on exercises for the lips, the tongue and the soft palate in this part of the warm up.

The *lips* are the free edges of the mouth and can be minutely shaped to form specific sounds. The *tongue* lies on the floor of the mouth and is rooted in the front wall of the upper throat or pharynx: it's the most active of the speech organs with movement varying between the tip, the blade, the front and the centre (or back of the tongue). The *soft palate* is a muscular flap at the back of the roof of the mouth and can move up and down, controlling the flow of air and sound through the nose or mouth, like a trap door. The trap door is closed for all sounds, except / m /, / n / and / ng /, when it then lowers so the sound vibrates through to the nasal cavities.

The box below includes aerobic exercises for the lips, tongue and soft palate, as well as exercises using specific sounds formed by them. I tend not to rely on tongue-twisters in articulation warm ups; however, there is no reason for you not to include a couple if you find them useful, but only after there has been some sort of muscular aerobic warm up.

Because you will be aiming for lip/tongue/soft palate muscularity with your actors, be aware that they could pick up some unnecessary jaw tension along the way. It's a good idea to get them to shake their jaws out gently in between exercises, which we explored in the section entitled *Release Exercises* (clasping hands together and shaking them up and down whilst letting the jaw go with some sound).

Articulation Exercises (some ideas)

GENERAL

- **Facial Mirroring.** Ask your actors to work in pairs, facing each other. One person should start by pulling various faces and the other person must follow their actions: the lead can change at any time. Encourage them to work with the facial muscles, lips and tongue. Sound can be added in at a later stage.

THE LIPS

- **Chewing.** Just in case you didn't do this exercise as part of the 'facial warm up' in *Resonance Exercises*, try it here. Get your actors to chew with their mouths open, using as much of the face as possible. Make sure they include chewing into the upper lip.

- **Sneering.** Likewise, if you didn't try this the first time around, ask them to sneer now (lifting what I call, the two 'sneer muscles' on the upper lip). Then ask them to try a one-sided sneer, using only one of the sneer muscles. Most people will have a strong side and a weak side. See if they can use their weaker side and swap between the two.

- **Stretching.** Now ask them to glide their tongue around between their gums and the inside of their lips.

- **Grinning and Pouting.** Try getting them to alternate between grinning and pouting. Move this into the vowel phrase 'ee – ah – oo', then 'tea for two and two for tea', gently exaggerating the lip movements.

- **Lip Explosions.** Now ask them to press their lips together so they're covered by each other, feel some breath pressure build up behind them and release into 'pah'. Repeat the exercise with 'bah'.

- **Rhythmic Lips.** Try some different rhythms on / p / and / b / (for example, ppp ppp ppp pah) aiming for crispness, lightness and speed. You could always ask your actors to come up with their own rhythms.

THE TONGUE

- **Tongue Aerobics 1.** Tongue aerobics is best done in front of a mirror although it's still a useful exercise without one (just a bit more difficult). Ask your actors to drop their lower jaw (and hold onto it with one hand if it's in danger of following the tongue around) and point the tongue out level from the mouth, away from the bottom lip. Then, get them to withdraw the tongue until it contacts the back of the lower teeth. Try alternating the movements a few times.

- **Tongue Aerobics 2.** Repeat 'tongue aerobics 1' but this time, instead of withdrawing the tongue back into the mouth, ask them to take it from side to side as slowly as possible and then up and down as slowly as possible. Make sure they stop, swallow and moisten the mouth with saliva in between each try.

- **Tongue Aerobics 3.** Now ask them to draw a small circle in the air with the tip of their tongue, the slower the better.

- **Rhythmic Tongue.** Placing the tip of the tongue on the gum ridge behind the upper front teeth, ask them to try some different rhythms on / t / and / d / (for example, ddd, ddd, ddd, dah) aiming for crispness, lightness and speed. You could always ask your actors to come up with their own rhythms.

THE SOFT PALATE

- **Soft Palate Aerobics.** Ask your actors to keep their mouth open and breathe in through the nose and out through the mouth. They should be able to feel the action of the soft palate. If they look in a mirror they might be able to see the movement. Now get them to hum on an / ng / sound and then cut it off with a breathy / ha /.

- **Back of the Tongue/Soft Palate Rhythms.** Ask them to try some different rhythms on / k / and / g / (for example, kkk, kkk, kkk, kah) aiming for crispness, lightness and speed. Repeat the exercise but this time ask them to place two fingers between their teeth, which will widen the gap in which the soft palate has to move, thereby making it work harder.

- **Sound, Word and Rhythm.** It's a good idea to finish the warm up with a group exercise that focuses on sound, word and/or rhythm so that your actors can (briefly) put into practice what they've achieved throughout the warm up. Try adding in one of the exercises listed in the box sections within the next three chapters, perhaps something that links with the work on text you wish them to undertake in the remainder of the class, workshop or rehearsal.

Warm up Objectives: A Summary

Time for a quick recap of the vocal objectives. Being clear about what you want to achieve will help you to structure the warm up appropriately. It may also help you add in other exercises you know and like that aren't listed here or develop your own. Whatever you decide to include, just make sure you keep the following objectives in mind.

1. To release unnecessary tension whilst retaining or building physical energy for the work to come.
2. To free up the flow of breath through the body.
3. To strengthen muscular support for vocalisation.
4. To intensify vibration in the resonating spaces.
5. To wake up the pitch range, easily and safely.
6. To ensure that the movable speech organs are muscularly free and flexible.

'Time is of the Essence': Another Approach

So you've read through this chapter and, although you can see the value in undertaking a detailed warm up, you still don't see how you're going to fit one into the time allocated to you in your class, workshop or rehearsal. If this is the case, then you'll need to work with exercises that cover a number of objectives at once. The following example is a speedier warm up that won't compromise your warm up objectives too much.

Warming up when 'time is of the essence'

- **Skin Stretch.**
  - Ask your actors to space out around the room so they can move freely. Coach them to ground, centre and align their bodies (refer to *Release Exercises*). It's best if they work with their eyes closed at the start of this exercise although if anybody in the group is prone to dizziness then ask them to keep their eyes open throughout.
  - Ask the group to imagine wearing a 'second skin', like an imaginary wetsuit that's a little too tight. It might feel a bit uncomfortable, which is fine (you should be able to see their bodies tense).
  - Now get them to start stretching the skin around their fingers and hands in any way they like in order to find some space. You'll need to give them a little bit of time for exploration. Then, ask them to start stretching the skin around their lower arms, followed by the upper arms, the shoulders, the upper chest, the rib cage, the abdominal area and the pelvis. Keep reminding them to focus on the objective of 'stretching the skin' and, again, give them a little bit of time to explore each body area before you move onto the next. When you get to the shoulders ask them to let go of their breath, which they've probably been holding because of the tension. Keep reminding them, through the remainder of the exercise, to breathe.
  - Now ask them to start stretching the skin around the toes, the feet (allowing them to move their feet) the ankles, the lower leg, the upper leg, the buttocks, up the spine, the neck, the jaw, the lips, the cheeks, the skin around the nose, the skin around the eyes, the forehead and the scalp. Again, don't forget to give them a little bit of time to explore each body area before you move onto the next, and keep asking them

to breathe. If necessary, add in some extra instructions for the neck and jaw to ensure that there aren't any full head rolls or jaw swings that work against natural movement. It's fine for them to open their eyes when they start stretching the skin around the facial area.

- When you've covered the body (front and back), ask them to get annoyed with this 'second skin' and stretch everything at once. Allow them some time to go a little bit mad, physically. Then, ask them to rip the imaginary skin off, being very specific ('between fingers', 'behind knees', 'at the back of the neck', etc). When they've finished, coach them to come back to a grounded, centred and aligned position with their eyes closed.

- They should now focus in on the tingly sensation as their new skin hits the air for the very first time. Coach them to feel their skin breathing, almost as if their breath is flowing in through all the skin pores and out again. Start them releasing each breath on an fffff sound, deepening and lengthening them as they work.

- **Focus Points.** Ask them to open their eyes and focus on a point just under the horizon, letting the breath 'drop in' to their body, quickly and easily, and releasing on the fffff sound to their point. Move on to sssss, vvvvv, zzzzz when you feel they are working from a low muscle base.

- **Focus Walks.** Then, ask them to walk to the point they've been focusing on (watching out, with their peripheral vision, for other people moving in the room). Ask them to turn, find a new point and walk to that. Coach them to find the most direct route there. After a few different walks, ask them to turn, find a new point, breathe in and release fffff all the way to their point. Repeat on sssss, vvvvv and zzzzz. Finally, ask them to work with 'blowing through the lips', ensuring that the sound is carried right through to the end of the phrase/walk.

Although this has taken up quite a bit of space on the page to explain, it will cover less time than you think, and just look at what you've already achieved: physical release, breath release, breath support and a facial warm up! Now for some resonance work:

- **Patting.** Ask your actors to gently pat their face and scalp so they become a little bit tingly. Now get them to pat all over their bodies. They can ask a partner to pat down their back for them. Finally, ask them to pat across their chest whilst vocalising an open vowel sound to wake up the powerful chest resonator.

- **Humming.** Get them to place their lips gently together, drop the back of the tongue and hum on any pitch (whatever comes to them naturally). They should try and think the sound forward onto their lips, concentrating on building the vibration there.

- **Hum on the Run.** Ask them to take that hum for a heavy jog around the room. Coach them to use the whole of their feet (they shouldn't be running on their toes) and ask them to drop their arms. Let them bounce around with the sound for a few minutes. Ask them to stop and flop over from the waist so that their breath centres before coming up through a spinal roll to standing. Make sure they reconnect to their breath with an fffff sound before trying the hum again. They should feel the sound is much easier to produce as the vibration has automatically bounced forward.

- **Placing the Hum.** Repeat the humming exercise on the lips and then move on to the cheekbones, bridge of the nose, temples, top of the head and the chest. Ask them to place their hands on each of these points in turn so that they can really think (and feel) the vibrations coming off their body. Make sure their spines stay aligned and that their hands come up to meet their faces rather than their faces sinking down to meet their hands.

- **Imaginary Writing.** Now get them to draw their names in the air, slowly, and hum. The pitch of their voice should follow the movement of their finger, which means they should be moving all over their range. Once they've finished, get them to rub their writing out with their hand(s), again using the humming sound.

If you still have time after all this then add some articulation exercises to finish. Of course the group have already done some lip work as part of the skin stretch but you'll still need a couple of exercises for the tongue and soft palate before you finish.

CHAPTER 2

SOUND

From our very beginnings, we have an emotional relationship with sound. Our first cries for food, warmth, sleep and comfort are open vowel sounds, shaped by the lips and tongue. Listen to very small babies and there are quite definite changes in their cries, depending on their needs or wants.

Soon we start to form consonant sounds by bringing the lips and tongue into contact with either each other or fixed parts within the mouth such as the gum ridge above the upper front teeth or the hard palate on the roof of the mouth. We spend a great deal of time practising, perfecting and enjoying these sounds over and over again. Part of this enjoyment is through listening to the sound we're making and then wanting to re-create it; the other part is gained through the actual physical act itself. Creating and relishing individual sounds is a satisfying and sensual experience for us.

Eventually we start to open up our ears to the sounds around us and mimic what we hear. When these unrelated sounds start to join up into words, we create meaning as well as emotion for the first time. The last stage is the realisation of the effect these sounds and words have on others around us, which inspires us to find new ways of expressing ourselves. It's an exciting journey.

It is in these early years that we truly understand the essence and interplay of individual sounds; however, as we develop into adulthood, and spend vast amounts of our time focusing on the written page in order to read and write, we lose some of this unconscious knowledge. Having said that, education in many societies has started to open out and include more opportunities for spoken communication in mainstream curriculum; however it is still in its infancy compared to the opportunities provided for written communication. We focus on the nuts and bolts of writing but not, necessarily, on the nuts and bolts of speaking aloud.

It is important for actors to take a journey back to their early experiences in sound so that, ultimately, they can re-discover and relish the power of words. Writers often link what they are describing with the sounds of the words with which they choose to describe it. Of course it is the words themselves that carry the meaning and not the separate sounds, but a writer's choice of sounds can provide us with all sorts of information, including the inner workings of character. If an actor can't access these sounds then the energy and drive of a character's speech may become blocked.

You will need to understand the effect, energy and interplay of individual sounds in order to re-create this experience for your actors: so let's get a bit more technical.

Consonants

Vowels release emotional energy, whilst consonants create definition and meaning. This is partially because vowels are formed by the lips and the tongue shaping the breath stream (modifying the space within the mouth), whilst consonants are formed by the lips and the tongue coming into contact with either each other or another speech organ (obstructing or narrowing the space within the mouth).

It is much easier to feel how consonants are formed in the mouth than vowels and it can be a useful exercise for actors to describe how different consonants are placed or created. For example, in Standard British Speech, or Received Pronunciation, / t / is created by the tip of the tongue coming into contact with the gum ridge above and behind the upper front teeth. Be aware that the positioning may change depending on accent: for example, in an Indian English accent, / t / is created by the tongue tip curling upwards and backwards towards the roof of the mouth. It is extremely important that you don't get hung up on what you believe is or isn't correct: there are only different accents. You may require an actor to work on a particular accent for a particular character at a later stage but the work, for now, is about playing with sound.

The second way in which consonants can be classified is by their *voicing*: some consonants are *voiceless* and others are *voiced*. *Voiceless* consonants occur when the vocal chords or folds are apart, whilst on *voiced* consonants the vocal chords or folds come together and vibrate so that the breath is vocalised. Many consonants have their *voiceless* and *voiced* equivalents, for example, p/b, t/d, s/z and f/v. This means that, in Standard British Speech or Received Pronunciation, / t / and / d / are created in exactly the same way in the mouth (tip of tongue coming into contact with the gum ridge), however one is voiceless and the other is voiced. You can get your actors to check on this by putting a finger on their voice boxes and trying each sound. If their finger feels a buzzing sensation then the sound is voiced, if there is nothing there, then it is voiceless.

The third way in which consonants can be classified is by the way in which they release the sound.

- *Plosives*

Plosives occur when the passage of air is totally blocked by two speech organs coming together, for example, the lips in the case of / p / and / b /, the tongue and gum ridge in the case of / t / and / d /, and, in the case of / k / and / g / the back of the tongue and the soft palate. Breath pressure increases behind the point of contact and a mini explosion (or plosion) is heard as the organs part.

- *Affricates*

Affricate consonants occur when two speech organs make contact but there is a gradual release, creating friction in the sound: for example, the initial consonants in 'child' and 'judge'.

- *Fricatives*

Fricative consonants occur when two speech organs are held close together, narrowing the air passage so that friction is created in the sound: eg / f /, / v /, / s /, / z /, / h /, the initial consonants in 'thin', 'those', 'shop', and the middle consonant in 'measure'.

- *Nasals*

Nasal consonants occur when the passage of air is completely blocked by the contact of two speech organs so that the air and sound have to travel out through the nose, creating a nasal sound. There are only three sounds in English where this occurs: / m /, / n / and / ng /.

- *Laterals*

Lateral consonants occur when the middle of the outgoing air passage is blocked by raising the tongue to contact the gum ridge, the sides remain lowered so the air escapes sideways or laterally. This happens on two sounds in Standard British Speech or Received Pronunciation: the / l / found at the start of the word 'little' and the / l / found at the end of the word 'little'. The former is called clear l, and, the latter, dark l, where the back of the tongue is raised.

- *Semi-vowels*

Semi-vowels begin in a vowel position but because this position can't be sustained they're classified as consonants, for example, / w /, / r /, / y /.

Plosive consonants are also known as *stops* because the sound is stopped by the speech organs: *affricate, fricative, nasal, lateral* and *semi-vowel* consonants are also known as *continuants* because the sound can be sustained or continued on.

Writers will use plosive consonants to create a particular effect, perhaps to slow the pace of delivery and/or sharpen the effect of the character's speech. Other combinations of consonants might help speech to flow, combining with vowels to create an emotionally charged lyricism.

Take a look at this speech by Lady Macbeth and her use of plosive stops, which sharpen the horrifying image she presents to her husband.

> I have given suck, and know
> How tender 'tis to love the babe that milks me:
> I would, while it was smiling in my face,
> Have **p**luck'**d** my ni**pp**le from his **b**oneless **g**ums,
> And dash'**d** the **b**rains ou**t**, had I so sworn
> As you have done to this.   (1)

In the second half of this excerpt, the hard plosive consonant sounds (both voiceless and voiced) create a brutal effect: the / p / in 'pluck'd' and 'nipple'; the / b / of 'boneless' and 'brains'; the / g / of 'gums'; the final / t / of 'pluck'd', 'dash'd' and 'out' (remember it is the sound not the spelling we are focusing on and although 'pluck'd' and 'dash'd' are spelt with / d /, the sound is actually / t /). The actor who bites into these sounds and explores them fully will find greater relish in the image, in keeping with Lady Macbeth's character, as well as communicating the full horror of it for Macbeth and the audience.

Dorimant in *The Man of Mode* by George Etheredge also uses the plosive / p / but in an entirely different way, evoking the hard, thrusting nature of sexual encounter with 'pluck', 'passion' and 'panting'.

> I had made her *p*luck off this mask and show the *p*assion that lies *p*anting under.   (2)

A more lyrical effect is created by Antonio in this extract from *The Changeling* by Thomas Middleton and William Rowley.

> I bring nought but Love
> And his *s*oft-wounding *sh*afts to *s*trike you with   (3)

The delicate use of voiceless consonant friction in 'soft', 'shafts' and strike' helps Antonio create a sensual image to woo Isabella. The actor who explores the gentle hiss of these sounds will bring to life the full extent of Antonio's feeling.

All of these examples can be described by the terms *alliteration* (a repetition of the same consonant at the beginning of a series of words), *consonance* (a repetition of the same consonant in the middle or at the end of a series of words) and *onomatopoeia* (when a word makes a sound similar to its meaning).

A word of warning, however: the actor who over-uses individual sounds at the expense of meaning will destroy the natural speech rhythm of the character. The audience will only hear the sound and not the effect it is intending to create or the thought inherent in the line. Therefore, working with sound must be carefully balanced with the character's thought process and emotional state.

Vowels

As we have already learnt, vowel sounds are free flowing and unimpeded in their passage through the mouth; however, they can also be different lengths, depending on how they are shaped in the mouth, and, depending on the other sounds surrounding them. Vowel length is of particular importance to the actor because writers often use it to create emotional depth, flow and lyricism.

Monophthongs (or pure vowel sounds) are made when the tongue, lips and lower jaw take up the one position to shape the vocalised breath, remaining in that position for the duration of the sound. Monophthongs can be long or short: in Standard British Speech or Received Pronunciation, long pure vowels can be found in the words 'mark', 'feed', 'tall', 'blue' and 'bird'; whilst short ones can be found in the words 'cat', 'get', 'hit', 'not', 'but', 'cook' and the final neutral sound in 'water'. If you try them aloud you'll be able to feel and hear the difference.

Diphthongs are made when the tongue, lips and lower jaw start in one position and glide immediately *towards* the position of another vowel sound. In Standard British Speech or Received Pronunciation these are the sounds in 'might', 'gate', 'note', 'how', 'boy', 'fear', 'there', 'tour' and 'roar'. If you try them aloud you'll be able to feel and hear the glide within them.

Vowels can be lengthened or shortened further depending on the surrounding consonants. If a vowel sound is followed by a voiceless plosive consonant then it will be shorter than if it is followed by a voiced continuant consonant, for example, try the difference aloud between 'heart' and 'harm'. Both use words with the same / ah / monophthong, in Standard British Speech or Received Pronunciation, but the final consonant alters its length.

Likewise a vowel sound may be longer if it is the final sound in a word, for example, 'far', although this really depends on where the word is placed within a phrase as the next sound in the following word may limit its length or the rhythm of the line may place it in an unstressed position, again altering its duration.

In Seamus Heaney's *The Burial at Thebes,* which re-tells the story of Antigone, the blind seer Tiresias tries to deliver some brutal advice to King Creon. He uses strong images to bring home his point and persuade Creon to change his decision about Antigone's death sentence.

> I know things once I sit in that stone chair
> And the birds begin to skirl above my head.
> But never in all my years have I heard the likes
> Of the screams and screeches that I heard this day.
> There was no meaning to them. I knew by the whirl of wings
> And the rips and spits of blood the birds were mad.　　(4)

The repetition of sounds (both vowel and consonant) in 'screams' and 'screeches' creates a chilling effect, and, the long pure vowel / ee / gives weight and emphasis to the sound and image (or sound image). In the final line the short vowel in 'rips' and 'spits' effectively creates the image of short, sharp, violent movement and provides the actor with an opportunity to fully create an image of mad birds in order to evoke a response from Creon.

Further on in the text, Creon accuses Tiresias of expecting a bribe, part of Tiresias' response is:

> Then tell me, when the lamentation starts,
> When woman-wail and man-howl rake your walls,
> Tell me I've been bribed.　　(5)

The long diphthongs in 'wail' and 'howl', if fully explored, give us a small insight into the actual sound lamentation or the keening that is about to take place.

These examples can be described by the terms *assonance* (a repetition of the same vowel in a series of words) and *onomatopoeia* (when a word makes a sound similar to its meaning).

Many classical writers use the long diphthong 'O' at the start of a line in order to convey the character's emotional response to a situation or to allow the character an emotional moment prior to intellectualising a situation. One of the most famous examples (and one that everybody seems to explore at some point in their training) is at the start of the Chorus speech in Shakespeare's *Henry V.*

> O for a muse of fire, that would ascend
> The brightest heaven of invention,   (6)

I have heard actors shy away from using the full weight of an 'O' sound because it makes them feel uncomfortable and they often pass over it quickly or de-voice on a breathy whisper, hoping that nobody will notice. A useful exercise is to take the 'O' away from its context in order to explore a series of emotional moments for the character in isolation from the text. It is important to use the diphthong glide fully in order to express the range of emotions that might be within it. Putting it back into context, clarifying the exact emotional reason for the sound and using it as a launch pad into the rhythmic thought, will strengthen the resolve of the whole speech.

After focusing on an individual vowel sound and exploring its emotional weight, always help actors to find a way back into the context of the word, thought and world of the play so that its use is balanced within the whole.

Playing with Sound (some ideas)

These exercises seem simplistic but they will help your actors to re-discover and relish sound in ways they may not have thought about since they were children. In addition, these exercises will act as a powerful wake-up call to the speech organs so that the later work on words will be underpinned and supported by the sounds within them, ultimately creating a much more powerful response to the text.

Because these exercises do seem basic, the way in which they need to be introduced to actors should be carefully planned. There will be a different way of implementing this work with amateur actors and actors-in-training as opposed to a trained professional acting company. For the latter, I would strongly suggest undertaking one or two of these exercises at the end of a warm-up, prior to working on the text, whereas, amateurs and students may need a more comprehensive focus during classes and/or rehearsals.

- **Creating Sound.** Ask your actors to lie on the floor in semi-supine (se Chapter 1 for details) with their eyes closed. Give them time and space to release into the floor and regulate their breathing. Provide them with a series of directions which will help them to explore the way in which human beings learn, create and enjoy sound, for example: sighing out, like a contented baby; laughing, like a tickled baby; speaking short vowels, then plosive consonants, followed by nasal consonants, like a baby experimenting with their first sounds. Ask them to try joining some of these sounds together and, finally, invite them to speak their first word (the choice should be theirs). Keep coaching them to relish the muscularity of the sounds they are creating.

- **Defining Sound.** Create a list of consonant sounds and ask your actors to work in pairs so they can test out and describe for each other exactly how each one is formed in the mouth. It's useful if actors with different accents work together so that they can discover any differences in placement. Swap the pairs around so they can compare their discoveries.

- **The Plosive Bite.** Create a list of plosive sounds (/ p /, / b /, / t /, / d /, / k /, / g /) and ask your actors to speak through all six, exploring the bite and (ex)plosive release of each one. Gradually get them to increase the pace of the list (without necessarily increasing in volume). Finally, place your actors in groups so that they can play with different rhythmic variations and create a sound poem, chant or rap. Allow them to add movement so that the sound rhythm is reinforced with a physical rhythm.

- **The Sound Song.** Ask one actor to start the song by creating a sound or a rhythmic sequence of sounds, either on a sung or spoken note. Ask another to join in with a different sound or rhythmic sequence of sounds to compliment the first singer or speaker. Gradually allow the rest of the group to join in, one by one. Allow them to find a natural finishing point by themselves.

- **The Sound Orchestra.** Set up your actors in rows with one person at the front as 'conductor'. The conductor then physically 'conducts' and the group must react with sound in accordance with his or her movement. The 'orchestra' might, naturally, choose to work only with long, open vowel sounds. If this is the case then allocate different sounds to different actors so that there is a balance between short vowel sounds, long vowel sounds, plosive consonants and continuant consonants.

- **The Sound Improv.** Create a simple scene topic, for example, a child's birthday party, or, create a scene around the characters of the play you are rehearsing. Allow the actors to improvise the scene but, instead of using words, they may only repeat a sound which you have allocated them, for example, the consonant / t /. Think carefully about how you allocate these sounds. For example, if a character in your play (and the improvised scene) is playing an aggressive objective then allocate a harder plosive sound, which will allow the actor to balance sound with emotion and meaning much more fully. As well as providing opportunities for playing with sound and warming up the speech organs, this exercise may help your actors to discover new layers to their work with the words of the text.

- **Isolating Sound.** Choose a short speech from a classical text, preferably one that marries sound with meaning (like the examples given in this chapter). Ask your actors to speak only the vowel sounds, isolating them away from the actual words and exploring their shape, length and weight. Then, ask them to speak the words of the text and forget about the previous exercise: they may find that the text will hold more emotional weight for them now. Repeat the exercise but with the consonant sounds so that the words are fully defined by the sounds within them.

- **The Emotional 'O'.** Choose a short speech from a classical text where the character uses an isolated 'O' to express an emotion, for example, the prologue speech by the Chorus in Shakespeare's *Henry V* that starts: *'O for a muse of fire...'* Create a list of different emotions for that 'O' and ask your actors to explore each one on the sound, either in isolation, in pairs or as a group. Make sure they stay on their feet, which will hopefully prevent them from falling into the trap of analysing the work rather than just 'doing' it. Then allow them to place the 'O' back into its original context and see if it holds any more weight or meaning for them. Give them an opportunity to share their thoughts.

- **Contextualising Sound.** Choose a nursery rhyme or short, simple piece of verse that uses sound to create a particular effect. I like *Fee Fie Foh Fum** from *Jack in the Beanstalk*, where the giant bites into sound in order to verbalise his threat. Teach the rhyme to your actors, line by line: it may not be familiar to speakers from a non-English background. Ask them to try it aloud a few times with a partner. Now ask the pairs to try it again but with the objective 'to threaten'. Their natural reaction will be to increase the volume, which will blur the specifics of meaning and simply create an emotional wash of sound. Ask them to speak the text quietly (without whispering it or devoicing it), relishing the sounds to create the threat. The effect will be so much more powerful.

---

*   *Fee Fie Foh Fum*
     I smell the blood of an English man
     Be he alive or be he dead
     I'll grind his bones to make my bread.

CHAPTER 3

WORD

So we've talked about how a focus on individual sounds and their length can underscore meaning, emotion and intention. Yet, of course, it is the words themselves that will define these elements within the text much more specifically.

Imagery
Imagery is the term used for descriptive words that appeal to our senses (sight, touch, taste, smell and hearing). The imagery within a text will help the audience to see a visual image with their mind's eye, hear a noise in their head, or imagine the feel, taste or smell of something. The more powerful the image, the more powerful the experience for the audience.

In 'Sonnet 130' Shakespeare appeals directly to our senses through the imagery, asking us to consider how his mistress looks, how she smells and how she sounds.

> My mistress' eyes are nothing like the sun;
> Coral is far more red than her lips' red

and

> And in some perfumes is there more delight
> Than in the breath that from my mistress reeks.

and

> I love to hear her speak, yet well I know
> That music has a far more pleasing sound.　　(7)

These images build a picture for us of a real woman whom Shakespeare loves and not the idealised poetic version of womanhood that many of Shakespeare's contemporaries created through their verse.

However, imagery also provides us with important clues about character. Almost every word that a character speaks will help to reveal his or her inner feelings, thoughts, motivations and preoccupations. In Ben Jonson's *Volpone*, the language throughout the play highlights a pre-occupation with animal-like greed and lust within the human race. Not only are some of the characters named for some not-very-nice animals in Italian (Volpone – the fox; Mosca – the fly; Voltore – the vulture; Corbaccio – the crow; and Corvino – the raven) but their speech is littered with animal imagery which emphasises their base desires and provides motive for their deeds. It is not just the absurdity within the story that creates the comedy but also the silliness within this imagery: we laugh at the characters and, ultimately, our own greed, lust and desire in the process.

A writer may also use individual words to reveal the background and status of a character. For example, Sir Fopling, in George Etheredge's *The Man of Mode*, uses specific words to try and show off his good breeding, including some in French; however, he mispronounces many of them and uses others in the wrong context, which not only creates humour but actually diminishes his worth.

In both these examples, understanding and relishing the language will help to reveal character and drive the humour and action through the play.

Rhetorical Devices
Rhetorical devices categorise the way in which a writer uses words. The most useful terms when working with the voice on classical play texts are: simile, metaphor, pun, personification, antithesis and repetition.

Similes and Metaphors
Similes and metaphors describe comparison: a simile likens one thing to another, more often than not using the words 'like' or 'as', whilst, a metaphor turns one thing into something else completely. Shakespeare uses both similes and metaphors to great effect.

In *The Tempest* Antonio uses the simile:

> They'll take suggestion as a cat laps milk;   (8)

And in *Othello*, Iago uses the metaphor:

> O beware, my lord, of jealousy!
> It is the green-eyed monster, which doth mock
> The meat it feeds on.   (9)

Each comparison uses a vivid visual image in order to strengthen the meaning and emphasise the point. If an actor pulls away from the image without vocally releasing its full intention then the meaning will be diminished and the point weakened. This means setting up exercises where actors can find the balance between breath, sound and meaning to bring the image to life.

Puns

A pun is created when a phrase or line exploits the confusion between two different meanings within a word, often humorously. For example, the very title of *The Importance of Being Earnest* by Oscar Wilde is a pun. 'Being Earnest' not only refers to the Victorian idea of being devoted to duty and working hard but also Cecily's and Gwendolen's obsession with marrying a man named Ernest, and, therefore, with Jack and Algernon's obsession with being called Ernest so that they may lay claim to these ladies' hearts. Indeed, Jack and Algernon are earnest about being Ernest.

The vocal delivery of a pun needs to be exercised with subtlety and care so that the point isn't over-played. We've all heard jokes whereby the teller ruins the telling by playing the humour too hard. A pun might not necessarily be humorous but the same concept operates in serious contexts as well. So the word itself needs to be lifted out gently and given a tiny bit of extra emphasis to indicate for the audience that there may be more to this than originally meets the eye (or ear). Technically, this translates into a light lift in pitch, a tiny lengthening of sound and a dash of extra breath force on the word, as well as a mental focus on the pun itself.

Personification

Personification is when inanimate objects or concepts are endowed with human qualities: Time and Death are two of the most common personifications, perhaps because of the emotional reaction they evoke. Shakespeare's sonnets are littered with the personification of Time, which are often capitalised like that of somebody's name. In 'Sonnet 19', Time is challenged to do its worst (ie move on forward to old age) as the speaker knows he will remain young through his writing, which will live on long after he is dead.

> Yet do thy worst, old Time; despite thy wrong,
> My love shall in my verse ever live young.   (10)

There is a particularly potent personification of Death in Shakespeare's *King John*, revealed by the distraught Constance who longs to feel Death's embrace after the loss and imprisonment of her son.

> Death! death, O amiable, lovely death!
> Thou odoriferous stench! sound rottenness!
> Arise forth from the couch of lasting night,
> Thou hate and terror to prosperity,
> And I will kiss thy detestable bones
> And put my eyeballs in thy vaulty brows,
> And ring these fingers with thy household worms,
> And stop this gap of breath with fulsome dust,
> And be a carrion monster like thyself:
> Come, grin on me, and I will think thou smil'st,
> And buss thee as thy wife. Misery's love,
> O, come to me.   (11)

Personification requires the actor to endow the object or concept with human characteristics by bringing to life the imagery that has been used to describe it. Constance's words not only describe the physical character of Death but also her own emotional relationship towards him: 'odiferous stench', 'sound rottenness', 'detestable bones', 'vaulty brows', 'household worms', 'fulsome dust', 'carrion monster', 'misery's love'. Each image needs to be specifically realised by the actor through a combination of breath, sound and meaning.

Antithesis

Antithesis is all about the juxtaposition of ideas, set against each other through the arrangement of contrasting words. Shakespeare's Romeo says to his friend Benvolio:

> Here's much to do with hate, but more with love.
> Why then, O brawling love, O loving hate,
> O anything of nothing first create!
> O heavy lightness, serious vanity,
> Misshapen chaos of well-seeming forms!
> Feather of lead, bright smoke, cold fire, sick health,
> Still-waking sleep that is not what it is!
> This love feel I that feel no love in this.
> Dost thou not laugh?   (12)

Romeo is learning that love and hate are often bound up together (love is not always wonderful and sometimes causes misery) and he finds himself loving where he should be hating (by rights he should hate Juliet because she is a Capulet) and quarrelling with those he should be loving. He uses contrasting imagery to communicate this confusion, for example, 'heavy lightness', 'feather of lead', 'bright smoke', 'cold fire', 'sick health', 'still-waking sleep'.

It is important that the actor finds the vocal contrast, the light and shade, in each contrasting image so that the weight of Romeo's inner turmoil can be heard and, ultimately, felt by the audience. However, it should be a subtle use of contrast so that the flow of his thoughts and the context of the speech are maintained.

Repetition

The repetition of a word in a phrase, line or speech is an important device when a character wants to emphasise a point. In Seamus Heaney's *Burial at Thebes,* when Antigone knows she is about to be walled up in a cave and left to die, the repetition of the word 'stone' reiterates the cold, hard reality of her fate.

> Stone of my wedding chamber, stone of my tomb,
> Stone of my prison roof and prison floor

Behind you and beyond you stand the dead.   (13)

Actors often worry that the repetition will come across as, well, repeti-
tive (in other words, boring) and so they pass over the words quickly
and lightly. However, the writer has used these words as a device for the
character and they just can't be ignored. Not only that, but in Heaney's
example, 'stone' has been placed in a position of rhythmic strength at
the forefront of three phrases so if the words are (vocally) ignored then
the overall sense will be lost.

Playing with Words (some ideas)

Again, like the exercises listed in the previous chapter, some of these
exercises are better applied to student actors and untrained actors, as
opposed to professional actors. I've used these exercises in all contexts;
however, it really does depend on the type of company you are working
with and whether they are open to playing with language in this way.
Test the water and tread carefully. These exercises might seem simple
but they have very big pay-offs in rehearsal.

- **Discovering Words**
  - Ask your actors to bring their favourite word, and the reason why they
    like it, to the next class, workshop or rehearsal. They shouldn't bring
    more than one word (which will really get them thinking) and need
    to know that they won't be 'censored' (so that they can include swear-
    ing). Their reason for liking a word could be related to the sound, the
    meaning or the way in which the word affects others when it's spoken
    aloud. It's important that this exercise is set as homework (rather than
    discussed on the spot) so that they'll have the time and space to explore
    different options and be able to really listen to the ways in which words
    are used in the world around them.
  - The exercise itself is relatively simple – they only need to share their
    word, and their reason for liking it, with the group. It's the actual
    thinking work away from the session that's important.
  - If you're rehearsing a play, a variation on (or addition to) this exercise,
    would be to ask your actors for a 'favourite' word from within the play
    text.

- **Physicalising Words**
  - Ask your actors to create a movement for their 'favourite word', which they will be able to physicalise at the same time the word is spoken. The movement should inhabit the essence of the word and mirror the energy of the sound, ie short, sharp sounds within the word may need a short, sharp movement, and, multiple syllables may need a series of movements. There is no need for them to use the literal meaning of the word within the movement although they may wish to do so.
  - Ask your actors to repeat the word and movement a number of times so that they can clarify, define and strengthen their execution of both elements.
  - Combine your actors in groups of four to five and ask them to 'teach' the other people in the group their word and movement as precisely and meticulously as they can.*
  - Now ask each group to create a poem by putting their words all together. They will need to decide on how many voices will be used at any one time and how many repetitions will be needed of a particular word to create the effect they desire. It's always interesting to explore two versions, one with movement and one without, so that the quality of the action is retained in the word. The movement often helps actors find an appropriate vocal dynamic.
  - Again, a variation or addition to this exercise, is working with individual words from the text that you're using in rehearsal.

- **Clarifying Imagery**
  - Choose a text (perhaps a piece of verse so that emotion and meaning is self-contained within a shorter space of time) and create a word list of all the visual imagery.
  - Ask your actors to lie on the floor in semi-supine (see Chapter 1 for details) with their eyes closed. Give them time and space to release into the floor and regulate their breathing.

---

* I love asking actors to 'teach' one another: it's a useful (and practical) way of getting them to really take something on board as they'll need to have sufficient clarity and vision about an exercise in order to impart it to another person. Sometimes the very act of 'teaching' will help actors gain that extra bit of clarity that previously eluded them.

THREE: WORD

— Feed them the words, one by one, allowing them time and space to breathe in the visual picture and release the word as they see it. Encourage them to try each word a number of times so that the visual picture is strengthened in the spoken word.

— If possible (within the framework of the verse you have chosen) repeat this exercise with sound imagery, taste imagery, touch imagery and smell imagery. Your actors will need to breathe in and hear the sound before they release the word, breathe in and taste the image before they release the word, breathe in and feel the image before they release the word, and, breathe in and smell the image before they release the word. The combination of breath connection and mental connection will help to strengthen the vocalisation of the image.

— Now allow your actors to slowly come to their feet (releasing and breathing in semi-supine may leave them light-headed and dizzy so take things slowly) and provide them with the list of words on a sheet of paper. You may wish to build in 'Physicalising Words' at this point (the previous exercise in this chapter); otherwise ask them to discuss, in groups of about three to four people, what they think the text may be about, based on their understanding of the word list. This will help them to share their visual pictures and clarify their understanding of the process they've just been through. Allow each group to share their thoughts with the whole group when they're ready.

— Provide them with a full copy of the verse and ask them to read it to themselves in their head*, then ask them to mouth it without sound† and then to vocalise it quietly (without whispering or devoicing).‡

---

*   There are two ways in which we read in our heads: one, to make sense of the meaning, which means scanning it quickly, and, two, as though the text is being read aloud internally, which means taking it slowly and with care. Ask your actors to try both ways.

†   Speaking is a physical activity and so our muscles need to know exactly what steps they will need to take (in the same way our bodies need to know the steps of a dance). Silently mouthing a text will help the speech organs through this process. Encourage your actors to really use their lips and tongue and feel the length and weight of the words in their mouth.

‡   Your actors will need to listen to what they're doing with the words on their first vocalisation of the text and this can be difficult if there is a room full of people doing exactly the same thing. A good way of helping them through this is to ask that they cup one hand a couple of centimetres away from their ear and cup the other hand a couple of centimetres away from their mouth. In this way they'll be able to focus in on what they're saying. Encourage them to actually vocalise: they may fall into a whisper or a breathy devoice on the first reading due to a lack of confidence, which will prevent them from dealing with the images specifically.

– Return them to their groups and ask one person to read the verse aloud to their partners. The speaker must work to bring each of the images to life within its context so that the listeners can visualise the pictures in their heads. Communicating to an audience and creating a context for the imagery will change the whole dynamic. Ask the listeners to close their eyes and explain that, if they lose the image or picture, they must ask the speaker to stop and start the text again. It's important that they don't discuss it at all or try to coach the speaker in any way: the word 'stop' is enough. This process may take time. Allow all of the group members a turn as 'speaker'. Sometimes speakers may increase their volume when asked to start the text again, subconsciously thinking that this will make the images easier to understand. You will need to coach them through this if you feel the noise in the room is beginning to grow. If it happens, ask them to work quietly (not on a whisper though) so that they are forced to rely on making the imagery specific rather than just louder.
– Finally, finish with a whole group discussion about which of the images appealed to them/affected them the most.

CHAPTER 4

RHYTHM

Rhythm is a part of our core: our hearts beat in a rhythm, we breathe in a rhythm, we eat in a rhythm and we walk in a rhythm. Each of us has a unique, internal rhythmic energy, which, in turn, creates our very own speech rhythm. This rhythm is then adjusted, depending on how we group, connect and arrange words for the meaning that we want to communicate and the context in which we find ourselves.

Therefore the grouping, connection and arrangement of words in dramatic text defines the individual speech rhythm of a character, whether in a sentence or phrase in prose drama or a line in verse drama. Understanding how this works will provide your actors with further clues about a character's inner thoughts, motivations and machinations.

Prose Rhythm

Words are grouped together into sentences or phrases in dramatic prose, which create particular rhythms. An understanding of how this works in a piece of text will help actors re-create the specific speech rhythm of a character speaking in prose.

Prose rhythm is formed by the construction and length of the sentence or phrase; by pauses which interrupt the flow of sound; and, in the arrangement of weak and strong stresses.

Sentences and Phrases

A sentence is usually defined as a grammatically complete group of words (often containing a subject, verb and object) beginning with a capital letter and ending with a full stop, exclamation point or question mark. However, a sentence could be made up of a number of sub-units or phrases. A phrase is usually defined as a group of words linked together by sense; otherwise called a *sense-group*. Sense-groups often introduce a fresh idea and may or may not be marked by punctuation.

The particular length of a phrase or sentence will create a particular rhythmic energy and, for the character, a particular speech energy. A writer may use short, simple phrases or sentences to suggest immediacy and directness or long complicated sentences to strengthen evaluation or reflection.

Oscar Wilde's dramatic prose has a rhythmic energy all of its own. He often uses long sentences, made up of smaller sense-groups, to create a light flippant quality, which drives the characters' speech forward. Slowing it down is almost impossible and would work against the rhythm of the wit. Take, for example, this speech from Mrs Allonby in *A Woman of No Importance*. Speak it aloud and you'll feel (and hear) the natural rhythmic drive.

> Oh, the Ideal Man should talk to us as if we were goddesses, and treat us as if we were children. He should refuse all our serious requests, and gratify every one of our whims. He should encourage us to have caprices, and forbid us to have missions. He should always say much more than he means, and always mean much move than he says.   (14)

How phrases and sentences are linked together will also drive the overall rhythmic energy of the prose. For example, a short phrase or sentence that comes after a series of longer ones draws attention to itself. Here, we find Mrs Arbuthnot appealing to Lord Illingworth in *A Woman of No Importance*. Notice the strength and forcefulness of 'Forget it' after a series of long emotional sentences. This provides us with information about Mrs Arbuthnot's emotional resolve.

> George, don't take my son away from me. I have had twenty years of sorrow, and I have only had one thing to love me, only one thing to love. You have had a life of joy, and pleasure and success. You have been quite happy, you have never thought of us. There was no reason, according to your views of life, why you should have remembered us at all. Your meeting was a mere

accident, a horrible accident. Forget it. Don't come now, and rob
me of…of all I have in the whole world.   (15)

Pauses

Pauses interrupt the flow of sound, whether it is a *terminal pause* at
the end of a sentence or a very brief *sense pause* to define or set up a
sense-group. The length and frequency of pauses are an important part
of prose rhythm.

Harold Pinter uses pauses in his plays for particular rhythm effect,
helping to establish the emotional inner life of his characters. In this
example from *Betrayal*, Jerry is talking to Emma, with whom he is
having a long-term affair. The written punctuation is married to the
oral punctuation, meaning that the text has been broken up into small
sense-groups marked by pauses. This helps to create a very natural
speech rhythm yet also illustrates perfectly Jerry's sense of discomfort
about how the relationship has changed over time.

> You see, in the past…we were inventive, we were determined,
> it was…it seemed impossible to meet…impossible…and yet
> we did.   (16)

Stress

Stress is created when a particular word or syllable is given prominence,
usually through a combination of extra breath force, a change in pitch
and a lengthening in sound.

Every word of more than one syllable has its own stress. For example,
a strong stress sits on the first syllable of '*dollop* and the second syllable
is weakened: in the word *in'tensity*, the strong stress sits on the second
syllable. In Standard British Speech or Received Pronunciation some
words can even change meaning according to word stress, for example,
'*subject/sub'ject*.

When words are grouped together, word stress can change under the
influence of sentence stress. Sentence stress depends on meaning and
context; the more important the word, the stronger is its stress. For
example: *He en'joyed his 'holiday but was 'glad to be 'back 'home.*

Here you can see that the pattern of weak and strong stresses is irregular because the positioning of strong stresses relies on the meaning

and context inherent within the sentence. The actual rhythm is created by the amount of variation between strong and weak syllables. Lots of strong syllables can create a heavier, stronger or sharper rhythm, naturally slowing speech down.

Lady Windemere's appeal to Lord Darlington in *Lady Windermere's Fan* by Oscar Wilde is strengthened by the final sentence in this example, which consists of one syllable words all with a strong stress. Their rhythmic and emotional weight means that they can't be rushed through or hurried.

> You are right – you are terribly right. But where am I to turn?
> You said you would be my friend, Lord Darlington – Tell me
> what am I to do? Be my friend now.   (17)

A different effect can be seen in this example from *The Country Wife* by William Wycherley. Harcourt is speaking to Horner about his friend's somewhat difficult relationship with women. Most of the words are one syllable, creating a sharp, staccato rhythm.

> Now your sting is gone, you looked in the box, amongst all
> those women, like a drone in the hive, all upon you; shoved and
> ill-used by 'em all, and thrust from one side to t'other.   (18)

Verse Rhythm

Many classical dramas are presented in verse, which heightens natural speech rhythm. The Greek and Latin poets of antiquity were interested in and experimented with heightening speech within a particular rhythmic framework, which in turn influenced the Elizabethan dramatists, who looked back to antiquity for inspiration.

It is imperative that actors come to terms with the nuts and bolts of verse rhythm when working with classical drama, even if a period production has been transplanted into a contemporary context, as the writer will have placed important clues about a character's speech energy within the rhythm. Ignoring or working against the verse rhythm will only muddy character and weaken the drama.

I've worked with professional actors and directors who've worried about focusing on the verse rhythm and consequently ignored it, placing their own natural speech rhythms on the text. This is quite a normal response, given all the seemingly hard and fast 'rules' about speaking verse rhythm but one that, ultimately, will cause problems in character development.

First, it is important to realise that we tend to think that our own natural speech rhythm is the norm and that everyone speaks this way; however, this is something peculiar to us. Therefore, trying to work with someone else's speech rhythm, particularly a character who is speaking in verse, can be daunting. You must help your actors to realise that their own natural speech rhythm is not necessarily the only way in which people speak (some of the exercises at the end of this chapter will help).

Secondly, the 'rules', as I call them, will not only provide your actors with important information about character but will also give them a framework and a freedom in which to fully explore the text: rather than stifling creativity, the 'rules' can provide a springboard for the imagination. Liken it to a game of football. Nobody questions that the rules of the game are an essential part of its framework. They allow the game to flow and develop and there is always space for creative, inspirational, individual performances.

If you do decide to break the 'rules', or allow your actors to break them, then make sure that you know them inside out and back to front first. Make the decision to break them as part of the creative process not because, you believe, they're there to hinder your creativity as a teacher or director.

Time to take a look at it all in a lot more detail.

Metre
So if English prose rhythm is formed (primarily) by an irregular combination of weak and strong stresses, English verse rhythm depends upon the arrangement of these stresses into patterns. When that pattern is regular and repeated it is called metre.

One bar or unit of a metrical form is called a 'foot' (the name comes from dancing in ancient Greece when the foot was raised and set down on the stressed beat of a musical bar) and a metric line is named according to the number of feet within it:

Monometer	=	one foot to a line
Dimeter	=	two feet to a line
Trimeter	=	three feet to a line
Tetrameter	=	four feet to a line
Pentameter	=	five feet to a line
Hexameter	=	six feet to a line
Heptameter	=	seven feet to a line
Octometer	=	eight feet to a line

A metric line can also be named according to the type of rhythm within the unit or bar. In English verse there are two main types: Falling Rhythm and Rising Rhythm.

Rising Rhythm

- Iambus (an iambic foot)

The pattern of an iambic foot consists of an unstressed followed by a stressed syllable.

> weak **strong** | weak **strong** | weak **strong** | weak **strong** | weak **strong**|

or

> de **dum**, de **dum**, de **dum**, de **dum**, de **dum**

It comes from the Greek word meaning 'to hurl' or 'to throw', used when writers of satire hurled their verse, like a weapon, at their enemies. The rhythm resembles the beating of a human heart and is very close to natural speech patterns. Although we may not be aware of it, everyday conversation frequently falls into an iambic rhythm. For example:

> The ticket isn't valid for today.

> The **tick** | et **is** | n't **val** | id **for** | to**day** |

The forward drive of the iambus also makes it ideal for ongoing narrative, which is another reason why the Elizabethan dramatists used it so consistently. Shakespeare's Romeo speaks in iambic pentameter as he waits below Juliet's window in *Romeo and Juliet*.

> But soft, what light through yonder window breaks? (19)
>
> But **soft,** | what **light** | through **yon** | der **win** | dow **breaks?** |

Notice how the metrical structure of the line gives emphasis to the words 'soft', 'light' and 'breaks'.

- Anapaest (an anapaestic foot)

An anapaestic foot consists of two unstressed syllables followed by a stressed syllable, which creates a rapid effect, driving the line of the verse forward.

> de de **dum** | de de **dum** | de de **dum** | de de **dum** | de de **dum** |

Take a look at the first foot of the second line in this speech from Shakespeare's *Macbeth*. The anapaest quickens the pace and helps to reveal Macbeth's internal nervous energy about murdering Duncan.

> If it were done, when 'tis done, then 'twere well
> It were done quickly: (20)
>
> If **it** | were **done** | **when** 'tis | **done,** then | 'twere **well** |
> It were **done** | **quick**ly |

Falling Rhythm

- Trochee (a trochaic foot)

A trochaic foot consists of a stressed syllable followed by an unstressed syllable.

> **dum** de | **dum** de | **dum** de | **dum** de | **dum** de |
> **Nev**er, | **nev**er, | **nev**er, | **nev**er, | **nev**er. | (21)

King Lear's response upon discovering his daughter, Cordelia, dead, is captured in the mournful, falling tone of the metre. Shakespeare often uses a trochee at the start of an iambic line, which gives extra weight to the meaning of the first word, for example, in 'Sonnet 27':

Weary with toil, I haste me to my bed,   (22)
Weary | with **toil,** | I **haste** | me **to** | my **bed,** |

- Dactyl (a dactylic foot)
A dactylic foot consists of a stressed syllable followed by two unstressed syllables.

dum de de | **dum** de de | **dum** de de | **dum** de de | **dum** de de |

In the following line from *Hamlet* the metre places stress on the word 'that', highlighting the reflective nature of the speech and drawing our attention to the 'question'. The use of two lighter syllables in the fourth foot rapidly moves the line forward to 'question'.

To be, or not to be – that is the question;   (23)

To **be,** | or **not** | to **be** – | **that** is the | **quest**ion; |

Other Rhythms

- Spondee (a spondaic foot)
A spondaic foot consists of two successive syllables with equal weight.

| **dum dum** |

In this example, *Hamlet* uses a spondee to reveal the strength of his anger towards his mother: she has just questioned his grief over his father's death. His speech immediately returns to an iambic rhythm in order to clarify and justify his anger.

'Seems', madam – nay, it is, I know not 'seems.'   (24)

'Seems', mad | am – **nay** | it **is,** | I **know** | not **'seems'.** |

Scansion
A succession of lines consisting of the same kind of metrical rhythm can become a bit tedious so many writers combine different rhythms to make it more interesting and to link the rhythm more precisely with the meaning they wish to convey. It's useful for actors to understand where these shifts take place so that they can bring the speech rhythm of the

character to life as it was intended by the writer. Sometimes (but not always) this means that actors need to 'scan' a piece of verse (working through it line by line, analysing the number of feet and marking the weak and strong stresses) so they have a firm grasp of the ways in which the verse structure links with the character's thoughts and emotions. In other words, actors sometimes need to become detectives, searching out the character clues within the verse structure. An understanding of metrical patterning can also provide the key to a passage that might at first seem difficult to comprehend. If you know where the stresses fall in a given speech then you may find it easier to locate the sense. A word of warning, however: it's important that the rules of verse form aren't isolated from thought and emotion. Working with the rhythm and metre must be connected to feeling and impulse, otherwise your actors will end up speaking the metre but not the sense.

Line Endings

In verse, an *end-stopped line* is where the sense and rhythm stop at the end of the line, which is often indicated by a punctuation mark in the writing. *Enjambment* is when the sense of a line of verse continues on into the next line without punctuation marks. Both types of line endings can be found in this speech by Doctor Faustus in Christopher Marlowe's play of the same name. Here, Faustus is thinking through the benefits of listening to the Evil Angel and following the necromantic books, which might give him what he wants: power and omnipotence.

> Shall I make spirits fetch me what I please,
> Resolve me of all ambiguities,
> Perform what desperate enterprise I will?
> I'll have them fly to India for gold,
> Ransack the ocean for orient pearl,
> And search all corners of the new-found world
> For pleasant fruits and princely delicates.
> I'll have them read me strange philosophy,
> And tell the secrets of all foreign kings.
> I'll have them wall all Germany with brass,

> And make swift Rhine circle fair Wittenberg.
> I'll have them fill the public schools with silk,
> Wherewith the students shall be bravely clad.
> I'll levy soldiers with the coin they bring,
> And chase the Prince of Parma from our land,
> And reign sole king of all the provinces.   (25)

I like the way in which all the lines are *end-stopped*, which helps to clarify Faustus' shopping list of desires, apart from

> And search all corners of the new-found world
> For pleasant fruits and princely delicates.

where the *enjambment* creates a sense of movement through the *new-found world.*

Dealing with *enjambment* and *end-stopped lines* is a matter of timing that is, essentially, created by pauses.

Pauses

• Rhythmical or Metrical Pauses

A *rhythmical* or *metrical pause* occurs, naturally, at the end of *end-stopped lines* to maintain the form and pattern of the verse. Actors need to mark these moments with silence in order to preserve the rhythmic timing of the verse. If they're held for too long though, the timing, as well as the momentum of the thoughts to come, will be lost. This is particularly true in the *Doctor Faustus* speech where the momentum of the list needs to be maintained. Occasionally, there will be enough space and time to take a breath but only if the sense and the rhythmic timing allow it.

• Caesural Pauses

A *caesura* or *caesural pause* occurs mid-line, usually indicated by a break in sense and sometimes indicated by a punctuation mark in the writing. Take a look at this scene between Alsemero and Beatrice in *The Changeling* by Thomas Middleton and William Rowley.

BEATRICE: You are a scholar, sir.

ALSEMERO: A weak one, lady.

BEATRICE: Which of the sciences is this love you speak of?

ALSEMERO: From your tongue I take it to be music.

BEATRICE: You are skilful in't, can sing at first sight.

ALSEMERO: And I have showed you all my skill at once.
       I want more words to express me further
       And must be forced to repetition:
       I love you dearly.

BEATRICE: Be better advised, sir:
       Our eyes are sentinels unto our judgements
       And should give certain judgement what they see:
       But they are rash sometimes, and tell us wonders
       Of common things, which when our judgements find,
       They can then check the eyes, and call them blind.

ALSEMERO: But I am further, lady; yesterday
       Was mine eyes' employment, and hither now
       They brought my judgement, where are both agreed.
       Both houses then consenting, 'tis agreed;
       Only there wants the confirmation
       By the hand royal, that's your part, lady.   (26)

Not only are there split lines, where Beatrice and Alsemero share the same speech rhythm (always an interesting revelation about character) but their later speeches in this example are littered with *caesural pauses*, indicated by punctuation in the middle of some of the lines. Although these breaks are tiny in order to maintain rhythmic flow, they shorten and sharpen their thoughts, helping the characters to think through the concept of love at first sight as they speak about it.

- Suspensory Pauses

When an *enjambed* line occurs actors need to preserve the meaning without losing the rhythm or form of the verse: a *Suspensory Pause* solves the problem. The final word of the first *enjambed* line needs to be carried over into the next line (suspended by pitch and length). In other words, rather than there being a pause of silence at the end of the line, there is a pause on the word itself, thereby doing away with the need for a silence. This means that the momentum of the rhythm is maintained without a beat being lost.

Take another look at the enjambed line in that *Doctor Faustus* example:

> And search all corners of the new-found world
> For pleasant fruits and princely delicates.   (27)

Using a *suspensory pause* on the final word of the first line (*world*) lengthens it and lifts it out ever so lightly, emphasising its sense and importance: a perfect marriage between form and meaning.

I know there are some professional directors and actors who don't like using *enjambed lines* or *suspensory pauses*, believing that they destroy the structure of the verse. In fact, I once worked with a professional actor who insisted on pausing at the end of every enjambed line, in other words breaking the flow of the thoughts. This not only sounded odd but also prevented the audience from truly understanding the specifics of what he was talking about. If an actor runs through enjambed lines without using a suspensory pause then the verse structure *would* be destroyed; however, it is the suspensory pause that is the key, strengthening the form and, therefore, the meaning.

Playing with Rhythm (some ideas)

- **Reading Other Texts.** Actors need to become familiar with the particular rhythmic patterns within classical drama if they are to make them their own in performance. Reading other texts from the period will help them to discover differences and variations in writing, which, in turn, will inform their understanding of rhythm in the play they are rehearsing. So set them a reading project at the start of rehearsals, which may include prose, verse and drama from the same period.

- **Speaking Aloud.** Ask your actors to spend as much time as possible speaking the texts aloud from their reading project. Reading in their heads will only turn the work into an academic exercise and the rhythmic energy within a text needs to be felt in the mouth and heard aloud, if it is to be truly understood.

- **Clapping Rhythms.** Choose some music that has a well defined rhythmic beat and ask your actors to clap along to it. Follow this up with music of a different rhythm and music that changes its rhythmic beat at some point. Allow your actors the opportunity to dance to it as well in order to feel the rhythmic beat through their whole body. These exercises sound simplistic but are particularly important for those actors who haven't studied music before.

- **Beating Verse Metre.** It's useful for actors to be able to mark the feet and rhythmic stresses in a verse text with a pencil so spend time showing them how to do this. However, they must be able to engage with the metrical pattern aloud so, once again, it can be felt and experienced. Make sure they spend time beating or clapping the metre, at the same time as speaking the text, so they understand the patterning of weak and strong stresses. This is particularly important in passages where there are variations to the metrical beat so they can focus on the motivational reasons why the character has altered his/her speech pattern.

- **Physicalising Verse Metre.** Once your actors know how to beat and speak the metrical rhythm and can handle any metrical variations successfully, ask them to walk the metrical pattern across the room, changing direction (and the rhythm of the walk) on any metrical variations. They may find this difficult on the first attempt but ask them to persevere: moving the metre in this way will help it to become a natural, unconscious part of performance. Finally, ask them to try some tougher physical variations, such as running or rolling around on the floor as they speak the text.

- **Physicalising Line Endings and Pauses.** Choose a piece of verse text that has a number of end-stopped lines, enjambed lines, suspensory pauses and caesural pauses. Ask your actors to try the text aloud but whenever a punctuation mark occurs they must take a step. It's important to ensure that they don't speak on the movement: that the movement is a silent action. Then, ask them to explore the timing of each pause so that their steps vary from tiny baby steps to large leaps, depending on the sense and the type of pause. After they've tried this a number of times, ask them to do a little jump on the final word of every end-stopped line. Finally, every time there is an enjambed line, ask them to turn around on the spot as they speak the final word of the line, thereby lengthening out that word into a suspensory pause. After they've practised and refined the whole sequence so that they're physically comfortable with it, ask them to drop all the movements and just speak the text in a still, centred position. Their work should hold onto the timing without them having to think about it, which will help to define and clarify meaning.

- **Driving the Thoughts to the End of the Line.** Ask the group to sit in a circle and, using a piece of dramatic verse, get each person to speak a section of the text from punctuation mark to punctuation mark (sometimes this may include just one word; in other cases, a number of lines). On the last word of their section, ask them to gently push their neighbour, which will ensure that they vocally drive through to the very last sound.

- **Breathing in Sync.** Sometimes it's useful for actors performing a duologue to work in each other's breath rhythm before they start speaking the text in rehearsal. Ask both actors to stand close to each other, face to face, eye to eye, and, palm to palm so there is some sort of physical contact (a variation can be made with both actors sitting back to back) and ask them to spend time listening to each other's breathing. They will find that the rhythmic timing of their in-breaths and out-breaths soon synchronises. Gently coach them to release an elongated 'f' sound, then an elongated 's' sound, followed by an elongated 'v' sound, and, finally, an elongated 'z' sound. When you feel that they are working in a comfortable rhythm, ask them to start speaking the text. This exercise may help them to find the natural timing of the piece they are rehearsing. If they do not know the words from memory, ask other actors to stand behind each of them and feed them the lines so that they're not bound by words on a written page.

NOTES

1. William Shakespeare, *Macbeth* (The Arden Shakespeare, 2002); Act I, Scene vii, Lines 54-59

2. George Etheridge, *The Man of Mode* (Norton Critical Editions, 1997); Act III, Scene iii, p. 132

3. Thomas Middleton and William Rowley, *The Changeling* (Penguin Books, 1982); Act III, Scene iii, Lines 135-136

4. Seamus Heaney, *The Burial at Thebes* (Faber and Faber, 2004); p. 43

5. *Ibid.* p. 46

6. William Shakespeare, *Henry V* (The Arden Shakespeare, 2001); Prologue, Lines 1-2

7. William Shakespeare, edited by John Kerrigan, *The Sonnets and A Lover's Complaint* (Penguin Books, 2005); 'Sonnet 130', p. 141

8. William Shakespeare, *The Tempest* (The Arden Shakespeare, 2000); Act II, Scene i, Line 289

9. William Shakespeare, *Othello* (The Arden Shakespeare, 2002); Act III, Scene iii, Lines 167-169

10. William Shakespeare, edited by John Kerrigan, *The Sonnets and A Lover's Complaint* (Penguin Books, 2005); 'Sonnet 19', p. 86

11. William Shakespeare, *King John* (The Arden Shakespeare, 2007); Act II, Scene iii, Lines 25-36

12. William Shakespeare, *Romeo and Juliet* (The Arden Shakespeare, 2002); Act I, Scene i, Lines 173-181

13. Seamus Heaney, *The Burial at Thebes* (Faber and Faber, 2004); p. 40

14. Oscar Wilde, *A Woman of No Importance* (Penguin Plays, 1977); Second Act p. 99

15. Oscar Wilde, *A Woman of No Importance* (Penguin Plays, 1977); Second Act p. 112

16. Harold Pinter, *Plays Four: Betrayal* (Faber and Faber, 1986); p. 198

17. Oscar Wilde, *Lady Windermere's Fan* (Penguin Plays, 1977); Second Act p. 37

18. William Wycherley, *The Country Wife* (Norton Critical Editions, 1997); Act III, Scene ii, p. 32

19. William Shakespeare, *Romeo and Juliet* (The Arden Shakespeare, 2002); Act II, Scene ii, Line 2

20. William Shakespeare, *Macbeth* (The Arden Shakespeare, 2002); Act I, Scene vii, Lines 1-2

21. William Shakespeare, *King Lear* (The Arden Shakespeare, 1997); Act V, Scene iii, Line 307

22. William Shakespeare, edited by John Kerrigan, *The Sonnets and A Lover's Complaint* (Penguin Books, 2005); 'Sonnet 27', p. 90

23. William Shakespeare, *Hamlet* (The Arden Shakespeare, 2006); Act III, Scene i, Line 55

24. *Ibid.* Act I, Scene ii, Line 76

25. Christopher Marlowe, *Doctor Faustus* (Penguin Books, 1983); Act I, Scene iii, Lines 78-93

26. Thomas Middleton and William Rowley, *The Changeling* (Penguin Books, 1982); Act I, Scene iii, Lines 65-83

27. Christopher Marlowe, *Doctor Faustus* (Penguin Books, 1983); Act I, Scene iii, Lines 83-84

PART TWO: GREEK TRAGEDY

CHAPTER 5

DEMANDS AND CHALLENGES

This chapter is about the vocal demands placed on actors performing in Greek tragedy. Given that many of these demands arose from either the physical conditions of the theatre at the time or the social context in which that theatre was placed, an understanding of historical context is important.

The Context

Formalised theatre in ancient Greece grew out of two annual religious festivals. The spring festival to honour the Greek god of fertility, Dionysus, was considered the more important event. Religion was firmly integrated into Greek society and, during the festival, playwrights re-told myths and stories relevant to the moral and spiritual life of Greek citizens. Their audiences were probably familiar with these stories but would have been interested in the viewpoint or angle from which they were told. The plays were presented in competition to one another and an elected jury awarded prizes to the best entry.

The most prolific time for playwrights was during the 5th Century BC when Athens linked up with other Greek states and became a rich trade city after success in a series of wars against the Persian Empire. Wealth gave Athenians the opportunity to develop more cultural and philosophical pursuits and the playwrights Aeschylus, Sophocles, Euripides and Aristophanes wrote during this time.

The Plays

Very few of the plays have survived: fourteen comedies by Aristophanes, seven tragedies by Aeschylus, seven tragedies by Sophocles and nineteen tragedies by Euripides (although we do know that Euripides wrote ninety-one plays).

Their structure developed out of epic poetry that had a strong narrative thread and religious rituals that relied on singing and dancing. Drama, as we know it, was born when playwrights started to alternate acted scenes with choral interludes.

Originally, there was only one actor and a chorus in each play; however, the playwright Aeschylus added a second actor and Sophocles added a third. Three actors and a chorus became the norm, which meant that playwrights could only place three characters on stage at any one time.

The Actors

When the first actor separated himself out from the chorus, a completely different type of performer was born, one who was required to interpret, create and communicate character. And, given that there was a restriction on how many actors could be used within a play, each actor needed to create multiple characters, using different masks to help distinguish between roles.

All actors were male citizens and, although they were paid, they were not full-time professionals, given that they were only required to perform a few weeks every year during festival time. However, they did spend time training for these theatrical events. They already had physical stamina from regular athletic exercise that prepared them for the possibility of war so much of their training focused on vocal development. An actor was given a good review if his performance voice was strong and expressive.

They were usually directed by the playwright (which is one of the reasons why the original Greek texts don't include stage directions) and there is reason to believe that they learnt their roles from hearing them recited.

The Chorus

The chorus played an important role in the drama, linking the story to its religious roots by ritualistically singing and dancing their way through the text.

However, its primary function was as the narrative voice of the collective community. The collective voice is a powerful force in any democracy and no less so in ancient Greece, where governance of the city-state relied on communal debate. When playwrights started developing more complex roles for actors, the chorus started to assume its own personality and character (for example, Corinthian women or Theban elders) which meant they could communicate more directly with the actors in the tragedy as well as the audience.

Chorus members were not professional actors but were trained especially for the festivals, and a certain number of citizens were selected each year to take part (eventually between 12 and 15 for tragedy and 24 for comedy). They wore matching robes and masks to emphasise their collective identity and were choreographed by the playwright himself.

They communicated their shared view of the world through dialogue with individual characters (thought to be spoken by the leader of the chorus, *the choruphaios*, on behalf of the group) and choral odes (thought to be sung and danced collectively). These odes were broken down into different verses, stanzas or sections: *strophe, antistrophe* and *epode*, which related to the dance executed by the chorus. *Strophe* means 'turn', *antistrophe* means 'counterturn' and *epode* means 'standing still'. The odes were lyrical in nature and provided a welcome relief from the dramatic tension; however, their reference to religious myth often strengthened and highlighted the tragedy.

The Original Vocal Demands

Ancient Greek actors needed strong technical skills in projection, a flexible range and precise articulation in order to fill vast spaces, deal with the sound limitations of wearing a mask, draw out the subtleties from texts written in structured verse and plumb the depths of tragic stories.

Space

The plays were written for performance in specific open air spaces called amphitheatres. The actors were placed on a raised wooden stage called the *skene* which had a single-storey building for exits and entrances. The chorus sang and danced in the *orchestra*, which was below the *skene.* Around the *orchestra* there were tiers of seats, rising upwards, often built into a hill, where the audience looked down on the drama.

These structures were enormous. The Theatre of Dionysus in Athens had room for 16,000 people, the theatre at Megalopolis in the Peloponnese could house 46,000 people, Epidaurus had a capacity of 20,000 and the theatre at Ephesus (now in Turkey) originally held 55,000 people. This meant that there was a considerable distance between the actors and the audience: in the Theatre of Dionysus, some 300 feet between the back seats and the stage.

Therefore, it wasn't possible for actors to incorporate subtle physical nuances into their performances (they just couldn't be seen very well) so they relied on their voices to communicate the details. Luckily these theatres possessed amazing acoustics and were structured in such a way that the audience in the back rows could hear almost equally well as those seated in the front. However, the actors did have to compete with significant background noise, given that the audiences were so massive and much of the seating, in the early days, was wooden.

Mask
Both the actors and the chorus wore masks. Unfortunately there aren't any surviving examples because they were made of wood, linen and cork, materials that don't have a particularly long life. However, surviving pictures have provided us with some idea of their shape, form and range.

Masks had a number of important functions:

— They helped the audience to identify different characters, making them more visually accessible in the large performance spaces.

— They made it easier for actors to play more than one part.

— They may have aided audibility, given that some had trumpet shaped mouths (although resonance must have been severely compromised with the face being covered and enclosed).

— They helped the actors create character through the embodiment of the emotional and/or physical elements portrayed on their masks.

Playwrights created roles with the particular attitudes of a mask in mind: this helped to mould a character's fate. Fate was a concept with which the ancient Greeks were familiar. They felt that human beings were subject to the laws of nature and the gods: a pre-destined plan was mapped out for each individual. Oedipus is a prime example of this concept: he tried to escape his fate (killing his father and marrying his mother) but was ultimately defeated by it. His mask is one of pride and self-belief (pride in his achievements and belief in his own identity and judgement).

Accepting the physical and vocal archetype of the mask, whether an actual mask is used or not, is an important part of the rehearsal process for actors working with ancient Greek texts.

Verse

All of the original Greek texts were written in verse. The stories presented by the playwrights were more suited to verse form: the scale and magnitude of the tragedies and their religious nature did not suit prose. Likewise, it was inconceivable that gods and heroes should speak the speech of ordinary mortals.

Having said that, in the original Greek texts character speech is written (primarily) in the verse metre closest to ordinary speech: the iambic (unstressed syllable followed by a stressed syllable – de dum – see Chapter 4: Rhythm for further details). However, the metre often changed to suit the mood, particularly in moments of high intensity. The choral odes, which are more lyrical, are broken down into quite different and complex metres in the original Greek, although usually the *strophe* and *antistrophe* metrically matched in some way.

The regular rhythm within verse also allowed playwrights to focus the tragedy much more acutely. This focus is broken when modern actors break up the verse naturalistically.

Word

The specific language used within the texts presented another set of vocal demands for the performer, primarily because the words explain everything. The playwrights wrote with the performance space in mind and, because it would have been difficult for audiences to understand complex or subtle physical action at such vast distances, let alone recognise different characters, the words tend to do all the work (which is why characters are always introduced verbally).

- Narrative speeches (with imagistic language)

Descriptive language can put powerful pictures in the minds of an audience. This would have been particularly true in tragic moments when horrific action just couldn't be staged. Some sort of violent tragedy usually takes place off stage, which is reported back by a messenger, often unwillingly because he is barely able to deal with the horror of what he has seen. The language he uses helps us to build up a gruesome visual image of what has happened.

- Character speeches (with philosophical, intellectual and/or
  imagistic language)

Character speeches often use language drawn from the public and political arena. Although they can be highly emotive in content, the words themselves do not leave much room for private internalised feeling, which often helps strengthen a character's emotional resolve.

- Dialogue (with verbal argument and/or enquiry)

The dialogue doesn't mirror the irregular conversational patterns of human speech. Characters speak in regular verse lines, which alternate only when a line has been completed. This type of dialogue is called *stichomythia*. It is interesting that the playwrights chose to use such a formal structure when they also chose to write their verse in an iambic metre, which does tend to mirror the rhythmic patterns of human speech. It seems as though the stichomythia and the iambic metre work against each other. Perhaps stichomythia helped the audience identify who was speaking. Speaker identification would have been difficult given the enormous distances between audience and actor, and given that the actors were wearing masks and the audience wouldn't have been able to see their lips moving. A regular and consistent exchange of lines between actors would have made the speaker clear. Stichomythia can be quite difficult for actors to bring to life so many translators have abandoned it and created more colloquial dialogue.

- Choral Odes (with lyrical language)

The choral odes, presented by the chorus, used poetic and lyrical language but their arguments strengthened and gave weight to the story being presented. This involved looking back on the previous scene as well as looking forward to the future and using myth to illuminate, explain and understand the situation that had arisen.

The Original Delivery

There was a strong tradition of speaking publicly in ancient Greece. Citizens spent a great deal of time in public discussion, particularly in the voting assembly (where much of the Greek city-state was run) and in the law courts. Good oratory was considered important because success or failure of an argument often depended on how that argument was delivered. This meant that average citizens were not only skilled speakers but good listeners as well.

There is evidence that orators received training from festival actors; however, public speaking and acting were still considered two very different types of presentation, given that the dramas relied on the communication of character. Although it seems as if there was less vocal realism required (speech patterns in the original play texts didn't change to show sex, age or social status and different types of dialect were only used in comedies), the actors still needed to deal vocally with vast changes in a character's emotional range that were part of the tragedy.

It's not known how the words were actually delivered: they may have been sung, they may have been spoken, or perhaps there was a combination. The most common assumption is that the actors and the choruphaios (leader of the chorus) spoke lines, whilst the chorus sang the choral odes.

The actors didn't just stand and deliver the words; they did rely on gesture as well, although it was simple, clear and defined, given the distance between audience and actor. This didn't mean that gesture was stiff and mechanical, as it flowed out from the character's emotional centre, giving it life and rhythm.

Unfortunately very little is known either about the actual choreographed dance of the chorus. Was the movement literal, acting out part of the story within the songs? Or was it metaphorical, creating visual concepts that simply illuminated the words? We just don't know.

Given the performance demands placed on the actors and the powerful public moments they were required to communicate, they could not rely on intimate vocal nuance. However, there is some evidence to suggest that they didn't just declaim the text like a public address. For example, Aristotle praised actors who were more vocally natural and used their voices to communicate a range of different emotions. Certainly actors who shouted rather than projected were severely criticised. This means that ancient Greek actors found a balance between projected vocal delivery and naturalistic vocal delivery, which freed the story for the audience. Something to think about in the work to come.

Past to Present

So what does all this mean for an actor presented with these texts today?

Unfortunately many modern productions of ancient Greek drama fall into the trap of a declamatory vocal style, bordering on shouting, as the actors try to meet the power of the tragedy. I call it 'funny voice acting'. This prevents them from truly engaging with the words of the text, which means the searing emotions become generalised and the audience is confronted with a tedious barrier of sound.

So the modern actor still needs to meet a variety of vocal demands. Certainly our theatre spaces might be smaller, but there is still the verse text in translation, the power of the tragedy, the concept of mask (whether one is worn physically or not) and the presentation of the chorus and their choral odes. Then, of course, what happens if you decide to stage a production out-of-doors: it creates a whole new set of challenges. Therefore, I've organised the lesson plans into the following sections:

- Acting in Translation
- Articulating the Tragedy
- Voicing the Mask
- Choral Thinking, Choral Speaking
- Performing Outside

CHAPTER 6

ACTING IN TRANSLATION

If you don't speak Greek then you'll be working with texts in translation, providing you with a whole new set of performance demands.

Unfortunately translation isn't an exact science, which is why
computer-generated translations can sound nonsensical. Translating a
dramatic text means *re-composing* the words of that text into another
language. A translator must interpret the meaning, make conscious
choices between words and place those words within the appropriate grammatical, syntactical and idiomatic conventions of the new
language, which might have very little in common with the original language. In other words, because of the different ways in which
human beings express themselves in different languages, the translator
will need to adjust the original text in order to bring it to life. This
means there will always be something 'lost in translation'.

In addition, because a translator must interpret what the playwright
means rather than just focus literally on the words that the playwright
has used, and, because it is difficult for any human being to divorce
their own personality from interpretation, there will always be two
voices present within a translated text – that of the playwright and
that of the translator. If you take a look at different translated versions
of the same text then you will begin to see how much a translator can
leave their mark on the original.

Translators are also influenced by the period of time in which they
live. Theatre is subject to different fashions and trends, like any other
art form, which often can be linked to the political and social context
of the day. A translated text published in 1910 looks and feels very
different from one published in 1994, as you can see from the boxed
texts. The modern texts use language more colloquially and directly,

whilst the older versions remind us of a more formal era influenced by texts from an earlier age (they seem almost Shakespearean in style).

As we learnt earlier, all of the original Greek texts were written in verse, which creates additional and (almost) insurmountable problems for translators. Verse is considered the most difficult form to translate because verse metre is made up of a regular patterning of sound (please refer to Chapter 4: Rhythm) and these metrical laws can't be recreated in another language if the power of the drama is to be maintained. Those translators who try to stick too closely to the original metrical patterns often turn the translation into an academic exercise that lacks the searing emotions of the original. Therefore it is usually the rhythm, and the lyrical quality inherent within the rhythm, that tends to suffer. It is the same type of loss that is experienced when Shakespearean verse is translated out of English. Some translations do find a metre, a rhythm, a lyricism, but it's just different from the original.

The ancient Greek playwrights were fond of using complex verbal patterns within the verse form as well, creating another hurdle for translators. In English we tend to repeat words in order to emphasise and/or clarify; however, in Greek a word in one line can emphasise another word further on through agreement in case and gender. This means that some translators have found dialogue difficult to translate so they often abandon the formal verse structure of the stichomythia and create a much more colloquial speech pattern.

However, it isn't all about loss: translators have added as much as they have taken away. The ancient Greek playwrights didn't include stage directions in their texts (probably because they directed productions of their own plays and didn't feel the need to record what they would be putting into practice personally). Many translators decide to clarify the text by including them.

What does all this mean for actors? Obviously the translation you choose for them to work with will have a direct bearing on their performances, given the wide variations in translation styles and forms. However, even though you might be married to one particular text, it's a useful exercise for actors to compare different translations as part of their workshop or rehearsal process. These are the pay-offs:

- To find out more about the original text.
  - A comparison of four to five different translations *may* bring the actor closer to the truth of the original text.

- To clarify meaning and emotion more precisely, ie what a character is thinking and feeling.
  - Rhythm and metre establishes word stress, which in turn reveals information about a character's particular emphasis. Different translations will use different rhythms thereby changing that emphasis. A comparison of different translations will provide the actor with a more rounded view of what the character is trying to say.
  - Some translations will be more cryptic than others and may not include as much information within the text. A comparison of different translations will provide the actor with much more detail about the story and the characters who live within it.

- To find an appropriate vocal level for the tragedy.
  - The dramatic impact of the tragedy will be different across translations, primarily because of the words a translator has chosen to use. The language may be more formal or emotionally heightened in some translations. A comparison of different translations will provide the actor with a way of voicing the tragic moments more appropriately.

Text Samples: Acting in Translation

Presented here are four different translations of the same speech spoken by Medea from Euripides' *Medea*. The first was translated by Gilbert Murray and published in 1910, the second by Philip Vellacott and published in 1963, the third by Alistair Elliot and published in 1992, and, the final speech was translated by Frederic Raphael and Kenneth McLeish and published in 1994.

It is an emotionally charged piece of writing in any language.

The story so far:

Medea was the daughter of Aeetes, King of Colchis (as well as niece of the sorceress, Circe, and granddaughter of the sun, Helios) and met and fell in love with Jason when he arrived in Colchis on a quest to steal the Golden Fleece. Because Medea had to betray her family and murder her brother to help, Jason swore that he would never leave her. They returned to Jason's home in Greece together. Unfortunately, Jason's uncle Pelias had taken the throne in his absence and refused to give it up so Medea cleverly conspired to have Pelias' own daughters kill him. Jason and Medea were forced to flee to Corinth for sanctuary.

King Creon of Corinth convinced Jason that he should marry his daughter to start a new life for himself and gain a political foothold in his new home. Of course, this meant banishing Medea. Jason tried to convince Medea that it was the right thing to do, particularly for their two young sons. However, Medea wasn't having any of it and plotted for the destruction of them all. First, however, she organised a safe passage and refuge for herself with King Aegeus of Athens, who happened to be passing through Corinth.

This speech is the moment when Medea rejoices about receiving help from Aegeus, because it means she can put her vengeance into action. She reveals her plans aloud, ostensibly to herself, although the chorus are always present. They include: lulling Jason into a false sense of security by telling him that she's changed her mind, sending poisoned gifts to Creon and his daughter to secure their deaths, and, finally, killing her own children to ensure Jason is left childless.

I.   God, and God's Justice, and ye blinding Skies!
       At last the victory dawneth! Yea, mine eyes
       See, and my foot is on the mountain's brow.
       Mine enemies! Mine enemies, oh, now
       Atonement cometh! Here at my worst hour
       A friend is found, a very port of power
       To save my shipwreck. Here will I make fast

Mine anchor, and escape them at the last
In Athen's walled hill. – But ere the end
'Tis meet I show thee all my counsel, friend:
Take it, no tale to make men laugh withal!
    Straightway to Jason I will send some thrall
To entreat him to my presence. Comes he here,
Then with soft reasons will I feed his ear,
How his will now is my will, how all things
Are well, touching this marriage-bed of kings
For which I am betrayed – all wise and rare
And profitable! Yet will I make one prayer,
That my two children be no more exiled
But stay... Oh, not that I would leave a child
Here upon angry shores till those have laughed
Who hate me: 'tis that I will slay by craft
The king's daughter. With gifts they shall be sent,
Gifts to the bride to spare their banishment,
Fine robings and a carcanet of gold.
Which raiment let her once but take, and fold
About her, a foul death that girl shall die
And all who touch her in her agony.
Such poison shall they drink, my robe and wreath!
    Howbeit of that no more. I gnash my teeth
Thinking on what a path my feet must tread
Thereafter. I shall lay those children dead –
Mine, whom no hand shall steal from me away!
Then, leaving Jason childless, and the day
As night above him, I will go my road
To exile, flying, flying from the blood
Of these my best-beloved, and having wrought
All horror, so but one thing reach me not,
The laugh of them that hate us.
                      Let it come!

The Medea by Euripides, translated by Gilbert Murray and first published in 1910.   (1)

2.   O Zeus! O Justice, daughter of Zeus! O glorious Sun!
Now I am on the road to victory; now there's hope!
I shall see my enemies punished as they deserve.
Just where my plot was weakest, at that very point
Help has appeared in this man Aegeus; he is a haven
Where I shall find safe mooring, once I reach the walls
Of the city of Athens. Now I'll tell you all my plans;
They'll not make pleasant hearing.

(*MEDEA's NURSE has entered; she listens in silence.*)

                                    First I'll send a slave
To Jason, asking him to come to me; and then
I'll give him soft talk; tell him he has acted well,
Tell him I think this royal marriage which he has bought
With my betrayal is for the best and wisely planned.
But I shall beg that my children be allowed to stay.
Not that I would think of leaving sons of mine behind
On enemy soil for those who hate me to insult;
But in my plot to kill the princess they must help.
I'll send them to the palace bearing gifts, a dress
Of soft weave and a coronet of beaten gold.
If she takes and puts on this finery, both she
And all who touch her will expire in agony;
With such a deadly poison I'll anoint my gifts.

However, enough of that. What makes me cry with pain
Is the next thing I have to do. I will kill my sons.
No one shall take my children from me. When I have made
Jason's whole house a shambles, I will leave Corinth
A murderess, flying from my darling children's blood.
Yes, I can endure guilt, however horrible;
The laughter of my enemies I will not endure.

Now let things take their course.

Medea by Euripides, translated by Philip Vellacott and first
published in 1963.   (2)

3.   O Zeus! O Justice of Zeus! O Helios!

Now we are winning; we shall stand in triumph
Over my enemies. We have begun to move.
Just when we seemed caught helpless in the storm,
This man appears, and offers me safe harbour.
Now I shall tell you what I'm going to do.

I'll send a servant who will ask for Jason
To come and see me; and when Jason comes,
I'll lull him with soft words and calmly say,
'Yes, I agree with you, it's quite the best decision
To leave us, to make a royal marriage:
It's in all our interests, a clever move.'
Then I shall ask him if our sons can stay –
I'll use them as messengers of death to Creon's child.
I'll send them to her with presents in their hands,
A long light veil and a wreath of beaten gold,
But I shall smear such ointments on each one
That when she takes these ornaments and puts them
Against her skin, she will die horribly –
And everyone who touches her will die.

All that is easy, but I weep
To think of what comes next, what must be done,
And done by me: I'm going to kill
My children. Nobody shall take them from me.
Then, with the house of Jason quite destroyed,
I shall escape from Corinth, and escape
The penalty of killing my dear sons,
The most unholy crime we can commit.
I cannot, will not tolerate the scorn
Of those I hate. So let it all come down.

Medea by Euripides, translated by Alistair Elliot and first published
in 1992 by Oberon Books.   (3)

4.   O Zeus! Justice of Zeus! Light of the Sun!
     My enemies are in my power.
     The road lies open – to victory.
     We were weak, and then he appeared:
     My harbour, my anchorage when the deed is done.
     Now my enemies will pay, and pay.

     Listen now. My plan. My dreadful plan.
     I'll send a slave inside to Jason.
     Beg him out here again –
     And when he comes, soft words:
     I've changed my mind; what he did was right;
     His new marriage, his treachery
     Were brave and right – good luck.
     One favour only: let the children stay.

     Oh it's not that I mean to leave them,
     Not here, ringed by my enemies.
     They're my trap, to spring on her.
     They'll take her my wedding gifts:
     A silken robe, a golden crown.
     Soon as the pretties touch her flesh, she dies,
     And all who touch her die as well.
     I'll poison them. I'll smear them. So.

     Then…then…
     I can't say it. Do such a thing. I must.
     I'll kill the children. My children. Mine!
     Then, when all Jason's hopes, his palace hopes,
     Are gone, I'll leave this land,
     I'll run. I'll kill my darling sons, and run.
     Vile. Vilest. Yes, I'll do it.
     I should bear their mockery? I won't.

     It's settled.

Medea by Euripides, translated by Frederic Raphael and Kenneth McLeish and first published in 1994 by Nick Hern Books.   (4)

Workshop Plan: Acting in Translation

OBJECTIVES

- To build an understanding of how different translations of the one piece of text can vary in style, form and tone.

- To clarify meaning and emotion more precisely through a comparison of different translations of the same text.

- To find an appropriate vocal level for the tragedy through a comparison of different translations of the same text.

MATERIALS

You will need separate copies of the four different translated texts from Euripides' *Medea* (as provided in the previous 'Sample Text' box) for each member of the workshop group.

Although these texts are spoken by a female character, for the purposes of this workshop, they are appropriate for a mixed gender group of actors. However, if you prefer to use text that is non-gender specific then look for different translated versions of a chorus speech or messenger speech.

You might also like to provide a handout with the group discussion questions.

WARM UP

Structure a warm up from the information listed in Chapter 1; however, make sure that exercises which focus on muscular support for breath are given priority, as the heightened emotions presented in the texts may require strong vocalisation during the course of the workshop.

ACTIVITIES AND EXERCISES

- Hand out one piece of text to each actor, making sure there are a number of different translations in operation around the group. You may wish to give some background detail about *Medea* at this point but try to avoid telling them what the speech is about. Or you could decide to add in information about the story later on in the workshop, when they've had a chance to discuss the text between themselves.

- Ask your actors to read through the words silently just to make sense of the meaning. Ask them to silently read through it again as if they are reading it aloud in their heads (transferring it into the tempo in which they would speak it aloud).

- Now get them to mouth the words silently to themselves. Speaking is a physical activity and their muscles will need to know exactly what steps they will need to take (in the same way a dancer's body needs to know the steps of a dance). Encourage your actors to really use their lips and tongue, and, feel the length and weight of the words in their mouth.

- Ask them to vocalise the words aloud in their own space and time. As the noise level will increase and you will need them to listen back to what they're saying, ask them to cup one hand a couple of centimetres away from their ear and cup the other hand a couple of centimetres away from their mouth so they can focus in on the words. Make sure they don't devoice into a breathy whisper – keep them on their voices.

- Ask them to repeat the text aloud again but this time separating each of the thoughts out with a step to one side on every punctuation mark. It's important to ensure that they don't speak on the movement: that the movement is a silent action. Then, ask them to explore the timing of each pause so that their steps vary from tiny baby steps to large leaps, depending on the sense and the type of pause. This will help them to find the rhythm and flow of the verse, whilst separating out and making sense of the words themselves. Once they've become physically confident with this exercise ask them to repeat the text without the movement, which should retain some element of the verse's structure, rhythm, timing and flow.

- Now that they've started to build up a better understanding of what the text is about through physically speaking and listening, place them into groups of four. Each person in the group should have been working on a different translation of the same text. Now ask each person to describe in detail what the text is about (without taking a look at the other versions). Ask the group to record any differentiation between versions and report these back to the group as a whole. If you haven't already, you may wish to add in the background details to Medea's story at this point in the workshop.

- Ask each person to try speaking aloud the other translations so that they can be fully informed for the discussion to come. If there is time, they should try out all the previous exercises on each different translation.

- Ask everybody to return to their original discussion group and provide them with a series of questions to discuss in detail.

  – Which version do you prefer? Why?

  – Which version is easier/harder to speak aloud? Why?

  – Which version has greater dramatic impact? Why?

  – What are the differences in meaning between the opening lines in each version?

  – What are the differences in meaning between the final lines in each version?

  – What are the differences in meaning/emotional impact between the sections where Medea talks about killing her children?

  – As a group, choose a line or word from each translation where you feel Medea expresses her revenge at its fiercest. Note any differences.

- If the discussion questions have been answered in depth then the appropriate vocal level for each different translation will have been revealed. Without discussing vocal levels, ask your actors to re-visit one translation of their choice and read it aloud to their group. They should work to bridge the divide (however small the distance) between themselves and their audience, both mentally and vocally. Make sure they're standing and, if it's easier, get one member of the group to stand behind each speaker and feed them the lines, one by one, so they're not restricted by the words on the written page.

- If you feel the noise level in the room rising because there is shouting or vocal pushing (in other words, they're playing an emotional state rather than engaging with the actual words) or they've fallen into 'funny voice acting' (in other words, they're playing the tragedy without engaging with the actual words) which is often the case with the 1910 version, then get everybody to stop what they're doing, flop over from the waist so they're hanging upside down, let go of their head, shake out their arms and roll up the spine gently releasing an elongated fffff sound. This will help them to centre physically and vocally before continuing.

- Alternatively, or in addition, try adapting the *contextualising sound* exercise from *Playing with Sound (some ideas)* in Chapter 2. Ask everybody to speak aloud the rhyme *Fee Fie Foh Fum* to a partner, verbalising the threat without using volume. This will help bring them back to the power of the words and take away a reliance on volume to communicate strong emotion. As soon as they've finished, bring them back to the *Medea* texts and note the difference.

- Make sure you allow time for everybody to de-brief in a whole group discussion. Ask the following questions:

  - What did you discover about the vocal levels in each translation? Can you articulate the differences?

  - What practical knowledge will you take away from this workshop (ie what did you learn)?

CHAPTER 7

ARTICULATING THE TRAGEDY

There is no doubt that the stories presented by the Greek dramatists were tragic, partially because of their focus on the relationship between man and the immortal gods. Human beings who try to follow their own passions, tempting or usurping the fate outlined for them by the gods, will always lose and the consequences of this loss will be destructive and tragic.

The Greek dramatists saw that staging the consequences of a tragedy (ie the violence) wasn't going to be easy. First of all there were practical considerations: if one character were to die and the 'body' couldn't be removed from the stage then only a limited amount of actors would be available to complete the remainder of the story (given that there were only three actors allowed in each play). Secondly, there were emotional considerations: the staging of violence can sometimes leave us cold (or even make us laugh) because it's so far removed from the horror of reality, and, given that the Greek theatres were so vast, visual violence could only ever have a limited impact. Faced with these dilemmas, the Greek dramatists avoided portraying actual gruesome events on stage. Instead they created characters whose specific function was to describe horrific events that happened off-stage, thereby placing powerful pictures in the minds of the audience. After all, the imagination can conjure up far more detail than can ever be visually portrayed. This is one of the reasons why we will never be entirely happy when our favourite novel has been adapted onto the big screen because we've created our own film of the story in our heads, linked primarily to the descriptive words provided for us in the book. Of course, it's very difficult for a film to compete with the depth, range and our own acutely personal take on these images.

Let's take this a step further into the murky world of the horror movie: there's a particular genre called the 'splatter movie', where numerous victims are always graphically and gorily dispatched. We may flinch but, more often than not, we aren't afraid. The scariest horror movies are those that leave more to our imaginations, just like the Greek dramatists did with their tragedies. Take, for example, *Seven*, released in the UK in 1996, directed by David Fincher and starring Brad Pitt, Morgan Freeman, Gwyneth Paltrow and Kevin Spacey. A serial killer sets out to punish people whom he sees as lost to one of the seven deadly sins: gluttony, greed, sloth, envy, wrath, pride and lust. We follow the two investigators who deal with the trail of horror he has left behind. However, what is powerful about the movie is that it doesn't show the details of what the killer's victims experienced; instead we are either told what happened to them or shown a small visual left over from the experience. The rest is up to our imaginations, which creates a truly horrible reality.

So a combination of narrative description and audience imagination effectively create the horror of Greek tragedy. The character usually designated to bring this to life is the 'Messenger' (although other characters sometimes deliver 'messenger' – type speeches as well), who has been entrusted to deliver a report on events he has personally witnessed. Of course the messenger will always bring his own emotions to the task in hand: he's often shocked by what he's seen or reluctant to speak because he knows what effect his words will have on the remaining characters. Whatever he feels though is secondary to the actual story he relates and its importance within the world of the play. He knows and understands his function, however emotional the moment might be for him.

This means that if the messenger's emotions are played out in full then the story will be lost and the tragedy eroded (in other words, avoid playing the tragedy or being tragic in order to bring the tragedy to life). The actor must work through the story, image by image, to ensure that it is received and understood by the other characters. This doesn't mean that the messenger will be emotionally disconnected from what he is delivering: far from it, given that much of the language in 'messenger speeches' involves highly charged description. However, it is only by being vocally specific with word and image that the actor will be able to bring the events to life in the mind's eye of the audience.

Text Sample: Articulating the Tragedy

The following text has been taken from *The Burial at Thebes* by Seamus Heaney. It isn't a direct translation of Sophocles' *Antigone* as Heaney doesn't read classical Greek. He relied on a number of different translations as poetic templates to create a powerful, fierce and urgent adaptation.

The story so far:
Eteocles, Polyneices, Antigone and Ismene were born to Queen Jocasta and King Oedipus of Thebes (who were actually mother and son but that's another story). After their parents died, Eteocles and Polyneices fell out over their inheritance rights and went to war with each other: both were killed on the battle field. Creon, Jocasta's brother, took control of the city after their deaths, being the closest surviving male heir to the throne. He ordered that Eteocles be given a full burial whilst Polyneices' body be left to rot, which effectively denied him entry into the world of the dead. Antigone defied his edict and attempted to bury her brother, covering his body with some dirt. When she returned to finish the job she was arrested by one of the guards. Creon condemned her to death in accordance with the law and would not listen to reason, either from the citizens in the chorus, his son Haemon (who was engaged to be married to Antigone) or the blind seer, Teresias, who predicted dire consequences if the edict was carried out. Eventually Teresias' words sank in and Creon changed his mind. He hurried out to reverse his decision but was too late; Antigone had already been buried alive in a walled up cave. The Messenger brings back an eyewitness account of what happened next. He speaks to Eurydice, Creon's wife and Haemon's mother.

MESSENGER: I can tell you the whole thing, ma'am. There's no
                                                sense
    In making a liar of myself.
    Right from the start I was at your husband's side,
    All of us climbing the hill. And sure enough
    It was still there, Polyneices' corpse,
    Or what the dogs had left of it. So we prayed
    To the goddess of the crossroads and to Pluto
    To hold their anger back and to ignore
    The pitilessness of that desecration.
    Then we washed the remains in purifying water,
    Gathered sticks and made enough of a fire
    To burn him decently. And as was right,
    We piled his home ground over him at last.

    Then on we went, right up to the cave mouth,
    And deep in that unholy vault we hear
    Such terrible howling we have to send for Creon.
    And when Creon comes, he howls himself and he
                                          knows.

    'O hide me, hide me from myself,' he cries,
    'For I face the saddest door I ever faced.
    I hear my son's voice in there. Come on,'
    He shouts, 'Tumble the stones, break through
    And look and tell me. Tell me if it's Haemon.'

    So we broke the barrier down as ordered
    And saw into the gallery. Antigone was there,
    Hanging by her neck from a linen noose,
    And Haemon on the ground beside her
    With his arms up round her waist, imploring
    The underworld, lamenting his dead bride
    And shouting execrations against Creon.

    But Creon couldn't help himself and went
    With open arms to the boy and started pleading,
    Calling him 'son', saying he'd had a fit
    And to watch himself. But Haemon spat in his face

And made a quick lunge with his two-edged sword
And would have got him if Creon hadn't dodged.
Then before we knew where we were, he had turned
The sword on himself and buried half the blade
In his own side. And as he was collapsing
His arms still clung to the girl and blood came spurting
Out of his mouth all over her white cheek…
That was the kiss he gave his bride-to-be.

(*EURYDICE begins her exit.*)

A wedding witnessed in the halls of death.
And one to teach us living witnesses
The mortal cost of ill-judged words and deeds.

The Burial at Thebes by Seamus Heaney, adapted from *Antigone* by Sophocles, and first published in 2004 by Faber and Faber.   (5)

Workshop Plan: Articulating the Tragedy

OBJECTIVES

- To work vocally in the moment, recreating an eyewitness event.

- To vocalise word, image and story within a piece of text, specifically and truthfully.

- To find an appropriate vocal level for the tragedy through the words and images of the text.

MATERIALS

You will need:
- A collection of old newspaper cuttings of dramatic/tragic events
- Copies of the Messenger speech from *The Burial at Thebes* by Seamus Heaney (as provided in the previous 'Sample Text' box) for each member of the workshop group
- Crayons and felt tip pens

- Sheets of blank drawing paper
- Recording equipment

WARM UP

Structure a warm up from the information listed in Chapter 1; however, make sure that exercises which focus on muscular support for breath and articulation are given priority so that sound and word can be explored fully and specifically.

ACTIVITIES AND EXERCISES

- Take a series of old newspaper cuttings and ask the group to choose one of them as inspiration for the imaginary re-telling of an event they have witnessed. It's a good idea to get them to prepare this as homework so they have time to develop and practice their story. Now ask them to present each of their stories as if they're late for the workshop/rehearsal and this incredible event prevented them from getting there on time. Get each person in turn to leave the room and enter with their particular version of events, starting with 'You're not going to believe what's just happened to me'. Although they'll be in an emotional state (from witnessing something tragic) they should remember to let the story shine through, building it image by image. Get the rest of the group (their audience) to repeat back the images that had the most impact on them.

- Hand out *The Burial at Thebes* text to each actor. You may wish to give some background detail about the story at this point but try to avoid telling them what the speech is about.

- Ask your actors to speak the text aloud in their own space. They may need to try it a couple of times through in order to clarify the sense for themselves.

- Get them to break the text down into separate images, marking each one with a pen or pencil. Hand out paper and pens and ask them to create a storyboard of the text, which means drawing a picture for each separate image. This will help them to build detailed visual pictures in their own heads, essential if they want to communicate the text images vocally to an audience. The quality of the drawings doesn't matter (stick figures are fine); it's the mental detail that's important.

- Now ask them to speak the text aloud again, but as they move from one image to another they must physically point to each of the pictures on their storyboard. They should then speak the text again but this time rely on the pictures within their head (without the storyboard) to bring the text to life. If they remain true to these pictures then the appropriate vocal energy, flow and impact will be found, without the actor having to think about it. For example, there is a change in vocal energy and pace when Haemon spits in Creon's face and lunges at him with his sword. If the actor has built up enough detail in the image and totally commits to what they've created then these vocal changes will happen automatically.

- Time to carry out a little test. Organise the group into pairs and ask one person in the partnership to speak the text aloud, image by image, to the other person. The listener must close their eyes and the speaker must allow time after each image for the listener to describe back the pictures they've seen in their head in response to what they've heard. There shouldn't be a discussion about the variation between the listener's pictures and the speaker's pictures as there will always be differences. All the speaker needs to know is that they've created some sort of detailed picture in the listener's mind. Once this has been achieved then the speaker can move on to the next image. If it hasn't happened then the speaker may need to repeat the previous image, strengthening their own visual pictures so that the image is clarified through the words of the text. Make sure both actors are given an opportunity to be both speaker and listener.

- Take this exercise one step further by asking the actors to imagine they're performing in a radio play as they speak the text aloud. This will help them to clarify word, image and story even more as they work to provide visual detail for an imaginary (and more distant) audience. Provide them with an opportunity to record the speech so that they can listen back to it with their partners, noting any differences they might hear from the previous exercise.

- Allow some time for a group de-briefing session. Use the following questions as a starting point for the discussion:

  - What did you discover about how human beings recreate and report tragic eyewitness events?

  - What were the vocal variations throughout the text? Describe how you brought them to life.

  - What practical knowledge will you take away from this workshop (ie what did you learn)?

CHAPTER 8

VOICING THE MASK

Every character in Greek tragedy possesses a universal human characteristic, which was physically represented on a mask that the actor wore in performance. This characteristic was usually the dominating value, attitude, drive or desire of the character, depending on the particular issues they faced. It didn't mean the characters were one-dimensional (far from it) because there is always a range of emotions dwelling within a dominant characteristic (for example, 'arrogance', 'uncertainty' and 'despair' can all develop out of 'pride').

It did mean, however, that playwrights were not so concerned with the minor individual or personal details within a character's life but more interested in the larger issues they faced as human beings and how they were affected by them. Of course the outcome of these issues usually brought characters into conflict with the gods and the pre-destined fate that the gods had mapped out for them.

Some contemporary productions of ancient Greek drama choose not to work with masks. It's a difficult decision for a director: masks can strengthen the character archetypes and, therefore, the impact of the story but they can also distract a modern audience who are used to seeing the detailed facial expressions of actors. Another consideration is that contemporary actors aren't always adept at utilising the physical properties of a mask so if you do choose to go down this road then you will need to allocate time for in-depth physical and vocal work.

A mask will help an actor to create a character but only if they fulfil what has been written into the mask by the playwright without imposing anything extra onto it. Of course there will be a range of human emotions to be explored but they must be all filtered through the archetype portrayed on the mask.

Physically, an actor must accept and inhabit the archetype of the mask and learn to communicate its expression through the whole body (excluding the face, of course).

Vocally, an actor must accept the mask through the language the playwright has used to express that mask. This means fully exploring the range and energy within the words if the mask is to be fulfilled.

Because the playwright has written the mask *into* story and character, this work becomes indispensable, whether you choose to work with the physical presence of a mask or not.

However, if full masks are worn then your actors will find their voices technically challenged. Resonance will be limited because the face is covered so it's important to increase vibration in other areas of the body to help compensate. Resonant vibration travels off the body and out into space but if this is blocked for some reason then vibration will be limited to other areas of the body. Consonant sounds may become muffled as well so articulation needs to be crisp, precise and muscular. A half mask will lessen the problem of articulation but resonance will still be limited. In all cases, clarity of thought and emotion will help to focus the sound.

Text Samples 1: Voicing the Mask

The following texts have been taken from *The Oresteia* by Aeschylus (comprising three plays: *Agamemnon, The Choephori* and *The Eumenides*) in a version by Ted Hughes, first published in 1999 by Faber and Faber. There are six pieces presented here, taken from the mouths of Agamemnon, Cassandra, Clytemnestra, Aegisthus, Electra and Orestes, which will provide you with a range of character archetypes to work with in a workshop situation.

The story so far:
The Oresteia tells the tale of the immediate aftermath of the Trojan War when the royal house of Argos succumbed to a family curse.

It all started back with King Atreus of Argos who was embroiled in a bitter feud with his brother, Thyestes. Thyestes slept with Atreus' wife so Atreus punished him by secretly killing his two eldest sons and serving them up for dinner. Needless to say Thyestes cursed his brother and family, a curse that was handed down to the next generation.

Atreus' two sons, Agamemnon and Menelaus, married Clytemnestra and Helen. When Helen was seduced and stolen away by Paris of Troy, Agamemnon and Menelaus organised an army to teach Troy a lesson and claim her back. Unfortunately, when they set out, the winds were not in their favour and Agamemnon was forced to sacrifice his eldest daughter, Iphigeneia, to ensure the goddess Artemis gave their fleet of ships a safe passage. Clytemnestra, bitter over the death of her daughter, took Aegisthus as her lover whilst Agamemnon was away. Aegisthus was the only remaining son of Thyestes so the two were united in their hatred.

Agamemnon returned from Troy ten years later, victorious and triumphant. Clytemnestra falsely welcomed him home as a hero only to stab him to death in his bath later as revenge. Agamemnon had brought Cassandra back from Troy as one of the spoils of war. Cassandra had been granted the gift of prophecy by Apollo but, because she had refused to sleep with him, her prophecies weren't believed. Clytemnestra murdered Cassandra as well but not before Cassandra had predicted the bloodshed. The two lovers, Clytemnestra and Aegisthus, ruled Argos together.

Agamemnon and Clytemnestra had two other children, Electra and Orestes. Orestes had been sent away from Argos as a child but Electra had witnessed her mother's and Aegisthus' atrocities. The god Apollo sent Orestes back to Argos to avenge his father's death and murder his mother and her lover. This invoked the wrath of the Furies, terrible creatures who lived under the earth, and Orestes was forced to seek protection at Apollo's shrine in Delphi.

AGAMEMNON: First, let me call on the gods that favour Argos.
You Gods, you shared the revenge I took on Troy.

You Gods, share my triumph.
Heaven heard the prayers of Argos, because they were
                                                          just.
But the prayers of Troy were empty. They were swept up
Like rubbish from the floors of heaven,
And dumped into the pit
As bedding for a slaughtered population –
Where the burial mound, over the mass graves,
Would be the city's ruins. Hope
Gave Troy energy to struggle awhile,
But in the end Troy was suffocated
In the smoke of its own burning wealth.
Troy's luxury glowed into embers of incense,
Mixed with the blue flame of melting corpses.
The smell spread over the sea, to neighbouring lands.
The gods can never be thanked.
Let everybody thank them.
Troy raped our woman. Troy no longer exists.
The lion of Argos, ablaze on our shields,
Burst from the belly of a horse, in pitch darkness.
Scattered the bones from the bodies of Troy's heroes,
Lapped up the royal lineage to the last drop
And left the city a bloody stain on the earth.

Agamemnon (*The Oresteia*) by Aeschylus in a version by Ted
Hughes. First published in 1999 by Faber and Faber.   (6)

CASSANDRA: You want to know?
          I'll rip away these bridal veils
          Where prophecy peeped and murmured.
          I'll let it go, like a sea-squall
          That heaps the ocean and piles towers
          Of thunder into the sunrise –
          I'll bring out a crime
          More terrible than my own murdered body
          Into the glare of the sun.

No more mystery. I will show you
How far back
The track of blood and bloody guilt
Began, that now sets me
And Agamemnon and Clytemnestra
Face to face today.
This house is full of demons.
The loathsome retinue
Of the royal blood.
Under these painted ceilings they flitter and jabber.
They huddle on every stair.
They laugh and rustle and whisper
Inside the walls.
They shift things, in darkness
They squabble and scream in the cellars.
And they sing madness
Into the royal ears. Madness.

Agamemnon (*The Oresteia*) by Aeschylus in a version by Ted
Hughes. First published in 1999 by Faber and Faber.   (7)

CLYTEMNESTRA: You heard me pronounce the words required by
                                            the moment.
          The moment has passed. Those words are meaningless.
          How else could I have killed this man –
          My deadliest enemy?
          Lies and embraces were simply my method.
          The knots in the net that enmeshed him.
          I pondered this for a long time.
          And when the moment for action came
          I made no mistake. See, my work
          Perfected. I don't disown it.
          Every possibility of error
          I wrapped in a great net –
          Not a fish could have slipped from the shoal.
          His struggles merely tightened the tangle.

Then, at my leisure, choosing the best places
On his helpless body
I pushed the blade into him. Once, twice.
Twice he screamed. You heard him.
Then his eyes stared elsewhere.
His body arched like a bow being strung,
Every muscle straining for life.
I placed the point for a third and final time
And drove the blade clean through him.

That was my thanks to God
For fulfilling my prayers.
I offered this murder up
To God – protector of the dead.
Then the blood belched from him with a strange
                          barking sound.
A foaming jet that showered the walls
And showered me, like a warm spring rain
That makes the new-sown corn swell with joy
And the buds split into blossom.
I felt my whole body exult.

Agamemnon (*The Oresteia*) by Aeschylus in a version by Ted
Hughes. First published in 1999 by Faber and Faber.   (8)

AEGISTHUS: Justice! At last the day of justice has dawned.
          This is perfect proof that the gods
          Watch men and punish evil.
          What a beautiful sight
          To see this man gagged and bound
          In meshes knotted by the Furies!
          To see his body
          Emptied of all its blood.
          At last he has paid
          For the inhuman crime his father committed
          Against my father. You should know
          His father and my father had quarrelled.

Agamemenon's father, Atreus,
Ruled Argos.
Atreus had driven out of the city
My father, his brother Thyestes.

Thyestes came back.
Forgave, begged to be forgiven,
Sat at the hearth of Atreus, a supplicant,
Happy simply to live in peace with his brother.
Happy simply to live.
Atreus hid his hatred.
He gave my father a banquet.
He took my two brothers,
The two eldest sons of Thyestes,
Cut their throats and bled them,
Butchered them, and stewed the meat.
The feet with their toes, the hands with their fingers
He hid at the bottom of the dish.
Over those he layered the steaks and collops,
The chopped livers and kidneys, the hearts, the brains.
Each guest had a separate table.
This was the dish set steaming before my father.

Agamemnon (*The Oresteia*) by Aeschylus in a version by Ted Hughes. First published in 1999 by Faber and Faber. (9)

ELECTRA: And now I pour out water of purification for my dead
father –

And I call on his spirit. Father –
Pity your children. Pity me. Pity Orestes.
Pity your son, Orestes, and your daughter.
We are disinherited and homeless,
Bartered by our own mother,
Sold off in exchange for Aegisthus,
Supplanted by your killer.
I live among slaves. I live the life of a slave.
Orestes is banished.

How shall we get our home back?
Aegisthus and your Queen, Clytemnestra,
Glitter among the luxury of your treasures
Like two serpents coiled together
In a gorged sleep.
Father, where is Orestes?
Guide him home.
Hear my prayer and answer it.

All I ask for myself
Is to be unlike my mother –
Hands, heart, thoughts clean,
Unlike my mother,
Conscience clean, undarkened by blood,
Unlike my mother.
These prayers are for us.

Now for our enemies –
Father, your avenger,
Let him come with a blade
Remorseless as the blade they pushed through you.
Let him measure it out, the length and the breadth
Of death for death,
Justice for murder.
What are your murderers hoping for?
Orestes' blade is my hope.
They curse you, and buried the curse to the hilt.
Orestes' blade is my curse.

The Choephori (*The Oresteia*) by Aeschylus in a version by Ted
Hughes. First published in 1999 by Faber and Faber.   (10)

ORESTES: Zeus, look down, look at us.
        Watch what we do now.
        We are the eagle's children,
        Bereft, in the nest fouled
        With the corpse of an eagle

Tangled in the meshing coils
Of the snake that struck.
See what deprivation
Has done to the helpless,
Strengthless fledgelings –
Yet the eagle's flight,
The eagle's prey, the eagle's nest, the highest eyrie
Belong to us.
Look at us, Zeus. Look at Orestes and Electra,
Orphaned and exiled.
King Agamemnon piled up sacrifices
And poured out libations
In a perpetual banquet
Of offerings to you.
If you let us perish
That banquet is over.
And when eaglets are dead
How shall men read
Your signals in heaven?
Who will honour
Your unresponsive altars?
Root out this evil monarchy.
Rescue this house.
Lift from its fall
Our tree of strength.
From the King's grave
Let our glory
Rise again.

The Choephori (*The Oresteia*) by Aeschylus in a version by Ted Hughes. First published in 1999 by Faber and Faber.   (11)

Text Samples 2: Voicing the Mask

An extract from Martin Luther King's speech on the steps of the Lincoln Memorial in Washington DC on 28th August 1963.

I say to you today, my friends, that in spite of the difficulties and frustrations of the moment I still have a dream. It is a dream deeply rooted in the American dream.

I have a dream that one day this nation will rise up and live out the true meaning of its creed: 'We hold these truths to be self-evident that all men are created equal.'

I have a dream that one day, on the red hills of Georgia, the sons of former slaves and the sons of former slave owners will be able to sit down together at the table of brotherhood.

I have a dream that one day even the state of Mississippi, a desert state sweltering with the heat of injustice and oppression, will be transformed into an oasis of freedom and justice.

I have a dream that my four little children will one day live in a nation where they will not be judged by the colour of their skin but the content of their character.

I have a dream today.

I have a dream that one day the state of Alabama, whose governor's lips are presently dripping with the words of interposition and nullification, will be transformed into a situation where little black boys and black girls will be able to join hands with little white boys and white girls and walk together as sisters and brothers.

I have a dream today.

I have a dream that one day every valley shall be exalted, every hill and mountain shall be made low, the rough places will be made plains and the crooked places will be made straight, and the glory of the Lord shall be revealed and all flesh shall see it together.

This is our hope. This is the faith with which I return to the South. With this faith we will be able to hew out of the mountain of despair a stone of hope. With this faith we will be able to transform the jangling discords of our nation into a beautiful symphony of brotherhood. With this faith we will be able to work together, to pray together, to struggle together, to go to jail together, to stand up for freedom together, knowing that we will be free one day. (12)

A speech by Elizabeth 1 to the troops about to enter into battle with the Spanish Armada in 1588.

My loving people, we have been persuaded by some that are careful of our safety, to take heed how we commit ourselves to armed multitudes, for fear of treachery. But I assure you, I do not desire to live to distrust my faithful and loving people. Let tyrants fear... I have always so behaved myself that, under God, I have placed my chiefest strength and safeguard in the loyal hearts and good will of my subjects, and therefore I am come amongst you as you see at this time, not for my recreation and disport, but being resolved, in the midst and heat of the battle, to live or die amongst you all, to lay down for my God, and for my kingdom, and for my people, my honour and my blood, even in the dust. I know I have the body of a weak and feeble woman, but I have the heart and stomach of a king, and of a king of England too, and think foul scorn that Parma or Spain or any Prince of Europe should dare to invade the borders of my realm, to which, rather than any dishonour shall grow by me, I myself will take up arms, I myself will be your general, judge, and rewarder of every one of your virtues in the field. I know already, for your forwardness you have deserved rewards and crowns, and we do assure you, in the word of a Prince, they shall be duly paid you... By your valour in the field, we shall shortly have a famous victory over these enemies of my God, of my kingdom and of my people. (13)

A speech by Neil Kinnock, Labour MP, delivered on the eve of a general election on the 7th of June 1983 in Bridgend. Labour lost the election but four months later Mr Kinnock was elected leader of the party.

If Margaret Thatcher is re-elected as Prime Minister,

I warn you

I warn you that you will have pain –
When healing and relief depend upon payment.

I warn you that you will have ignorance –
When talents are untended and wits are wasted, when learning is a privilege and not a right.

I warn you that you will have poverty –
When pensions slip and benefits are whittled away by a Government that won't pay in an economy that can't pay.

I warn you that you will be cold –
When fuel charges are used as a tax system that the rich don't notice and the poor can't afford.

I warn you that you must not expect work –
When many cannot spend, more will not be able to earn. When they don't earn, they don't spend. When they don't spend, work dies.

I warn you not to go into the streets alone after dark or into the streets in large crowds of protest in the light.

I warn you that you will be quiet –
When the curfew of fear and the gibbet of unemployment make you obedient.

I warn you that you will have defence of a sort –
With a risk and at a price that passes all understanding.

I warn you that you will be home-bound –
When fares and transport bills kill leisure and lock you up.

I warn you that you will borrow less –

When credit, loans, mortgages and easy payments are refused to people on your melting income.

If Margaret Thatcher wins, she will be more a Leader than a Prime Minister. That power produces arrogance and when it is toughened by Tebbitry and flattered and fawned upon by spineless sycophants, the boot-licking tabloid Knights of Fleet Street and placemen in the Quangos, the arrogance corrupts absolutely.

If Margaret Thatcher wins –

I warn you not to be ordinary.

I warn you not to be young.

I warn you not to fall ill.

I warn you not to get old.   (14)

Workshop Plan: Voicing the Mask

OBJECTIVES

- To build resonant vibration in the body to cope with the demands of wearing a mask.

- To explore the range and energy of the language which expresses a character's mask.

MATERIALS

You will need:
- Copies of the texts provided in the 'Text Samples 1' box from Ted Hughes' version of *The Oresteia* by Aeschylus.
- Copies of one of the famous speeches provided in the 'Text Samples 2' box.
- Neutral masks made from wood, plastic, cardboard or papier mache (although this workshop also works without using actual physical masks).

VOICING THE MASK

TIMING

This plan will need to be broken down into at least three separate sessions to allow your actors time to absorb and explore the work appropriately. More sessions should be added if you intend to incorporate extensive physical work with the masks.

WARM UP

Structure a warm up from the information listed in Chapter 1; however, make sure that exercises which focus on muscular support for breath, resonance and range are given priority in preparation for wearing a mask (because resonance will be limited by the face being covered). Don't forget to add in some articulation exercises so that consonant sounds are crisp, precise and muscular (because individual sounds may be muffled by the mask).

ACTIVITIES AND EXERCISES

- Start with an exercise that will help your actors create a character mask using the language within a piece of text that isn't related to Greek tragedy but embodies many of its ideals. Ask them to lie down in semi-supine, release into the floor and connect with the breath low in their bodies (see Chapter 1 for further instruction). Start feeding them, line by line, part of a famous speech, such as one by Martin Luther King, Queen Elizabeth I or Neil Kinnock in the 'Text Samples 2' box. Encourage them to breathe the words silently into their body then speak them aloud on the outgoing breath. As they work through the lines ask them to feel their energy and power, however quietly they're working volume-wise. They should choose one of the lines that has a particular resonance for them and repeat it a number of times through (it doesn't matter if they paraphrase). Now ask them to think of one word that describes that person's attitude, drive, desire or ambition (ie the character's mask) and get them to vocalise that word a number of times on their outgoing breath. Hand each actor a full copy of the speech to try all the way through.

- Whilst they're still on the floor, hand out copies of the character text from the 'Text Samples 1' box, making sure there are a number of different characters in operation around the group. You may wish to give some background detail about the story at this point but try to avoid telling them what the speeches are about. Ask them to read the text through silently in their heads just to make sense of the meaning and then again, transferring it into the tempo in which they would speak it aloud. Make sure their breath keeps flowing as they read (watch out for breath holders). Now get them to mouth the words silently to themselves, really using their lips and tongue, and, feeling the length and weight of the words in their mouth. Ask them to vocalise the words aloud in their own space and time: again encourage them to breathe each line or thought silently into their body then speak it aloud on the outgoing breath. They should now take their time coming up off the floor through the prayer position and a spinal roll (see Chapter 1 for further instruction).

- Set up small discussion groups (those with the same characters should work together). Ask them to start by comparing the words they chose to describe the character mask in the 'famous speech' exercise. Then they should come to a group consensus about the character mask in their Aeschylus text (ie the character's attitude, drive, desire or ambition) that they might have discovered whilst connecting to the words in semi-supine. It may help if they listen to each other speaking the text. Here are some suggestions:
  Agamemnon – proud and triumphant
  Clytemnestra – relieved and triumphant
  Aegisthus – defiant and triumphant
  Electra – vengeful conviction (grieving but hopeful)
  Cassandra – vulnerable conviction (grieving but resigned to her fate)
  Orestes – hopeful conviction

- Before working with the masks, take some time getting the actors to re-connect back to sound vibration. Ask them to gently pat all over their bodies, starting from the feet up and not forgetting the face and skull. They can team up with someone else so that their back can be done as well. Their bodies should now feel warm and tingly. Now ask them to try some humming and blowing through the lips across their pitch range (see Chapter 1 for further instruction). They can also try speaking the words of their text up and down their pitch range, which, of course, will sound strange but will help to loosen it up. Keep getting them to reconnect back to their breath on an fffff sound to ensure that the work is supported.

Finally, get them to speak their text aloud, exaggerating the consonants so that their words will have shape and definition once they're wearing the mask.

- Now it's time to start working with the masks. It's important to instil into your actors a sense of respect for their mask by providing them with opportunities for exploring its ritualistic nature and accepting its power. So:
  (1) Always ask them to put on their mask as if it's a sacred object.
  (2) Allow time for the neutrality of the mask to inform their whole bodies (so they're neutrally centred and focused).
  (3) Set-up physical activities and situations that will help them to express themselves through their whole body (rather than just the face).

- As part of this process, build in sound rituals that will also have a technical pay-off (helping them to release sound freely and easily whilst wearing the mask). For example, ask them to vocalise the same sound or rhythmic set of sounds, each time they place the mask on their face (they can develop their own idiosyncratic versions). Also ask them to create another sound which will help them find their neutral centre, like a calming hum or a vocalised release sigh or an elongated fffff that reconnects them back to the breathing muscles low in the body. Give them time to build confidence in vocalising and verbalising through the mask. Be patient.

- Now allow your actors to come back to the text but wearing their mask. If there is time, you might like to have them make their own masks, which portray the particular attitude of the character they're focusing on. If this isn't possible, then just for the purposes of this exercise, stick with the neutral masks. As they put them on ask them to endow their 'putting on the mask sound' with the particular attribute they decided on in their group discussion eg triumphant. This will also help them to take on the attribute physically. Now they should try the text aloud in their own space and time, building their confidence in expressing the words and thoughts through the mask.

- Time to carry out a little test. Organise the group into pairs (each actor must have worked on a different piece of text/character to their partner) and ask one person to speak the text aloud, thought by thought, to the other person. Allow some time for discussion so that the listener can describe back to the speaker what they believe the attribute to be. This will help the speaker to really clarify their attribute through the words and thoughts of the text. Now get them to swap over and repeat the exercise.

- Allow some time for a group de-briefing session. Use the following questions as a starting point for the discussion:

  - What did you discover about your character's voice after using the mask?

  - Did your character's voice change in any way as you worked your way through the text? Can you pinpoint it on the page?

  - How did you mark this change vocally?

  - What practical knowledge will you take away from this workshop (ie what did you learn?)?

CHAPTER 9

CHORAL THINKING, CHORAL SPEAKING

The primary function of the chorus was as the voice of a collective community of people who had a like-minded interest (or stake) in the story being presented. In *The Women of Troy* by Euripides the chorus have lost their husbands, fathers and sons and await their fate from the conquering Greeks. Of course each woman will have had an individual experience in the war but their communal commentary on the action is a collective pain, which ultimately strengthens the horror of their individual stories.

The collective voice that continuously breaks the dramatic flow with long choral odes is a challenge to produce on the modern-day stage. Consequently some productions reduce the chorus to one individual actor, cut the lyrical verse and play the text more naturalistically. However, this tends to weaken the tragedy (and the politics within the tragedy) because the chorus heightens the tension much more acutely by focusing on how that tragedy has affected a community of people.

So your actors should come to an understanding of the collective voice they are portraying by interpreting the text as an ensemble. Of course this doesn't mean that lines can't be delivered individually by members of the chorus or the leader of the chorus (the choruphaios), but it must be clear that any individual voice is speaking for the group as a whole.

Ultimately, collective understanding will only come from group experimentation with the words of the text. By grappling with the language as a group, your actors will come to a deeper understanding of the story (and their place within it) as a whole. Of course, you can always provide guidance during this process to ensure that the focus/

objective of the production is being met, but try to avoid choreograph-ing every single vocal nuance. Although this can create some very pretty vocal patterns it will remain, ultimately, an empty experience for actor and audience as it bypasses story, meaning and emotion.

This doesn't mean that there can't be ritualistic vocal elements within the chorus – a combination of singing, chanting and speaking (individual and group) can help open out the religious and mytho-logical significance within the story, as well as strengthen the tragedy. Encourage your actors to experiment with different types of vocalisa-tions. Vocal changes can help mark shifts in emphasis between sections which are more reflective in nature and those which comment more directly on the action.

Likewise you may wish to incorporate some ritualised and choreo-graphed dance into the chorus sequences. However, movement should always develop out of word and context so keep coming back to the text.

And a final word on group games. These are an important part of developing an ensemble mentality within your chorus but don't rely on them too heavily. Group games won't automatically create the collec-tive voice without group experimentation with the actual words.

Text Samples: Choral Thinking, Choral Speaking

The following text has been taken from *The Women of Troy* by Euripides in a version by Don Taylor, published by Methuen Drama in 2007. The piece could be spoken by one person but it also offers up wonderful opportunities for a collection of voices, movement and sound.

The story so far:
Helen, the most beautiful woman in the world, was lured away from Greece by Paris of Troy. When Helen's husband, Menelaus, found out, he declared war on Troy and set out with his brother Agamemnon and the Greek army to bring her back again.

The Trojan War lasted ten long years and was finally won by the Greek army sending an enormous wooden horse into the besieged city, which was filled with Greek soldiers. When the Trojans were lulled into a false sense of security, the soldiers sprang forth from the belly of the horse and took control of the city, killing the men and raping and imprisoning the women.

When the play opens the women are awaiting their fate as slaves and prostitutes for the Greeks. Hecuba, Queen of Troy and mother of Paris, and her daughter, Cassandra, are among them. Also imprisoned is Andromache, the wife of Hecuba's son Hector, and her baby son, Astyanax. The Greeks decide to kill the baby to ensure that he won't grow up to avenge his father's and family's deaths.

The following excerpt is a painful and bitter commentary by the women of the chorus on the final moments of war when the giant wooden horse entered the city so it has a strong narrative thread. The piece appears in the play not long after the virginal Cassandra has been taken away to become the 'bride' of Agamemnon.

CHORUS: Teach me, gods of song, some harsh lament
       Dissonant with tears and howls,
       Help me to sing Troy's sorrows, invent
       New sounds for my grief: the Greek horse on wheels
       Has ruined me, brought me to the edge of the grave
       Made me a slave.
       Unguarded they left it, by the main gate,
       Its gold cheek pieces gleaming,
       And from its belly the clash of armour plate
       Rumbled like thunder, muffled and threatening./
       So we ran to the rock of the citadel
       The whole population, shouting,
       'Come out everybody, all
       Our troubles are over, wheel
       This wooden offering for Zeus' daughter,
       Athene of Troy, inside the wall!'

And who ran from their houses the faster,
The young men or the old? All high
On the singing and the joy, as they laid hands on the
　　　　　　　　　　　　　　　　　　　monster
That was more than it seemed, and would doom them
　　　　　　　　　　　　　　　　　　　all to die./
Then it seemed the whole nation of the Phrygians ran
To the gates, eager to bring
That smooth planed icon of mountain pine
And the Greek ambush within it, as an offering
To the virgin who drives the immortal horses of
　　　　　　　　　　　　　　　　　　　heaven –
For the Trojans, destruction.
Roped with cables of twisted flax
They heaved it, like a black ship,
To the stone shrine at the heart of the temple complex
Of Pallas Athene – altars soon to drip
And smooth floors run slippery with Trojan blood./
Then the melodious African pipe
Honeyed the air, as the dark hood
Of night enfolded Troy. In celebration
After the day's exhaustion, the whole city was singing,
Dancing feet stamping in exhilaration
To the rhythm of young girls' voices, flickering
Torches casting puddles of light
In the darkened palaces, and on the faces sleeping,
And in eyes wide awake and glittering in the pitch dark
　　　　　　　　　　　　　　　　　　　night,/
At that time in our great hall
With the others, I was singing
All our favourite songs to Artemis, Zeus' daughter,
Virgin of the mountains, and joining in the dancing;
When suddenly I heard a terrible howl,
The unmistakable sound of murder,
A terrified scream rising from the streets of the whole
City. /Children grabbed hold of their mothers'

Skirts, their pale hands plucked at her gown,
Fluttering with fear. The god of war
Had sprung his trap, the ambush strategy
Worked perfectly, thanks to Pallas Athene, whose power
Secretly inspired it. The Trojans were cut down
In their own homes, in sanctuary, beheaded where they
lay
Sleeping, a whole generation of women raped in their
own
Bedrooms, breeding bastards for the Greeks, desolation
for Troy./

The Women of Troy by Euripides in a version by Don Taylor. First published in 2007 by Methuen Drama.   (15)

The following text has been taken from *Oedipus Tyrannos* by Sophocles, translated by Timberlake Wertenbaker, published by Faber and Faber in 1992. Much of the text is in prose except for some of the chorus pieces, which provide evocative commentary on the action.

The story so far:
Oedipus was abandoned at birth and left to die by his father, King Lauis of Thebes, because of a prophecy claiming that the son would grow up to kill the father. The baby was rescued by a shepherd and adopted by the King and Queen of Corinth, who didn't have any children of their own and so brought him up as their heir.

On reaching manhood, a stranger told Oedipus that he was not the real son of his parents. To discover the truth he went to Delphi to consult the oracle where he learnt that he was destined to kill his father and marry his mother. He resolved never to return to Corinth to save the people he believed to be his parents.

On his wanderings he had an argument with a man who tried to push him off the road. There was a fight and he killed him, not knowing that this was his real father, King Laius. He pressed on to Thebes where he ended up saving the city from the Sphinx (part woman, part animal) by solving a riddle.

In thanks the city made him King and he married Queen Jocasta, his mother.

Afterwards the city was struck by a terrible plague and when Apollo's ocacle advised that it was because Thebes was polluted by King Laius' murderer, Oedipus was blinded by his pride and self-belief (pride in his achievements and belief in his own identity and judgement). He refused to consider that the King and Queen of Corinth were not his parents or that he had killed his real father and married his mother and became arrogant and dismissive towards those witnesses who tried to tell him the truth.

This is the first choral ode in the play, where the Citizens of Thebes appeal to the gods to help them in their misery and send away the plague.

CHORUS: Welcome voice of Zeus, come
to famous Thebes from
gold-rich Delphi. But for
what?

Fear: my heart beats,
shakes. This fear: torture.
Terror racks me.

Delian healer,
awe-cloaked.
Is this a new calamity,
unknown? Or the return,
seasonal, revolving, of
something past?

Tell me, deathless voice,
child of golden hope

We call on you first,
daughter of Zeus, eternal
Athene.
And then on your sister,
earth-encircling Artemis,

whose throne dominates our
marketplace.
And on Apollo, whose darts
no one escapes.
You can turn fate back –
away.
Come to me
If you ever drove suffering
from our borders once
before, then come again
now.

I bear countless sorrows.
All my citizens ill. No
spear-like thought to cut
us free. Nothing grows in
the earth, nothing in the
wombs of women. Look: one
life after another flies off,
swifter than a bird.
Death speeds, with the
crackle of a forest fire.

The city dies again and
again. Offspring lie on the
ground spreading death. No
one pities their pain. No
one laments their end.
Wives, mothers, grey-
haired, come from all parts
to the steps of the altars,
crying out the bitterness
of pain.
Prayers for healing – cries
for the dead – mount in
unison.

From all this, golden

daughter of Zeus, friend,
defend us.
Give us strength.

Let the plague-bearing God
Ares – appearing not in
the bronzed glitter of
war, but in a mantle of
screams – let him turn
back, away from our
borders, blown over the
Atlantic, or sent north to
the black shores of Thrace.

Whatever escapes
destruction at night
succumbs by day.
Zeus, master of lightning,
of fire, smash this god of
plague with your thunder.

Apollo, god of light, defend
us with your golden arrows.
Artemis, defend us with the
hunting flares that sparkle
on your hills.

And Bakchos, companion of
the maenads, Bakchos of
the golden headband and
face flushed with wine,
defend us with the flame of
your torches –
You three gods,
come and defend us against
this ungodly god.

Oedipus Tyrannos by Sophocles, translated by Timberlake Wertenbaker. First published in 1992 by Faber and Faber.   (16)

Workshop Plan: Choral Thinking, Choral Speaking

OBJECTIVES

- To develop the sensitivity required to work as part of a vocal ensemble.

- To bring word, image and story to life within a piece of text as part of a vocal ensemble.

- To understand and communicate a collective character through a collective voice.

MATERIALS

You will need:
- Copies of one of the texts provided in the 'Text Samples' box, depending on the gender of the group you are working with. *The Women of Troy* text is more appropriate for work with a female group and the *Oedipus Tyrannos* text is useful if you have an all male or mixed gender group.

WARM UP

Structure a warm up from the information listed in Chapter 1; however, make sure that exercises which focus on a communal experience of breath, resonance, range and articulation are given priority.

ACTIVITIES AND EXERCISES

- Start with some games/exercises that will help your chorus to establish themselves as an ensemble. Some of the ones listed in Part 1 of this book are ideal: for example, from Chapter 2 try the *Sound Song* and the *Sound Orchestra*. You might also like to try another exercise called *Thunderstorm*. Ask the group to sit cross-legged on the floor in a circle. Their knees should be touching and their eyes should be closed. Now ask them to move from clicking their fingers to light clapping to heavy clapping to patting their knees to slapping their thighs to banging the floor in front of them (creating the sound of a growing thunderstorm). Repeat the exercise but this time anyone in the group can take responsibility for moving on from one sound to another or back again. As soon as the group hears a new sound they should move onto it as quickly as possible. This means that the group will be required to listen carefully and work together: it's a simple but effective way of focusing the group in on themselves.

- Ask the group to remain in a circle and read through the text together as one voice. It may become monotonous or sing-songy, which is fine for the moment. Avoid making any comment.

- Now ask one person to read to the first punctuation mark, followed by the person next to them to the second punctuation mark and so on around the circle until the text is finished. Coach them to balance a breath with each thought.

- Repeat the exercise but this time ask the group to voice aloud any individual words that stand out or affect them emotionally as they listen to each speaker. For example, in *The Woman of Troy* excerpt, they may choose to repeat: *lament, tears, howls, sounds, grief,* etc.

- Now get them to read through the text as a group again. You may find that their breathing automatically starts to follow the thoughts of the text and the words start to come to life.

- Break the group into smaller groups and allocate each group a portion of the text. For example, in *The Woman of Troy* excerpt you could break it up like this:

> 'Teach me…' to '…threatening.'
> 'So we ran…' to '…doom them all to die.'
> 'Then it seemed…' to '…Trojan blood.'
> 'Then the melodious…' to '…pitch dark night.'
> 'At that time…' to '…of the whole/City.'
> 'Children…' to '…Troy.'

Try to keep a minimum of three people to each group. If your overall chorus is quite small then give them bigger chunks of text to work with.

- Now ask each group to spend some time working out how their portion of the text should be vocalised. Initially they will need to make some decisions: whether there should be individual and/or group voices speaking and whether particular words/lines should be chanted, spoken or sung (depending on the subject matter, sounds, words and rhythm of their portion of the text). Encourage them to try different types of vocalisation aloud as opposed to discussing the text and intellectualising the exercise.

- Following on from this, give each group time to 'put the text up onto its feet', ie find a physical response. This may be simple in some portions, where stillness is key, but other portions may benefit from movement. Again, encourage them to try things out rather than sitting down and discussing it.

- Finally, ask them to add in extra sounds, if appropriate. This may mean taking the text literally and creating a series of vocal sounds underneath the spoken words that illuminate the meaning of the text. Or, it could mean just adding in sounds that evoke a particular mood or emotion. Give them the option of repeating words as well (as long as it doesn't break the overall rhythm or flow of the piece).

- Ask each group to present their work so that one portion follows on from the next. Repeat the performance but ask them to watch and listen critically so that they can analyse what works and what doesn't work for the text. Allow them some time to discuss their thoughts. Go back and adjust the performances if anything useful is revealed in the discussion.

- The last step in the process is for each group to 'teach' the other groups how to perform their portion of the text as a whole ensemble. This may take some time, as voices will need to be adjusted and any movement re-directed. The act of 'teaching' will help your actors to consolidate their clarity and vision of the text.

- Finish the workshop with a full group performance of the text.

- Allow some time for a group de-briefing session. Use the following questions as a starting point for the discussion:

  – Describe the way in which your group came to performance decisions.

- What did you discover about the collective voice or collective character within the text?

- Can you pinpoint the vocal changes you were required to make within the text?

- How did you mark these changes vocally?

- What practical knowledge will you take away from this workshop (ie what did you learn)?

CHAPTER 10

PERFORMING OUTSIDE

The play on which you are working may not be designated for an outside performance. However, it's an interesting exercise for your actors to workshop the text in the open air as it may help them to clarify their use of the text. The original plays were written for performance in specific open air amphitheatres and working with them outside often forces actors to simplify their delivery, vocally and physically, in order to ensure they are heard and understood.

As part of this process, I believe it is important to help actors come to a practical understanding of basic space acoustics so they will know where they are sending their voices and if the sound and meaning will carry without some sort of vocal adjustment.

Vibration carries sound through space. When this vibration hits a solid object it bounces off it and back to whence it came. So in enclosed theatre spaces we are able to hear ourselves as the sound travels back to us. Of course this varies depending on the materials within a theatre, for example, wood is a better sounding board than concrete and stone. However, in the open air the sound may have very little to bounce off and so doesn't necessarily return to us, which is why the Ancient Greek amphitheatres were structured upwards in a circular fashion to aid audibility. But outside an amphitheatre we may not hear ourselves very well, which means we often tend to push our voices too hard and too high in the mistaken belief that we'll be heard better (which, of course, has the opposite effect). So actors must learn to trust that the audience will receive the sound without it being pushed at them.

Your choice of open air space will affect the outcome of the work. However, if you're rehearsing or teaching in the inner city then don't discount car parks and squares. When I was at Rose Bruford College and working at the Deptford site (now gone) we were lucky enough to have Greenwich Park at our disposal. My favourite place to run this block of work was the small garden at the back of the Royal Observatory, which is often used by open-air theatre companies in the summer. Some of the best workshops were undertaken braving the elements (wind and drizzling rain). The presence of the occasional curious tourists helped to heighten the stakes as well so don't be put off by onlookers.

Text Sample: Performing Outside

The following text has been taken from the *Bacchai* by Euripides, translated by Colin Teevan and first published by Oberon Books in 2002. One of the reasons why this excerpt is useful is because of the constant references to natural forces, which may help your actors to connect to the environment in which they're working.

The story so far:
Dionysus, the god of ecstasy, was fathered by Zeus who fell in love with a mortal woman, Semele of the royal house of Thebes, and made her pregnant. Dionysus is angry with his cousin Pentheus, the ruler of Thebes, and Pentheus' mother, Agave, who refuse to acknowledge his parentage. So Dionysus gathers together the women of Thebes and takes possession of their souls. The women leave the city for Mount Cithaeron where they indulge in Dionysian worship and become known as the 'Bacchai'. Some herdsmen disturb them and the women, in ecstatic rage, tear their herd apart with their bare hands. The following piece is, essentially, a messenger speech, where the Herdsman reports back to Pentheus what he has seen, felt and experienced.

HERDSMAN: I saw them sir, up there, our womenfolk
        Who have abandoned their own homes and run
        Up to the mountains like some psychotic army.
        I saw them and have come to tell you of actions
        Shocking, brute, beyond all belief.

...
At dawn, as I led my herd of cattle
Towards the mountain pastures, I first saw them;
The women, the Bacchai as some now call them,
Because they cry Iacchus Evoe
When they call upon their god and Iacchus,
I suppose, sounds similar to Bacchus,
And they being plural feminine are called Bacchai.
Sorry. Yes. They were in three companies,
When I saw them first – dawn, in the mountains –
One led by Autonoe, the second
Led by Ino and the third, commanded
By their sister, your own mother, Agave.
When I first saw them, they were all asleep
On beds of oak leaves or just bare earth.
All were calm, all quiet, all seemed so innocent,
Not as you've described them, all drunk with wine,
Dancing wild to the music of the pipe,
Or indulging their desires in the solitary woods, but like
                                    I said, at peace.
Just then, with a start, Agave awoke,
She'd heard the distant sounds of men and beasts;
Herdsmen and their herds. Us. She woke the others.
They rubbed their eyes, stretched, soon all were
                                    standing.
At such a time and place, it was a sight;
Their hair free and wild about their shoulders
And teeming with wild snakes that licked their cheeks.
Those who'd left their newborn babes at home
Took up in their arms wild fawns or the whelps of
                                    wolves
Which they suckled to their milk-laden breasts.
All wore wreaths of ivy or of oak leaf.
One took her ivy-covered shaft and struck a rock
And from it sprang a spring of fresh water.
Another dug her shaft into the ground

And out flew a fountain of the god's own wine.
If one wanted milk, she just scratched the earth
With fingers, and the earth flowed with it,
While from each sacred shaft honey poured.
If you'd been there you would now praise this god
Whose rites and rituals you try to stop.
We mountain cattleherds and shepherds met up
To swop tales of the wonders we had seen.
One, who'd just returned from town said,
'Listen my mountain friends, what say you all
That Agave, Pentheus' own mother,
We hunt down from this place to please our lord.'
This seemed a good idea so we hid
Amongst the trees and, in ambush, waited.
When they'd had their fill someone gave the sign,
They came together as one company,
Their shafts aloft, they called in one loud voice:
'Dionysus Iacchus, son of Zeus.'
The whole mountain resounded to their cry,
Or so it seemed. The trees, the wild beasts shook,
The rocks themselves seemed to come to life
To the beat of the dance they then began.
All led by Agave who, in her whirl,
Whirled near to me so I jumped to catch her,
But she cried out, 'Sisters, my Bacchai,
These men would make prey of us. Come quick, come
With your ivy-covered shafts attack them.'
We turned and ran for it, for we have heard
How the Bacchai, when their god is with them,
Will eat raw the flesh from still-living beasts.
We escaped but they found our grazing herds.
They slaughtered them with nothing but their hands.
One dragged a calf from its own mother's teat
And tore it, as it bellowed, clean in two,
While others pulled apart whole heifers,
The woods soon seemed a bloody abattoir.

Even one proud-horned bull was dragged to earth,
His flesh, by fingernails, scratched from his bones
And the scrag ends hurled high into the trees.
All done by the hands of girls and women,
And quicker than a wink from a royal eye.
Then, as birds skim the surface of a lake,
They flocked down through the fruit-rich mountain
glens,
All our women running in wild rampage,
Across the plains where the broad river flows,
To the low-lying village of Erythrae
Which they fell upon like sworn enemies.
They plundered pots and pans and knives and forks
And wrenched babies from their mother's breasts
And, without strap, bore all off upon their backs.
The villagers, enraged by these actions,
Seized sticks and stones and fired them at the Bacchai.
But then a sight beyond belief, my Lord,
The shower of sticks and stones drew not one single
drop of blood
But the ivy shafts, which our womenfolk fired back,
Felled so many men, those who still stood took flight.
Surely some god must work with them when
Women fight like men and men flee like little girls.
As for the Bacchai, sated, for the moment,
They returned to where we first had seen them,
To where the god had poured forth earth's plenty.
They washed the blood from their hands, their faces
Were licked clean by snakes till their cheeks glowed.
Lord, whoever this god, this spirit is,
His power is great, accept him in your city.
Besides, he's given us the gift of wine,
Without which man desires nor endures not.

Bacchai by Euripides, translated by Colin Teevan and first published
by Oberon Books in 2002.   (17)

Workshop Plan: Performing Outside

OBJECTIVES

- To understand the challenge of vocalising a performance in an outdoor space.

- To work towards supporting and releasing the voice freely in the open air.

- To work towards clarifying word, image and story in an outdoor space.

MATERIALS

You will need:
- Copies of the Herdsman speech for each member of the workshop group, taken from the *Bacchai* as provided in the previous 'Sample Text' box.

OR
- One of the texts used in a previous workshop or rehearsal that would benefit from further work in a different space. Chorus speeches can be particularly demanding in this context as they may involve more complex physical elements which muffle vocalisation in the open air. However, don't shy away from using them, as the experience will help your actors to clarify and de-mystify the text.
- An outside space in which to work. A space within a park is ideal although a theatre or rehearsal space car park can provide a useful learning experience as well.

WARM UP

Structure a warm up from the information listed in Chapter 1; however, make sure that exercises which focus on centring and grounding, anchoring breath support, securing forward (mask of the face) resonance and developing strong, muscular consonant sounds are given priority. Think carefully about when and where you intend to hold the warm up: before you leave the building when the group will be more focused or when you first arrive in the open air space to benefit the work more directly.

ACTIVITIES AND EXERCISES

- If you decide to use the *Bacchai* text for this workshop then try to allow some time to explore some of the exercises/activities listed in the workshop entitled *Articulating the Tragedy*. This means that your actors will have an understanding of the text as a tragic eyewitness report before they explore it in the open air.

- Get your group to spend some time in different-sized spaces before you venture out of doors: they need to develop an understanding about spatial acoustics first. Your chosen spaces should range from a very large theatre auditorium down to a smaller rehearsal room. Undertake some vocal acoustic 'checks' in each auditorium/room in order for them to experience how sound bounces around or is absorbed by the space. This means checking on the amount of echo present. Place your actors around the space and get them to clap in turn and listen for how much of an echo follows the sound. Then ask them in turn to send out sounds into the space (such as a 'bah', 'mah' and 'vah'), once again checking on the echo. Now ask them in turn to send out some individual words from the text. Allow time for them to report back on what they discovered about the echo and whether this had an effect on their voice (enlivening it or deadening it). Point out some of the materials used in the space that might have helped to create this effect.

- Now ask them to send out some of the lines of the text to a partner at the opposite end of the space (ensuring that the breath is supporting their delivery). Allow each partnership time to get together to discuss how their voice might be adjusted to accommodate the spatial acoustics before trying again. Too much echo may need to be balanced out with crisper articulation, too little echo might need more forward facial resonance and, therefore, vocal energy. Remember to remind them that the acoustics will change again with the presence of an audience.

- Time to venture outside to the space in which you've chosen to work. Ask the group to take a good look around it and pick out objects that might reflect sound back to them eg buildings, trees, rocks, etc. Get them to try the clapping exercise once again to check on the echo. If there aren't many objects around to reflect the sound back to them then, of course, there will be no echo.

- Now ask your group to spend five minutes listening in silence to check the sounds they might have to compete against, eg traffic, aircraft. Also, get them to listen and feel how strong the wind is (and which way it's blowing) as this will also affect their vocal delivery.

- Explain that because the sound will not be reflected back to them they won't be able to hear themselves very well (their audience will hear them better than they hear themselves). This means they will need to trust in the sound they are sending out rather than trying to strain or push it out to be heard. Remember, if you go off your support while you're explaining this then they will, unconsciously, mimic you later so try to stay connected to your lower breathing muscles and avoid a rise in pitch.

- If you decided to hold a warm up prior to leaving the rehearsal room then it's time to reconnect to the warm up principles through a few additional exercises. In order to ground, centre and anchor the breath, get them to do some heavy stamping into the ground with the flats of their feet and ask them to throw their hands away (down to the ground). Now try some swings (first one arm and then the other with the knees bending on the downward movement). Encourage their breath into a rhythm with the physical action (see Chapter 1 for further details). Finish with some blowing through the lips up and down the range to ensure breath connection and mask of the face resonance.

- Keep the group standing but bring them into a close-knit circle. Feed them evocative phrases/images from the text to speak aloud as a group around the circle. Ask them to work for the visual image but also play with the sound (which will help them find a more muscular articulation for the space). If you're using the *Bacchai* try them with:

  – dancing wild
  – indulging their desires
  – whelps of wolves
  – milk-laden breasts
  – spring of fresh water
  – wild beasts
  – bloody abattoir
  – surface of a lake
  – fruit-rich mountain glens

– running in wild rampage
– shower of sticks and stones
– licked clean by snakes

- Divide your actors into groups of three to four and give each group a section of the text to work with. This means there will be a number of herdsmen coming back to tell their story rather than just one. Instruct your actors to work out a way of speaking the text as a group first of all (perhaps jumping in on each other as though keen to take up the reins of the story) and then ask them to breathe down to their strong support muscles and simply tell the story directly to the audience. They should avoid over-complicating it physically so that their voices remain clear in the open air. If you do choose to work with a more physical piece of text, perhaps a chorus speech, then allow them the time to speak it in stillness first so they can experience and feel their voices travelling out of their bodies into the elements without being compromised by the action. It can be an interesting exercise to compare the vocal variations between the 'still' performance and the 'physical' performance.

- Allow some time for a group de-briefing session. Use the following questions as a starting point for the discussion:

  - What did you hear and what didn't you hear?

  - What needed to be vocally adjusted in your own performance? How did you do this?

  - What practical knowledge will you take away from this workshop (ie what did you learn)?

NOTES

1. Euripides, translated by Gilbert Murray, *The Medea* (Allen and Unwin, 1910); p. 45-46

2. Euripides, translated by Phillip Vellacott, *Medea* (Penguin Books, 1963); p. 40-41

3. Euripides, translated by Alistair Elliot, *Medea* (Oberon Books, 1992); p. 39-40

4. Euripides, translated by Frederic Raphael Kenneth McLeish, *Medea* (Nick Hern Books, 1994); p. 26-27

5. Seamus Heaney, *The Burial at Thebes* (Faber and Faber, 2004); p. 50-52

6. Aeschylus, version by Ted Hughes, *Agamemnon (The Oresteia)* (Faber and Faber, 1999); p. 39-40

7. *Ibid.* p. 57

8. *Ibid.* p. 68-69

9. *Ibid.* p. 80

10. Aeschylus, version by Ted Hughes, *The Choephori (The Oresteia)* (Faber and Faber, 1999); p. 95-96

11. *Ibid.* p. 102-103

12. Brian MacArthur (ed.), *The Penguin Book of Twentieth Century Speeches* (Penguin Books, 1993); p. 333-334

13. Brian MacArthur (ed.), *The Penguin Book of Historic Speeches* (Penguin Books, 1996); p. 40-41

14. Brian MacArthur (ed.), *The Penguin Book of Twentieth Century Speeches* (Penguin Books, 1993); p. 429-431

15. Euripides, version by Don Taylor, *The Women of Troy* (Methuen Drama, 2007); p. 26-27

16. Sophocles, translated by Timberlake Wertenbaker, *Oedipus Tyrannos* (Faber and Faber, 1997); p. 7-9

17. Euripides, translated by Colin Teevan, *Bacchai* (Oberon Books, 2007); p. 41-44

BIBLIOGRAPHY

General

Peter Arnott, *Public and Performance in the Greek Theatre* (Routledge, 1995)

John Burgess, *The Faber Pocket Guide to Greek and Roman Drama* (Faber and Faber, 2005)

Jonathan Croall, *Peter Hall's Bacchai* (Oberon Books, 2007)

Nicholas Dromgoole, *Performance Style and Gesture in Western Theatre* (Oberon Books, 2007)

Simon Goldhill, *How to Stage Greek Tragedy Today* (The University of Chicago Press, 2007)

John Harrop, & Sabin Epstein, *Acting with Style* (Prentice Hall, 1990)

Brian MacArthur (ed.), *The Penguin Book of Twentieth Century Speeches* (Penguin, 1993)

Brian MacArthur (ed.), *The Penguin Book of Historic Speeches* (Penguin, 1996)

Patsy Rodenburg, *The Actor Speaks* (Methuen, 1997)

Patsy Rodenburg, *The Need for Words* (Methuen, 1993)

Patsy Rodenburg, *The Right to Speak* (Methuen, 1992)

Peter Walcot, *Greek Drama in its Theatrical and Social Context* (University of Wales Press, 1976)

Plays

Aeschylus translated by Ted Hughes, *The Oresteia* (Faber and Faber, 1999)

Euripides translated by Colin Teevan, *Bacchai* (Oberon Books, 2002)

Euripides translated by Gilbert Murray, *Medea* (George Allen and Unwin, 1910)

Euripides translated by Philip Vellacott, *Medea* (Penguin Books, 1963)

Euripides translated by Alistair Elliot, *Medea* (Oberon Books, 1992)

Euripides translated by Raphael and McLeish, *Medea* (Nick Hern, Books 1994)

Euripides translated by Don Taylor, *The Women of Troy* (Methuen Drama, 2007)

Seamus Heaney, *The Burial at Thebes*; (Faber and Faber, 2004)

Sophocles translated by Timberlake Wertenbaker, *Oedipus Tyrannos* (Faber and Faber, 1992)

PART THREE:
JACOBETHAN DRAMA

CHAPTER II

DEMANDS AND CHALLENGES

The Context

The reigns of Queen Elizabeth I and her successor, King James I, were a heady period in the history of English drama, where Thomas Kyd, Christopher Marlowe, William Shakespeare, Ben Jonson, Thomas Dekker, John Marston, Thomas Heywood, Francis Beaumont, John Fletcher, Thomas Middleton, William Rowley, John Webster and John Ford, among others, all flourished as playwrights.

Their experimentation with dramatic form grew out of new cultural movements that swept across Europe. Medieval religious studies were abandoned for a more humanist approach, which placed man's ability to reason at the centre of a secular world. Artists, writers, scholars, philosophers, rulers, entrepreneurs and explorers focused back on the Greek and Roman classics for inspiration, adapting their principles to meet a new and changing world. It became known as the Renaissance, which literally means *re-birth*: Europe was classically inspired out of the ashes of medievalism.

The Renaissance did embrace some medieval concepts but they were re-focused or re-designed for the new world. It had been thought that everything in the universe was placed in a particular hierarchy called *The Chain of Being*. Basically, God was at the top of the hierarchy, followed by the angels and ether, stars and fortune, the elements, man, animals, plants and minerals. Each of these categories had their own internal hierarchy: the monarch was at the top of the humans, the lion was the king of the beasts, the eagle was the chief of the birds, the rose was considered to be the most beautiful flower, whilst gold was the most important metal. Each creature, object or element was thought to be interdependent on the other and was also expected to know and accept its place within the chain. The Elizabethans and Jacobeans (Jacobethans) were most interested in the placement of man within this framework. Tillyard in *The Elizabethan World Picture* says:

> He was the nodal point, and his double nature, though the source of internal conflict, had the unique function of binding together all creation, of bridging the greatest cosmic chasm, that between matter and spirit. During the whole period when the notion of the chain of being was prevalent…it was man's key position in creation – a kind of Clapham Junction where all the tracks converge and cross – that so greatly exercised the human imagination.   (1)

The Jacobethans feared disorder, which could be caused by the chain becoming unbalanced, and many plays of the period exploited this. The Gunpowder Plot, a plan drawn up by Catholic recusants in 1605 to blow up James I and his parliament, was considered sacrilegious (the monarch being God's representative on earth) and the popular imagination was horrified. Therefore, the killing of King Duncan in Shakespeare's *Macbeth* (which echoed elements of the Gunpowder Plot) and the decision by *King Lear* to give up his place within the chain were considered equally shocking However, the chain didn't just inspire plot-lines, it also had a direct bearing on the descriptive language playwrights chose to use within their dramas.

The Original Vocal Demands

Most of the vocal challenges for actors working with Elizabethan and Jacobean (Jacobethan) texts lie within the language and the way in which that language is structured. If you haven't already looked over Chapters 2, 3 and 4 then please go back and do so now. An understanding of how *sound, word* and *rhythm* function in drama are essential when working with Jacobethan texts. In summary:

- *Sound* – the length, weight and energy of individual sounds support sense and emotion.

- *Word* – the imagery and rhetorical devices build layers of meaning, strengthening situation, story and character.

- *Rhythm* – the rhythmic form frames a character's speech, helping to clarify their thoughts and feelings.

Jacobethan Words

Rhetoric (the art of speaking and writing effectively in order to persuade or dispute) had a direct effect on the way in which Jacobethan playwrights used and developed language. The study of rhetoric was drawn from the Ancient Greeks and Romans and became very popular in the Renaissance, which revived scholarly activity based on classical sources. Every boy who underwent a Grammar School education in Jacobethan England would have studied rhetoric; therefore it isn't a surprise to find ornate, heightened, formalised language in plays of the period.

So getting your mouth and mind around the words of a Jacobethan text can sometimes be tricky. It's highly likely that audiences of the period experienced some difficulties listening to it as well, given that the Jacobethan playwrights had a tendency to invent new words or create new senses from existing words. Martin White in *Renaissance Drama in Action* estimates that over 10,000 new words were introduced in plays written between 1550 and 1650 (2). However David Crystal in *'Think on my words': Exploring Shakespeare's Language* debunks the myth that most of these were coined by Shakespeare and believes that about '1700 are plausible Shakespearean inventions' (with about half of them remaining in use) (3).

Whatever the number, Jacobethan playwrights did make a serious contribution to the evolvement of the English language as we know it today. The playwright Thomas Heywood wrote *An Apology for Actors* in 1612 (edited for publication by the Shakespeare Society in 1841) and claimed that Jacobethan playwrights were responsible for moving language on from the idiosyncracies of medieval Middle English.

> our English tongue, which hath ben the most harsh, uneven,
> and broken language of the world, part Dutch, part Irish, Saxon,
> Scotch, Welsh, and indeed a gallimaffry of many, but perfect in
> none, is now by this secondary meanes of playing continually
> refined, every writer striving in himselfe to add a new florish
> unto it; so that in processe, from the most rude and unpolisht

tongue, it is growne to a most perfect and composed language, and many excellent workes and elaborate poems writ in the same, that many nations grow inamored of our tongue (before despised).   (4)

However, playwrights didn't just use heightened language, invent new words or create new meanings from existing words to further the cause of the English language within a new Renaissance model. Their primary motivation for stretching and re-inventing linguistic boundaries was in order to meet the needs of story, situation and character, adjusting language to meet the moment. For example, there was a tendency to formalise and elevate the language of noble or upper class characters in order to clarify their place within society for an audience. Nowadays English actors tend to use variations of Received Pronunciation to convey class but, given that Received Pronunciation wasn't around in Jacobethan England, a character's words had to do the job instead. Another example can be found in Jacobean revenge tragedies, where language was adjusted to deal with the extreme emotions being presented. These plays offered up a new linguistic energy, packed with dark, dense and violent imagery.

Jacobethan Rhythms
The majority of playwrights used combinations of *blank verse, rhyming couplets* and *prose* to organise their words and construct their stories.

- *Blank verse* first appeared in Italian plays of the early 1500s and was probably brought to England by the Earl of Surrey, who applied it to his translations of parts of Virgil's *Aeneid*. Christopher Marlowe and William Shakespeare used it extensively, setting the standard for other dramatists of the period.

  Structurally, it's composed of unrhymed lines of iambic pentameter: each verse line has ten syllables which alternate between unstressed and stressed syllables (de dum de dum de dum de dum de dum). As we learnt in Chapter 4, the iambic metre often mirrors the rhythmic beat of everyday speech; however, blank verse formalises it a little more, framing and heightening a character's inner thoughts and feelings. In other words, it helps to intensify ordinary speech, raising it above the ordinary without making it sound superficial.

Playwrights often varied the pattern, changing the metre here and there, in order to avoid it sounding tedious and to link meaning much more precisely to what they wanted to convey. However, the basic configuration tended to remain the same.

- *Rhyming couplets* were used by almost all the Jacobethan playwrights for particular emphasis. They were most commonly placed at the end of dramatic speeches to punch a point home or finish with a flourish. Prologues, epilogues, masques, plays-within-plays and rituals all tended to use rhyming couplets as well.

  To be precise, a rhyming couplet is made up of two lines of verse, usually written in the same metre, with end-rhymes. This means that the last two words of each line rhymes with each other. The lines can either be end-stopped or enjambed (where the thought runs on from the first line into the second without punctuation: again, see Chapter 4). Those couplets written in iambic pentameter are called *heroic couplets*.

- *Prose*, as we learnt earlier, is made up of irregular arrangements of weak and strong stresses, dependent on meaning and context. Playwrights tended to move from prose to verse and back again to suit a particular purpose or character.

  There are literally thousands of works that discuss the reasons why Shakespeare used prose in his plays. The old view was that he tended to save prose for lower class characters, who weren't elevated or cultivated enough to speak in verse. However, this is easily disproved as so many of his nobles used prose as well, for example, Henry and Katherine in *Henry V*. He tended to use prose in situations when speaking in verse might seem inappropriate, therefore suiting the rhythmic form to the situation or moment. Some of these include: the reading of a letter, the making of a proclamation, a particularly cynical comment, broad comedy, a lively conversation, the thinking aloud of a difficult concept or the portrayal of simple, everyday life. Some characters move into prose as they lose their sanity: verse becomes too ordered for Lady Macbeth, Hamlet, Ophelia, Edgar and King Lear. Middleton used prose extensively as well, particularly in his city comedies and Jonson wrote *Bartholomew Fair* entirely in prose.

The Original Delivery

The Jacobethan playwrights tended to write for specific acting companies; however, this did mean their plays became the property of the company with which they were associated (although directing and/or acting in their own plays helped many of them gain greater artistic control over their work). Despite the popularity of particular companies with audiences, playwrights and actors were not highly regarded, especially by the Puritans, who thought theatre an incitement to vice as a whole. An actor not associated with a company could be arrested as a 'rogue and vagabond' under the Statute of 1572.

Although women weren't legally banned from the stage, their presence wasn't socially or morally accepted. This meant that young boys were apprenticed to companies to perform in a range of female roles. Most were no older than twelve years old to ensure their voices hadn't broken, which helped them create the vocal illusion of a higher-pitched female sound. Although a number of these boys received rave reviews in their day, it's doubtful they were ever able to meet the vocal demands of some of the more complex female roles of the period. Some of these characters require a vocal weight or vocal maturity in performance, such as Shakespeare's Cleopatra, that simply would have been beyond the physical limitations of a young boy.

Many academics assume that performances by Jacobethan actors were over-stylised and formal; however some original sources speak otherwise. Shakespeare's much quoted advice to the actors in *Hamlet* mentions some important aspects of dealing with text vocally, which most voice coaches would approve of today. Hamlet's speech to a group of travelling players visiting Elsinore in Act III, Scene ii talks about vocal lightness, quickness and fluency (avoiding the over-articulation of individual consonant sounds, which can sound false and unnatural in speech) as well as committing to the meaning of the words within the text.

> Speak the speech, I pray you, as I pronounced it to you
> – trippingly on the tongue. But if you mouth it as many of our
> players do, I had as lief the town crier spoke my lines… Suit
> the action to the word, the word to the action, with this special
> observance – that you o'erstep not the modesty of nature.   (5)

Thomas Heywood's *An Apology for Actors* provided a response to Puritan attacks on the theatre. He focused on the relationship between rhetoric, oratory and acting, highlighting what was expected from a vocal performance of the period. Like Shakespeare, he talks about drawing vocal performance from the text without imposing a 'voice' over the top of it. However he also championed a free release of projected sound, vocal fluency, clarity of articulation and delivery at an appropriate pace.

> To come to rhetoricke, it not onely emboldens a schollar to
> speake, but instructs him to speake well…to keepe a decorum
> in his countenance, neither to frowne when he should smile,
> nor to make unseemely and disguised faces in the delivery of his
> words, not to stare with his eies, draw awry his mouth, confound
> his voice in the hollow of his throat, or teare his words hastily
> betwixt his teeth…It instructs him to fit his phrases to his action,
> and his action to his phrase, and his pronuntiation to them
> both.   (6)

In 1615, John Webster, another playwright, added to Sir Thomas Overbury's prose collection *Characters*, publishing *New Characters (drawne from life)*. His analysis was supposedly based on the performances of Richard Burbage, an actor linked with a number of different companies but most famously associated with the Lord Chamberlain's Men, who performed many of Shakespeare's plays for the first time.

> An excellent Actor
> …He doth not strive to make nature monstrous: she is often
> seen in the same scene with him, but neither on stilts nor
> crutches; and for his voice, 'tis not lower than the prompter, nor
> lowder than the foil and target.   (7)

Richard Flecknoe also wrote about Burbage's vocal performance in his essay *A Short Discourse of the English Stage*, published in 1664 with his play *Love's Kingdom*.

> It was the happiness of the actors of those times to have such poets as these to instruct them and write for them; and no less of those poets to have such docile and excellent actors to act their plays, as a Field and Burbage; of whom we may say he was a delightful Proteus, so wholly transforming himself into his part…there being as much difference betwixt him and one of our common actors as between a ballad singer, who knows all his graces and can artfully modulate his voice, even to know how much breath he is to give to every syllable. He had all parts of an excellent orator (animating his words with speaking, and speech with action) his auditors being never more delighted than when he spake, nor more sorry than when he held his peace. (8)

It seems that Burbage's voice was well modulated, supported by his breath and matched the rhythm to the sense: all elements required from actors performing text from this period today.

Past to Present

So what does all this mean for an actor working with Jacobethan texts today?

First of all, there is the problem of the ornate and heightened language that might be unfamiliar to a contemporary actor.

Some of the words within Jacobethan writing may no longer be in common usage or they may have changed their meaning over time. For example, nowadays we think of 'humour' as something funny but in Jacobethan England it could have related to one of the four fluids in the body (blood, phlegm, choler and black bile), the balance of which determined a person's emotional and physical state. Therefore, more often than not, 'humour' was used to describe a character's temperament (often in a negative, unfunny way).

Some of the imagery within Jacobethan writing may also have been drawn from concepts and ideas that are no longer relevant or recognisable today. For example, metaphors and similes often refer back to

The Chain of Being (discussed earlier in this chapter) which would have been very familiar to Jacobethan audiences as part of their world view. Given that the Jacobethans were predominantly interested in man's place within the Chain, it was a convenient way of describing or reinforcing a particular character type. Aufidius in Shakespeare's *Coriolanus*, uses the image of a small eagle (osprey), who was king of the birds, to emphasise Coriolanus' regal nature.

> I think he'll be to Rome
> As is the osprey to the fish, who takes it
> By sovereignty of nature.　　(9)

In this instance, the fish (below birds on the Chain of Being) willingly yield themselves up to the eagle, meaning that Rome will readily, inevitably and naturally offer itself to Coriolanus. Only by understanding the Chain of Being can this image be brought to life.

In places where unfamiliar words or imagery coincide with an unusual grammatical syntax then the text may feel like a foreign language on first reading. By grammatical syntax I mean the way in which the words are ordered across a phrase, sentence or verse line. Sometimes a poet or playwright may alter usual grammatical word order so that a verse line scans, ie meets the demands of the particular metre they're using. For example, in *The Changeling* by Middleton and Rowley, Alsemero says to Beatrice Joanna:

> Oh, the place itself e'er since
> Has crying been for vengeance,　　(10)

A simple change to the grammatical syntax helps Alsemero maintain the strength of the iambic line so that he can drive his point home after the discovery of Beatrice Joanna's crimes.

Speaking the text aloud a number of times will help an actor make sense of the language, unravel any difficult grammatical syntax and place unfamiliar words in a helpful context. Remember these texts were written to be spoken and academic internalised study can defeat them. Allow your actors time to feel the weight of the language in their mouths and listen to the sound it makes in the rehearsal space. Given the variations of meaning over time, it's also important to have a good glossary close to hand for further research.

Translation of the text into contemporary speech isn't necessarily a useful exercise. This means your actors will lose the energy, impetus and nuance of the language that was formulated as speech for a particular character. The rhythmic flow of the words will be lost as well, which creates the character's thought rhythm, breath rhythm and, therefore, speech rhythm. Keep introducing and devising exercises for your actors that will bring the text to life.

Dealing with metrical form in verse drama can be a difficult hurdle for contemporary actors, particularly those who are more familiar with performing modern naturalistic texts. They must be able to *feel* the rhythm, drawing the through-line of a character's thoughts from the structure of the text. Again, speaking the text aloud will help, as will any exercise that explores the drive, flow and rhythm of the drama.

Jacobethan drama, and more particularly Jacobean drama, often requires vocal courage to release some of its extreme and horrific images into space. For this reason, it's very easy for contemporary actors to pull back and devoice into a breathy whisper or push the words out so their impact is lost. They will need exercises that engage with this type of imagery head-on.

For all of these reasons I've organised the workshop plans into the following sections:

- Speaking Sonnets
- Playing Detective (with a monologue)
- Playing Detective (with a duologue)
- Relishing Revenge

CHAPTER 12

SPEAKING SONNETS

Shakespeare's sonnets are a wonderful proving ground for actors: they need to dive into intense emotions, clarify complex thoughts and illuminate evocative imagery, all within the space of a mere fourteen lines and a specific verse structure.

I know of no better starting point for working on verse drama than speaking Shakespeare's sonnets. It helps actors find their feet, particularly if they had a less than positive experience with Shakespeare in English classes at school (usually by studying him academically) and feel weighed down with the unfamiliarity of his texts and his reputation as a whole within Western society. The vocal demands of Shakespeare's plays aren't explored in this book as there are many practitioners who have done that successfully already (for example, Cicely Berry, Patsy Rodenburg and Kristin Linklater). However, most of the exercises and activities in the workshop plan can be adapted to working with his drama.

Form and Structure

Shakespearean sonnets are primarily composed of iambic pentameter. This means that each verse line has ten syllables which alternate between unstressed and stressed syllables (de dum de dum de dum de dum de dum) as we learnt in Chapter 4. Occasionally the metrical rhythm varies to pinpoint meaning more accurately but the iambic pentameter does dominate.

The fourteen lines are broken down into three sets of four lines, called quatrains, and a final set of two lines, called a couplet, each of which have their own rhyme scheme (ABAB CDCD EFEF GG). The structure evolved from sonnets written by a fourteenth-century Italian poet called Petrarch, although his fourteen lines were divided into an eight-line octave and a six-line sestet, both with different rhyme schemes.

The way in which the sonnets are structured tends to determine the shape of the thoughts presented. New ideas, or ideas following on from the original premise, tend to start at the beginning of the next quatrain. A resolution or conclusion is usually presented in the final couplet, often with a twist in the tail. This means that an actor will need to keep sight of what's coming at the end in order to make sense of the sonnet as a whole.

Themes and Content

There are 154 sonnets in the Shakespeare canon and no one is entirely sure that the sequence they've been published in is correct (ie, did Shakespeare place them in this order or was it an editorial decision by the publisher?). Even if Shakespeare never intended them to be published in this way, it's still a useful exercise to read them in the order presented as some of the premises seem to flow on from sonnet to sonnet, creating a kind of mini-drama.

Sonnets 1 to 126 are addressed to a beautiful young man (could this be the 'Mr WH' in the original dedication?). The initial sonnets present the relationship between the poet and this young man as one of friendship, in particular an older man giving advice to a younger one with the wisdom of age. For example, the early sonnets talk about the young man's beauty and the poet urges him to have children in order to perpetuate himself and make his beauty immortal.

> And nothing 'gainst Time's scythe can make defence
> Save breed to brave him when he takes thee hence.   (11)

However, by 'Sonnet 18' the poet's feelings have moved on to romantic love for the young man. By 'Sonnet 20', it's clear that the poet also harbours lustful sentiments, with a homoerotic play on words.

> But since she pricked thee out for women's pleasure,
> Mine be thy love, and thy love's use their treasure.   (12)

The young man and the poet fall out around 'Sonnet 33' and it seems as though the young man is responsible. He is forgiven by the poet but in sonnets 40 to 42 the young man creates another problem by sleeping with someone else. Despite further forgiveness the poet is parted from the young man and desires him from a distance.

Around 'Sonnet 78' we find the poet jealous once again but this time because of the young man's connection with a rival poet. The friendship or relationship resumes around 91 but the poet expresses doubt (and paranoia) about the young man's ability to stay faithful. However, this time it is the poet himself who lapses into infidelity around 'Sonnet 117', which he bitterly regrets.

Sonnets 127 to 152 refer to a seductive but treacherous dark lady and are more sexually explicit than previous sonnets. The poet becomes consumed and obsessed with her and, when it appears that she is unfaithful to him with the young man of the earlier sonnets, he suffers deeply.

> Two loves I have, of comfort and despair,
> Which like two spirits do suggest me still;
> The better angel is a man right fair,
> The worser spirit a woman coloured ill.　　(13)

The final sonnets, 153 and 154, are written in the style of a classical Greek epigram about the nature of love and desire, bringing the soap opera to a fitting end.

Love and lust, and all this might entail (passion, desire, longing, obsession, jealousy, paranoia and pain), are certainly the primary themes of the sonnets, which does explain their universal appeal. However, along the way they also delve into issues such as morality, mortality, the nature of beauty and the power of poetry. Yet it is their ability to speak to us personally and intimately that draws us in. Unlocking this intimacy will be one of the key challenges for both you and your actors.

Text Sample: Speaking Sonnets

In 'Sonnet 130', the poet pinpoints what it is he loves about his mistress: the fact that she's a real woman and not a conventional image of beauty. He's also making a statement about the way in which he loves her by refusing to place her on a pedestal and worshipping her from afar: his love is real and defies comparison. At the same time he has a dig at the other poets of his day, who tended to describe their women in high-flown, non-realistic terms that didn't match genuine love for another human being. Note the use of images derived from the Chain of Being, for example, the sun and the rose were considered quite high up on the chain but, of course, inadequate comparisons for how the poet feels about his love.

The final couplet tells us everything. If we take it away then it's very easy for the sonnet to end up as a criticism of his mistress: after all, who wants a lover with smelly breath? (Although this would have been quite normal in Shakespeare's day without proper dental care!) So it is that the couplet turns the inverted images on their head.

Sonnet 130
My mistress' eyes are nothing like the sun;
Coral is far more red than her lips' red;
If snow be white, why then her breasts are dun;
If hairs be wires, black wires grow on her head.
I have seen roses damasked, red and white,
But no such roses see I in her cheeks,
And in some perfumes is there more delight
Than in the breath that from my mistress reeks.
I love to hear her speak, yet well I know
That music hath a far more pleasing sound.
I grant I never saw a goddess go;
My mistress when she walks treads on the ground.
    And yet, by heaven, I think my love as rare
    As any she belied with false compare.

The Sonnets and A Lover's Complaint by William Shakespeare, edited by John Kerrigan and published by Penguin. (14)

Workshop Plan: Speaking Sonnets

OBJECTIVES

- To explore the imagery, form and structure of a Shakespearean sonnet in preparation for working on Shakespearean drama.

- To allow imagery, form and structure to inform the communication of meaning, mood and emotion.

- To find vocal intimacy within heightened Jacobethan text.

MATERIALS

You will need separate copies of 'Sonnet 130' (as provided in the previous 'Sample Text' box) for each member of the workshop group.

WARM UP

Structure a warm up from the information listed in Chapter 1; however, make sure that exercises which focus on muscular support for breath and articulation of consonant sounds are given priority so that the workshop participants can be specific as possible with the words and images.

ACTIVITIES AND EXERCISES

- Hand out copies of 'Sonnet 130' to each actor and ask them to silently read through the words just to make sense of the meaning. Then ask them to silently read through it again as if they're reading it aloud in their heads (transferring it into the tempo in which they would speak it aloud).

- Now get them to mouth the words silently to themselves. They should really use their lips and tongue, and, feel the length and weight of the words in their mouth.

- Ask them to vocalise the words aloud in their own space and time. As the noise level will increase and you will need them to listen back to what they're saying, ask them to cup one hand a couple of centimetres away from their ear and cup the other hand a couple of centimetres away from their mouth so that they can focus in on the words. Make sure they don't devoice into a breathy whisper – keep them vocalising sound.

- Generate a discussion on what the sonnet is about but let your actors come up with the answers. Do provide them with some background information at the end of the discussion, though, so that the sonnet is placed within its context.

- Ask your actors to put the text away, lie on the floor in semi-supine, close their eyes, release into the floor and regulate their breathing (see Chapter 1 for details). Choose words from the sonnet that relate to the five senses and feed them to your actors, one by one. Give them time to breathe in the picture, smell or sound before they release the word into the space. Encourage them to try each word a number of times so that the pictures, smells and sounds are fully visualised, smelt and heard, connecting into the spoken word.

  Seeing = *sun, coral, red, snow, white, dun, black, wires, roses*
  Smelling = *perfumes, breath, reeks*
  Hearing = *music, pleasing sound*

- Allow them to get slowly to their feet through a spinal roll (see Chapter 1 for details) and ask them to come back to the full sonnet text, verbalising it into the space and placing the imagery back into its context (they will need to adjust their delivery of the imagery to make sense of the piece as a whole).

- Organise the group into pairs and ask one person in the partnership to speak the sonnet aloud to the other person. The listener must close their eyes and, when their partner has finished, list the images that were most effectively brought to life. Allow time for the roles to be reversed so that the listener has a chance to read the sonnet as well.

- Rhythm and Metre: Now ask the pairs to speak the sonnet together and clap at each strong beat of the metre so they understand the patterning of weak and strong stresses. This will also help them identify the variations to the iambic metre and why they're there. (There's a trochaic foot at the start of line 2, which emphasises the comparison between 'coral' and 'red', and, there's an extra syllable in line 13 at the end of the word 'heaven', creating an anapaestic foot, which drives the couplet forward to its final resting place on 'compare'.) Let them share their discoveries with the whole group. Ask them to repeat the sonnet to their partner again but, this time, they should allow the metre to support the sense.

- Line Endings: The last word of a verse line often summarises the whole thought, for example, 'sun', 'red', 'dun', 'head', 'white', 'cheeks', 'delight', 'reeks', 'know', 'sound', 'go', 'ground', 'rare', 'compare'. Indeed, the final word of a sonnet can often sum up the entire concept, for example, 'compare'. Get your actors to separate out from their partner into their own space in the room and focus on the line endings by reading the text silently through in their head except for the final word of each line, which should be verbalised out loud. Now ask them to verbalise the whole text but punch the fist of one hand into the palm of the other hand on every final word of a line.

- Shape: Back to their partners to repeat the sonnet out loud to each other but this time taking an extra long pause at the end of each quatrain to think through what they're about to say next. This is especially important at the end of the third quatrain before they enter into the couplet. Human beings don't always like silence so ask them to be brave and hold the pauses for longer than they think could be possible. Now ask them to put the whole thing back together but just remain aware of the changes to come at the start of each quatrain and couplet.

- Final Thought: A final couplet can often hold the key to a sonnet. If you take away the final couplet of 'Sonnet 130' then it seems as if the poet is just summarising everything that's wrong about his mistress; adding in the couplet makes it a sonnet about the poet's love. This means that your actors must be aware of the final couplet before they even start to speak. As an exercise, get them to verbalise the final couplet before they start. Then, get them to think it over silently in their head before they commence speaking. Finally, ask them to just find the feeling within the couplet before they start. However, they must still work to make the imagery throughout the sonnet specific, otherwise it will be awash with (inappropriate) emotion.

- You've dealt with imagery, form and structure, now it's time to focus on the intimate voice within the sonnet. Ask your actors to return to their partners and set up a scenario for them to play out to each other whilst speaking the text. For 'Sonnet 130' I usually ask them to imagine that they're best friends confiding in each other, quaffing some ales in an Elizabethan tavern.

- Allow some time for a group de-briefing session. Use the following questions as a starting point for the discussion:

  - Did the final exercise make a difference? How did it change the way in which your partner delivered the sonnet?

  - What practical knowledge will you take away from this workshop (ie what did you learn)?

- If you have the time, set up a sonnet project with your actors, following on from this workshop. For homework, ask them to read through all 154 sonnets and choose one they'd like to work on. Before bringing it to class they should try to do some of the 'Sonnet 130' exercises to draw out the imagery, form and structure. They must be prepared to read it aloud to the rest of their group. You may need to allocate a few classes or rehearsals so there is enough time to hear all of the sonnets and for the group to air their thoughts about each one. Try to hear them in their numerical order as, even if there are only ten to fifteen actors in the group, the story within the sonnets will emerge. Finally, ask them to come up with their own intimate scenario for their sonnet, to be played out with other members of the group. It doesn't have to be placed within a Jacobethan setting, they may choose to transfer the words to a more contemporary context. The very act of contextualising their work will help them to personalise their communication.

CHAPTER 13

PLAYING DETECTIVE (WITH A MONOLOGUE)

You and your actors will need to become detectives, searching out character clues within the text in order to bring it to life for an audience. This will mean focusing on the way in which the playwright has played around with sound, word and rhythm to reveal the thoughts and feelings of an individual human being within a given moment of time. Here are some questions you may need to answer before you embark on the workshop process, whatever text you decide to use.

Sound
- What do the combination, length and weight of individual sounds within the text tell you about the character's emotional energy and drive?

Word
- What does the language (more particularly the imagery and rhetorical devices) tell you about the character's inner thoughts and feelings?

Rhythm
- What does the rhythmic flow of the words tell you about the character's energy and drive?
- If the text is in verse, how does the verse structure heighten, frame and strengthen the character's thoughts and feelings?
- If the text is in verse, how does the metrical beat pinpoint the sense of the character's speech?

- What do rhythmic changes tell you about the character's thoughts and feelings?

As a little test, let's read aloud the following excerpt from Christopher Marlowe's *Edward the Second* and embark on a process of discovery by focusing on some of these questions.

Text Sample: Playing Detective (with a monologue)

The following text has been taken from Act Five, Scene One of Christopher Marlowe's *Edward the Second*, edited by J B Steane and published by Penguin. The first performance probably took place in 1592 with publication in 1594 after Marlowe's death (entitled *The Troublesome Reign and Lamentable Death of Edward the Second, King of England, with the Tragical Fall of Proud Mortimer*). The play is an intense and highly charged account of Edward's reign in the fourteenth century, primarily drawn from Raphael Holinshed's *Chronicles*, published in 1587, with a few embellishments.

The story so far:
The play opens with Piers Gaveston rejoicing over a letter from Edward II, inviting him back to court. Gaveston had been banished by Edward's father, the old king, and now that he is dead and Edward has the throne, they are able to openly pursue their friendship. Edward bestows honours, titles and riches on the low-born Gaveston, much to the annoyance of the other nobles at court. He also neglects many of his kingly duties whilst pursuing his passion, despite constant threats to the realm from Scotland, Ireland and France. Hatred for Gaveston builds and the nobles pressurise Edward into exiling him once again. Isabella, Edward's lonely and neglected wife, persuades Mortimer (one of the court nobles) to recall Gaveston. She hopes that Edward will look on her more favourably for interceding on Gaveston's behalf. The nobles agree in order to carry out a plot to murder him on his return.

When Edward refuses to pay a ransom for Mortimer's father, who has been captured in Scotland, there is open rebellion and Gaveston is seized and executed. Utterly bereft, Edward seeks vengeance, defeating the rebellious nobles in battle, executing some, imprisoning and exiling others. Mortimer escapes to France, where he meets up with the disillusioned Queen and becomes her lover. He raises an army and this time defeats the King, who is eventually imprisoned by the Earl of Leicester at Kenilworth Castle. Edward is forced to abdicate in favour of his young son with Mortimer as his Protector. Edward predicts that Mortimer is the one who will hold true power and be king in all but name. It is only a matter of time before Edward is secretly murdered by Mortimer.

This monologue takes place in Kenilworth Castle where King Edward, the Earl of Leicester, the Bishop of Winchester and Sir William Trussel are present. The Bishop and Trussel are in charge of obtaining Edward's crown and delivering word of his abdication to parliament. Leicester asks him, once again, if he will yield the crown.

EDWARD: Ah, Leicester, weigh how hardly I can brook   51
      To lose my crown and kingdom without cause;
      To give ambitious Mortimer my right,
      That, like a mountain, overwhelms my bliss;
      In which extreme my mind here murder'd is!
      But what the heavens appoint I must obey.
      Here, take my crown; the life of Edward too:

(*Taking off the crown.*)

      Two kings in England cannot reign at once.
      But stay a while. Let me be king till night,
      That I may gaze upon this glittering crown;   60
      So shall my eyes receive their last content,
      My head, the latest honour due to it,
      And jointly both yield up their wished right.
      Continue ever, thou celestial sun;
      Let never silent night possess this clime;

Stand still, you watches of the element;
All times and seasons, rest you at a stay,
That Edward may be still fair England's king!
But day's bright beams doth vanish fast away,
And needs I must resign my wished crown.   70
Inhuman creatures, nurs'd with tiger's milk,
Why gape you for your sovereign's overthrow?
My diadem, I mean, and guiltless life.
See, monsters, see! I'll wear my crown again.

(*Putting on the crown.*)

What, fear you not the fury of your king?
But, hapless Edward, thou art fondly led;
They pass not for thy frowns as late they did,
But seek to make a new-elected king;
Which fills my mind with strange despairing thoughts,
Which thoughts are martyred with endless torments; 80
And in this torment comfort find I none,
But that I feel the crown upon my head;
And therefore let me wear it yet a while.

Edward the Second by Christopher Marlowe, edited by J B Steane
and published by Penguin.   (15)

These are a few of my discoveries.

Sound

Marlowe uses alliteration, assonance and onomatopoeia within the text
to help Edward release his torment vocally. For example:

– The concentration of long pure vowels and diphthongs, particularly
   in lines 51-55, sit heavily in the mouth with an emotional weight
   that's almost satisfying to speak aloud.

   Ah, Leicester, weigh how hardly I can brook
   To lose my crown and kingdom without cause;
   To give ambitious Mortimer my right,
   That, like a mountain, overwhelms my bliss;

> In which extreme my mind here murder'd is! (16)

- The repetition of / k / in lines 51 and 52 (broo**k**, **c**rown, **k**ingdom and **c**ause) reinforce this weight and add a bitter twist or bite.
- The soft repetitious murmur of / m / in lines 53-55 provide some comfort (a**m**bitious, **M**orti**m**er, **m**y, **m**ountain, overwhel**m**s, **m**y, extre**m**e, **m**y, mind, **m**urder'd).
- The repetition of / g / in line 60 (That I may **g**aze upon this **g**litter-ing crown.), the / s / in line 64 (celestial **s**un) and the / b / in line 69 (**b**right **b**eams) bring some of the imagery to life.
- The friction of the / f / sounds in line 75 (What, **f**ear you not the **f**ury of your king?) strengthen Edward's anger.

Word

Edward's language continually reflects the momentous act he is about to take so he uses large images to help him through, such as 'kingdom', 'mountain', 'heavens' and 'celestial sun'. In fact he makes a point of calling on the 'celestial sun', the 'silent night', the 'watches of the element', the 'times' and 'seasons' to not move forward, thereby stopping what is about to happen. The divine right of kings to rule is very much part of his belief system, therefore the natural world and its forces should be against his abdication and those attempting to take the crown from him are 'inhuman creatures, nurs'd with tiger's milk' and 'monsters'.

He is clearly in torment and throws out emotionally dramatic words and phrases to describe his inner turmoil, such as 'my mind here murder'd is', 'strange despairing thoughts' and 'martyred with endless torments'.

The pain of losing his crown, the symbol of his kingship, is reflected in its repetition. The word 'crown' is used six times throughout the monologue, twice at the end of iambic lines, giving it even more weight and emphasis rhythmically.

Rhythm

Metre

It was Ben Jonson who coined the phrase 'Marlowe's mighty line'. Whatever else he had to say about Marlowe, he certainly gave him his due when it came to writing blank verse. Marlowe was a master of the form, using it to great theatrical effect in all of his plays. This monologue is no exception, written in pure blank verse (line after line of unrhymed iambic pentameter) with very few variations. So we are given the impression that Edward's mind is still in an ordered state despite his predicament. However, the heaviness of the regular strong stresses also give weight to his torment. It's only towards the end of the speech that he changes the metre dramatically for emphasis (lines 74 and 80) so that we sense his despair finally taking over.

Take a look at this scanned version of the text. The syllables in bold are the strong stresses and the slashes separate out each foot.

> Ah, **Leices** / ter, **weigh** / how **hard** / ly **I** / can **brook** / 51
> To **lose** / my **crown** / and **king** / dom **with** / out **cause**; /
> To **give** / am**bit** / ious **Mort** / imer / my **right**, /
> That, **like** / a **moun** / tain, **o** / ver**whelms** / my **bliss**; /
> In **which** / ex**treme** / my **mind** / here **mur** / der'd **is**! /
> But **what** / the **heav** / ens ap**point** / I **must** / o**bey**. /
> Here, **take** / my **crown**; / the **life** / of **Ed** / ward **too**: / (17)

Note that the 'Leices' of 'Leicester' in line 51 is one syllable and the extra weak syllable in line 56 ('heavens appoint') drives Edward's thoughts forward to 'obey'.

> Two **kings** / in **Eng** / land **can** / not **reign** / at **once**. /
> But **stay** / a **while**. / Let **me** / be **king** / till **night**, /
> That **I** / may **gaze** / up**on** / this **glitt** / ering **crown**; / 60
> So **shall** / my **eyes** / re**ceive** / their **last** / **content**, /
> My **head**, / the **la** / test **hon** / our **due** / to **it**, /
> And **joint** / ly **both** / yield **up** / their **wish** / ed **right**. /
> Contin / ue **ev** / er, **thou** / ce**lest** / ial **sun**; /
> Let **nev** / er **si** / lent **night** / possess / this **clime**; /

Stand **still**, / you **watch** / es **of** / the **el** / ement; /
All **times** / and **sea** / sons, **rest** / you **at** / a **stay**, /
That **Ed** / ward **may** / be **still** / fair **Eng** / land's **king**! /
But **day's** / bright **beams** / doth **van** / ish **fast** / away, /
And **needs** / I **must** / re**sign** / my **wish** / ed **crown**. /   70
In**hu** / man **crea** / tures, **nurs'd** / with **ti** / ger's **milk**, /
Why **gape** / you **for** / your **sov** / ereign's **ov** / er**throw**? /
My **di** / adem, / I **mean**, / and **guilt** / less **life**. /
See, mon / sters, **see**! / I'll **wear** / my **crown** / a**gain**. /   (18)

There is an extra syllable in line 60 because of 'glittering' that drives
the energy of the line forward to 'crown'. This also creates a light, glit-
tery feeling in the rhythm, which matches the sense. The metre tells
us that 'wished' in line 63 and 'wished' in line 70 become two syllables
rather than one. However, the biggest change occurs in line 74 with
'See, monsters, see!' where the first foot is trochaic rather than iambic
(a strong stress followed by a weak stress – 'dum de' rather than 'de
dum'), placing the strong stress on the first word 'See'. This strengthens
Edward's hatred towards those who are about to take his crown away.

What, **fear** / you **not** / the **fu** / ry **of** / your **king**? /
But, **hap** / less **Ed** / ward, **thou** / art **fond** / ly **led**; /
They **pass** / not **for** / thy **frowns** / as **late** / they **did**, /
But **seek** / to **make** / a **new-** / elect / ed **king**; /
Which **fills** / my **mind** / with **strange** / despai / ring **thoughts**, /
Which **thoughts** / are **mar** / tyred with / **end** less / **tor**ments; /80
And **in** / this **tor** / ment **com** / fort **find** / I **none**, /
But **that** / I **feel** / the **crown** / u**pon** / my **head**; /
And **there** / fore **let** / me **wear** / it **yet** / a **while**. /   (19)

The most significant change to the metre in this section of the text is
in line 80 with 'endless torments', where the final two feet are trochaic
rather than iambic (strong stresses followed by weak stresses – 'dum de'
rather than 'de dum'). Such a massive change to the metre really drives
home Edward's 'endless torments'.

Actors performing this monologue will need to go with the flow
of the regular strong beat in order to define the rhythm of Edward's

thoughts, the flow of his breath and therefore his individual speech patterns. However, it's important that the rhythm doesn't overtake the emotional weight, otherwise the audience will simply listen to the metrical beat rather than what Edward has to say. They will need to let the rhythm simply support meaning and emotion.

Line Endings and Pauses
Edward's speech is primarily made up of end-stopped lines, giving him the time and space to deal with each thought before moving onto the next. The only exception is right at the very beginning of the monologue where an enjambed line occurs (the sense of 51 flows into 52 without final punctuation). When Leicester asks him 'will you yield your crown?' Edward realises that this is it, the final moment, when he must give up everything. His words spill out and over each other as he responds.

There are quite a few caesural pauses throughout the speech, breaking up the sense even further. Also, there are a number of lines that begin with one word followed by a comma, where Edward seems to create an emotional moment before diving into the thought as a whole. Here are a few examples:

Ah, Leicester,   (20)

Here, take my crown;   (21)

See, monsters, see!   (22)

What, fear you not the fury of your king?   (23)

It's possible that the first feet of these lines are spondees (a double strong stress – 'dum dum') because of the extra weight given to the initial word by the space and time of the comma. The words then become a little like emotional launch pads for the thoughts that are about to follow.

Now it's time to open up the text for your actors through a process of practical discovery. You will need to offer up exercises that will help them to explore sound, clarify word and focus on speech rhythm so that Edward's horrific moment can be brought to life.

Workshop Plan: Playing Detective (with a monologue)

OBJECTIVES

- To discover how sound, word and rhythm within a Jacobethan monologue reveals the inner voice of the character.

- To create an unconscious connection to the metrical rhythm in order to
realise the character's speech rhythm.

MATERIALS

You will need:
- Separate copies of the *Edward the Second* excerpt (as provided in the
previous 'Sample Text' box) for each member of the workshop group.
- Handouts of words from the text that have long pure vowels and diphthongs (see Chapter 2 for further information about these sounds).

WARM UP

Structure a warm up from the information listed in Chapter 1; however, make
sure that exercises which focus on breath, resonance, range and articulation
are given priority so that the workshop participants can be specific as possible
with sound, word and rhythm within the text.

ACTIVITIES AND EXERCISES

- Ask your actors to lie on the floor in semi-supine, close their eyes, release
into the floor and regulate their breathing (see Chapter 1 for details).
Choose a series of words from the *Edward the Second* excerpt that have
long pure vowel sounds and diphthongs and feed them to your actors,
one by one. Coach them to breathe in each word and explore the length
and weight of the vowel sound on release. They should try each word a
number of times to strengthen the work before moving on to the next.
This will help them to find the emotional weight of Edward's vowel
sounds when they start exploring the text as a whole later in the work-

shop. You may decide to use: 'weigh', 'lose', 'crown', 'cause', 'right', 'mountain', 'overwhelms', 'extreme', 'mind', 'murder'd', 'resign', 'overthrow', 'fear', 'fury', 'despairing', 'martyred', 'torment'.

- Allow them to get slowly to their feet through a spinal roll (see Chapter 1 for details) and give them a handout containing a list of the words you used in the previous exercise. Now ask them to work through the list, creating a different movement for each word, to be physicalised at the same time the word is spoken. The movement should inhabit the essence of the word and mirror its energy. There is no need for them to use the literal meaning of the word although they may wish to do so. Encourage them to find the length and weight of the vowel sound within their movement. Now ask them to repeat each word and movement a number of times so that they can clarify, define and strengthen their execution of both elements.

- They now need to find a space of their own to work in and spend a few moments grounding, centring and aligning their bodies (see Chapter 1 for details). Coach them to breathe to their centre and release the breath on an elongated fffff sound. They should then try the word list aloud in stillness, retaining the energy and drive of the movement, vocally.

- Ask them to remain where they are (grounded, centred and aligned in stillness) and verbalise some ideas into the space as to what they think the text might be about, based on their understanding of the word list and bearing in mind that it was written during the Elizabethan Age.

- Ask them to remain where they are (grounded, centred and aligned in stillness) and hand out copies of the text. Encourage them to read it silently in their heads before verbalising it into the space. They will now need to place each of the words from the previous set of exercises into a specific context. Coach them to read it aloud from thought to thought (with a new breath for each new thought).

- Generate a discussion on what the text is about but let your actors come up with the answers. Do provide them with some background information at the end of the discussion, though, so that the excerpt is placed within its context.

- Now ask them to take just two words from the text – 'crown' and 'kingdom' – breathe the thought of each one down to their centre and find the differences between them on release. Encourage them to try the words a few times through. When the words seem clear to you, add in the concept of 'loss' (ie as a King, ask them to think about losing their 'crown' and 'kingdom'). They should now breathe this sense of loss down to their centre before releasing each word verbally into the space. This will help them to find the value and worth of these words within the text.

- Ask them to check they're still grounded, centred and aligned in stillness. Now get them to read the text aloud thought to thought again but this time incorporating this sense of loss through the words of the whole text.

- Time to find the rhythm of Marlowe's 'mighty line', which establishes Edward's speech rhythm. Ask everyone to speak the text together and clap at each strong beat of the metre so they understand the patterning of weak and strong stresses. This will also help them to find the variations to the iambic metre. Let them share their discoveries.

- Time to physicalise the verse metre a little more so that Edward's speech rhythm inhabits their bodies and becomes a natural, unconscious part of their performance. Ask them to choose a point across the other side of the room and walk towards it in the most direct route (keeping peripheral vision open so there aren't any accidents). Now ask them to turn, find a new point and walk towards that (most direct route again), this time taking an fffff sound all the way there. Repeat the exercise with sssss, then vvvvv, then zzzzz and then a line of their choice from the excerpt. In this way, body, breath, sound and thought will connect.

- Now ask them to take the whole text and walk each new thought to a new point in the room, taking the most direct route. Repeat the exercise but this time ask them to walk and speak in the metrical beat. When you feel their bodies and mouths are in sync (this may take a little time), then ask them to change direction on any metrical variations. When this has become comfortable for them, increase the pace until they're into a run.

- Finally, ask them to return to a centred, grounded and aligned position in their own space. Connect their breath again with an fffff sound from their belly and ask them to speak the text in their own time, just letting the metre support the sense and emotion. Encourage them to find the energy and drive through the vowels so that Marlowe's 'mighty line' doesn't plod along.

- Now engage your actors in a group discussion of the text, using the following questions as a starting point.

    - Did you discover any combinations or patterns of vowel and consonant sounds that helped you find the character's emotional energy and drive?

    - Which words within the text helped you to pinpoint the character's inner thoughts and feelings most accurately?

    - What did the rhythmic flow of the words tell you about the character?

    - What did the most obvious rhythmical/metrical changes tell you about the character?

- Give your actors an opportunity to repeat the final exercise so that the outcome of the discussion can inform their performance. You could ask them to perform it in pairs so that they have a final focus for their work.

- Allow some time for a group de-briefing session. Use the following questions as a starting point for the discussion:

    - What changed for you in the final performance?

    - What practical knowledge will you take away from this workshop (ie what did you learn)?

CHAPTER 14

PLAYING DETECTIVE (WITH A DUOLOGUE)

If Jacobethan playwrights define individual characters through sound, word and rhythm, what happens when characters exchange speech in a duologue? The same investigation applies, although the focus will shift onto the interplay of sound, word and rhythm between characters, depending on what they want from each other and how they decide to go about achieving it. Therefore, the questions from Chapter Thirteen need to be adjusted.

Sound
- What do the combination, length and weight of individual sounds tell you about what the characters want from each other within the scene?

Word
- What does the language (more particularly the imagery and rhetorical devices) tell you about the relationship between characters and what they want from each other within the scene?

Rhythm
- What does the rhythmic flow and drive of the words tell you about what the characters want from each other within the scene?
- How does the verse structure heighten, frame and strengthen each character's thoughts and feelings in relation to what they're trying to achieve within the scene?
- How do the rhythmic changes define what the characters want to achieve within the scene?

- What does the exchange or change of rhythm between characters tell you about their relationship and what they want from each other within the scene?

Read aloud the following excerpt from *Volpone* and embark on a process of discovery by focusing on some of these questions.

Text Sample: Playing Detective (with a duologue)

The following text has been taken from Act Three, Scene Two of Ben Jonson's *Volpone*, edited by Michael Jamieson and published by Penguin. A black comedy, first produced in 1606, *Volpone* satirises animal-like greed and lust in human beings. This is not perhaps the best scene to showcase Jacobean comedy, given that it revolves around the potential seduction and attempted rape of a virtuous woman by a man ruled by his greedy, lustful desires; however, it is beautifully constructed with luxurious images, perfect for practical analysis in a workshop context.

The story so far:
Volpone (the fox) is a rich Venetian aristocrat, obsessed with his wealth and its increase. Consequently he devises a cunning plan with the help of his servant, Mosca (the fly), to deceive three noblemen out of their money. Voltore (the vulture), Corbaccio (the raven) and Corvino (the crow) all hope to be declared sole heir to Volpone's vast fortune so Volpone pretends he's ill and the three men dutifully offer up fabulous gifts in the hope of impressing him before he dies. However, when Volpone finds out that Corvino has a beautiful, young wife, Celia, he must possess her as well. Mosca tells Corvino that Volpone has partially recovered and that his physicians now prescribe a young woman 'lusty, and full of juice, to sleep by him'.

Assured by Mosca that Volpone is impotent, Corvino offers up Celia in order to ingratiate himself further. The virtuous Celia is appalled at the prospect and begs her husband to reconsider but he is unmoved, threatening her with violence if she disobeys him and leaving her alone with the supposedly ill and incapable Volpone.

However, Volpone springs from his sick-bed, reveals himself as a potential lover and tries to persuade Celia to his side. His promises of a rich, luxurious and fantastical lifestyle fall on deaf ears. Thwarted, Volpone attempts to rape her, but she is saved by Corbaccio's son, Bonario, who hears her cries for help.

CELIA: Some serene blast me, or dire lightning strike
This my offending face.

VOLPONE: Why droops my Celia?
Thou hast in place of a base husband found
A worthy lover; use thy fortune well,
With secrecy and pleasure. See, behold,
What thou art queen of; not in expectation,
As I feed others, but possessed and crowned. 190
See, here, a rope of pearl, and each more orient
Than that the brave Egyptian queen caroused;
Dissolve and drink 'em. See, a carbuncle
May put out both the eyes of our St Mark;
A diamond would have bought Lollia Paulina
When she came in like star-light, hid with jewels
That were the spoils of the provinces; take these,
And wear, and lose 'em; yet remains an ear-ring
To purchase them again, and this whole state.
A gem but worth a private patrimony   200
Is nothing: we will eat such at a meal.
The heads of parrots, tongues of nightingales,
The brains of peacocks, and of estriches
Shall be our food, and, could we get the phoenix,
Though nature lost her kind, she were our dish.

CELIA: Good sir, these things might move a mind affected
With such delights; but I, whose innocence
Is all I can think wealthy, or worth th'enjoying,
And which, once lost, I have nought to lose
                                   beyond it,
Cannot be taken with these sensual baits.   210
If you have conscience –

VOLPONE: 'Tis the beggar's virtue.
If thou hast wisdom, hear me, Celia.
Thy baths shall be the juice of July-flowers,
Spirit of roses, and of violets,
The milk of unicorns, and panthers' breath
Gathered in bags and mixed with Cretan wines.
Our drink shall be preparèd gold and amber,
Which we will take until my roof whirl round
With the vertigo; and my dwarf shall dance,
My eunuch sing, my fool make up the
                           antic.   220
Whilst we, in changèd shapes, act Ovid's tales,
Thou like Europa now, and I like Jove,
Then I like Mars, and thou like Erycine;
So of the rest, till we have quite run through,
And wearied all the fables of the gods.
Then will I have thee in more modern forms,
Attirèd like some sprightly dame of France,
Brave Tuscan lady, or proud Spanish beauty;
Sometimes unto the Persian Sophy's wife,
Or the Grand Signior's mistress; and, for
                         change,   230
To one of our most artful courtesans,
Or some quick Negro, or cold Russian;
And I will meet thee in as many shapes;
Where we may so transfuse our wand'ring souls
Out at our lips and score up sums of pleasures,
                   That the curious shall not know

How to tell them as they flow;
And the envious, when they find
What their number is, be pined.

CELIA: If you have ears that will be pierced, or eyes   240
That can be opened, a heart may be touched,
Or any part that yet sounds man about you;
If you have touch of holy saints, or heaven,
Do me the grace to let me 'scape. If not,
Be bountiful and kill me. You do know
I am a creature hither ill betrayed
By one whose shame I would forget it were.
If you will deign me neither of these graces,
Yet feed your wrath, sir, rather than your lust,
(It is a vice comes nearer manliness)   250
And punish that unhappy crime of nature,
Which you miscall my beauty: flay my face,
Or poison it with ointments for seducing
Your blood to this rebellion. Rub these hands
With what may cause an eating leprosy,
E'en to my bones and marrow; anything
That may disfavour me, save in my honour,
And I will kneel to you, pray for you, pay down
A thousand hourly vows, sir, for your health;
Report, and think you virtuous –

VOLPONE: Think me cold, 260
Frozen, and impotent, and so report me?
That I had Nestor's hernia thou wouldst think.
I do degenerate and abuse my nation
To play with opportunity thus long;
I should have done the act, and then have
                            parleyed.
Yield, or I'll force thee.

(*He seizes her.*)

CELIA: O! just God!

VOLPONE: In vain –

Line 184 – *serene* – 'A light fall of moisture or fine rain after sunset in hot countries, formerly regarded as a noxious dew or mist.' OED.

Line 191 – *more orient* – of greater value.

Line 192 – *Than that the brave Egyptian queen caroused* – Pliny records that Cleopatra once, as an extravagant gesture, drank priceless pearls dissolved in vinegar. Volpone suggests that Celia does the same with a whole rope of pearls.

Line 193 – *a carbuncle may put out both the eyes of our St Mark* – perhaps a gem exceeding both those set in the statue of St Mark – or, possibly, a gem which would dazzle even our patron saint of Venice.

Line 195 – *Lollia Paulina* – mistress of the Emperor Claudius (eventually murdered by Agrippina)…the point is that Volpone sees her (as he sees everyone) as someone to be 'bought' – a prostitute.

Line 215 – *panther's breath* – this reference is not just exotic, panthers were thought to attract their prey by sweet and alluring breath.

Line 220 – *antic* – grotesque dance.

Line 221 – *Ovid's tales* – the *Metamorphoses,* which deal with transformations – Zeus, disguised as a bull, carried off by Europa; Erycine is another name for Venus.

Line 230 – *the Grand Signior* – the Sultan of Turkey.

Line 262 – *Nestor's hernia* – Nestor, ancient and wise Greek in *The Illiad*. His hernia (an invention of Juvenal's) here suggests sexual incapacity.

Volpone by Ben Jonson, edited by Michael Jamieson (including notes) and published by Penguin.   (24)

These are a few of my discoveries.

Sound

Jonson uses alliteration, assonance and onomatopoeia within the text to heighten meaning and strengthen both characters' emotional resolve. For example:

– The repetition of / d / in 'dissolve and drink 'em' (line 193) sharpens Volpone's command to Celia that she can decadently dissolve pearls in vinegar, like Queen Cleopatra, and drink them.

– The repetition of / j / in 'juice of July-flowers' (line 213) intensifies the sensuality within the image so that you can almost feel its stickiness and juiciness as Volpone tries to draw Celia into his web.

– The repetition of / f / in 'flay my face' (line 252) creates a friction as if Celia is trying to lash her face off with the words, which reinforces her desperate state.

– Celia tends to use long pure vowels and diphthongs when trying to appeal to Volpone's better nature, which heightens her emotional state and emotional resolve.

> If you have ears that will be pierced, or eyes
> That can be opened, a heart may be touched,
> Or any part that yet sounds man about you;   (25)

> And I will kneel to you, pray for you, pay down
> A thousand hourly vows, sir, for your health   (26)

Word

Volpone's language reflects that of his motivating drive: 'possession'. He believes that everybody has their price so tries to seduce and possess Celia with imagery drawn from tangible goods and riches. He even starts by describing her new life as if he's describing his gold, comparing her old life to that of 'base' metal.

> Thou hast in place of a **base** husband found
> A **worthy** lover; use thy **fortune** well,   (27)

His repetition of the word 'See', reinforces his need for her to actually visualise the rich life he is offering.

> Use thy fortune well,
> With secrecy and pleasure. **See**, behold,
> What thou art queen of; not in expectation,
> As I feed others, but possessed and crowned.
> **See**, here, a rope of pearl, and each more orient

> Than that the brave Egyptian queen caroused;
> Dissolve and drink 'em. **See**, a carbuncle
> May put out both the eyes of our St Mark; (28)

Much of his imagery is not only luxurious and sensual but fantastical and excessive as well. Take for example the rich meal that he envisages them sharing, with rare animals served up:

> The heads of parrots, the tongues of nightingales,
> The brains of peacocks, and of estriches
> Shall be our food, and, could we get the phoenix,
> Though nature lost her kind, she were our dish. (29)

Celia isn't impressed so Volpone sensualises his imagery even further:

> Thy baths shall be the juice of July-flowers,
> Spirit of roses, and of violets,
> The milk of unicorns, and panthers' breath
> Gathered in bags and mixed with Cretan wines. (30)

The 'gold and amber' drink (line 214) links back to his obsession with tangible wealth and the mistaken belief that Celia will be drawn in by riches as well.

Volpone also describes how they could play the parts of classical lovers from antiquity and lists the various roles that Celia could take on to spice up their time together: 'dame', 'lady', 'beauty', 'wife', 'mistress' and 'courtesan'. This gives us an insight into Volpone's sexual fantasies in order to 'score up sums of pleasures' (line 235).

The language Celia uses is confined to rejecting Volpone's advances, appealing to his better nature (which he doesn't possess) and asking him to punish her beauty which caused the seduction in the first place. This latter request reveals Celia's desperation through some appalling images:

> flay my face,
> Or poison it with ointments for seducing
> Your blood to this rebellion. Rub these hands
> With what may cause an eating leprosy,
> E'en to my bones and marrow; (31)

Rhythm

Metre

Jonson has devised the scene primarily in blank verse. This gives us the impression that Volpone is still in control of his desires: using an ordered verse structure to frame the excessive images means that he never loses sight of his objective (to seduce and own Celia).

However, there are quite a few variations to the metre. Some of these include feminine endings, where an extra weak syllable has been added to the pentameter line, which slightly softens and lightens some of his more lyrical and poetical images. For example:

> A diamond would have bought Lollia Paulina   (32)
>
> Thy baths shall be the juice of July-flowers,   (33)
>
> Our drink shall be preparèd gold and amber,   (34)

However, the boldest changes to Volpone's metre come after a series of verse lines in formulaic iambic pentameter. Note the difference in the second line of the example, where the change into dactylic feet not only makes it stand out from the previous lines but also rapidly moves the line forward, almost like an elegant galloping horse. In this way we get the impression that the 'sprightly dame of France' will move differently to the 'brave Tuscan lady' and 'proud Spanish beauty'.

> Attirèd like some sprightly dame of France,
> Brave Tuscan lady, or proud Spanish beauty;   (35)

Another bold change comes at the end of Volpone's major seducing speech, where he moves into two sets of rhyming couplets. He's not only showing off his artistry but is also summarising and finalising his wooing. We know and understand as listeners that he has completed the seduction and expects his reward.

> That the curious shall not know
>   How to tell them as they flow;
> And the envious, when they find
>   What their number is, be pined.   (36)

Although Celia speaks in verse she is less inclined to speak in formulaic iambic pentameter as her feelings of fear and desperation to escape increase. However, she pulls herself together for the final appeal and her thoughts become more ordered and in control. Some of her lines are even spoken in pure iambic pentameter. A bold change to the metre comes at line 258 when Celia offers to pray for Volpone:

> anything
> That may disfavour me, save in my honour,
> **And I will kneel to you, pray to you, pay down**
> A thousand hourly vows, sir, for your health;
> Report, and think you virtuous –   (37)

Celia's faith and belief are the cornerstones of her virtue so she changes her speech rhythm to mark the offer out from the rest of her appeal.

Line Endings and Pauses
Both characters use enjambed lines, where the sense flows on from one line to the next without final punctuation; however, they have different reasons for doing so. Volpone uses it to allow his images to flow, one upon the other, which builds his excitement:

> Our drink shall be preparèd gold and amber,
> Which we will take until my roof whirl round
> With the vertigo;   (38)

Whilst Celia's thoughts run on rapidly as she endeavours to save herself:

> Good sir, these things might move a mind affected
> With such delights; but I, whose innocence
> Is all I can think wealthy...   (39)

and

> You do know
> I am a creature hither ill betrayed
> By one whose shame I would forget it were.   (40)

The running on of thoughts from one line to the next increases the use of the caesural pause within the middle of verse lines, which can also be seen in the examples above. This adds to Celia's mental and emotional discomfort – her thoughts running on in one moment and pauses breaking up the lines internally in another. Volpone uses internal line pauses for particular affect, for example, when he is asking her to envisage her future life with him.

> Use thy fortune well,
> With secrecy and pleasure. See, behold,
> What thou art queen of; not in expectation,
> As I feed others, but possessed and crowned. (41)

Through pauses their thought lengths and breath lengths vary, defining their particular idiosyncratic speech rhythms.

Split Lines and Shared Rhythms
In line 185, Volpone leaps in with 'Why droops my Celia?' to stop her negativity and turn the situation around to his advantage. In line 211, he interrupts her, dismissing 'conscience' as something that only beggars can afford to adhere to (we have the advantage of being wealthy so our rules are different).

At line 260, Volpone loses his patience. He has no wish to be 'virtuous' so dives in with an angry response. Finally, in line 266, he attempts rape and the line is split three ways as the physical tension increases.

Once again it's time to open up the text for your actors through a process of practical discovery. Exercises that focus on sound, word and rhythm will help them to realise their character and their character's objective within the scene.

Workshop Plan: Playing Detective (with a duologue)

OBJECTIVES

- To discover how sound, word and rhythm within Jacobethan text create character and define character objective(s).

FOURTEEN: PLAYING DETECTIVE (WITH A DUOLOGUE)

- To clarify the vocal differences between complex images.

MATERIALS

You will need:
- Separate copies of the *Volpone* excerpt (as provided in the previous 'Sample Text' box) for each member of the workshop group. Include the footnotes.
- Pens and paper.

WARM UP

Structure a warm up from the information listed in Chapter 1; however, make sure that exercises which focus on breath, resonance, range and articulation are given priority so that the workshop participants can be specific as possible with the complex words and images.

ACTIVITIES AND EXERCISES

- Hand out copies of the *Volpone* excerpt to each actor and ask them to silently read through the words on their paper just to make sense of the meaning. Then ask them to silently read through it again as if they're reading it aloud in their heads (transferring it into the tempo in which they would speak it).

- Separate the group into pairs, with one person taking on the role of Volpone and the other Celia. Ask all those playing Celia to sit in a circle and ask all those playing Volpone to sit in a circle around the outside of the Celia circle. This will create an inner (Celia) circle and an outer (Volpone) circle, physically trapping Celia. Now ask everybody to breathe down to their belly and then release a long fffff sound to their partner, wherever they may be in the configuration. This will help them to regulate, support and centre their breath before they start speaking. They now need to try out a group reading with all the Volpones reading the Volpone text and all the Celias reading the Celia text. It doesn't matter if they aren't speaking in time (which can be more powerful). Ask them to try it through a couple of times.

- Generate a discussion on what the text is about but let your actors come up with the answers. However, do provide them with a context for the piece as well as some background information for the more complex images, particularly those bound up in classical antiquity.

- Now ask all those playing Volpone to separate out into their own group in order to discuss and agree the primary objective they believe Volpone is trying to pursue with Celia (for example, to seduce). Likewise, ask all those playing Celia to separate out and agree on her primary objective (for example, to reject).

- Get them to return to their inner and outer circles and once again take their breath down to their belly and release a long fffff sound to their partner, wherever they may be in the configuration. Ask them to repeat the exercise but this time breathe in the thought of their objective to their belly and release the power of it onto the fffff sound.

- Now they can repeat the text together as before but this time playing the objective through the consonant sounds. Encourage them to find their bite and muscularity. They can then repeat the exercise through the vowel sounds, finding their weight and length. A final repetition should simply focus on the objective and hopefully their lips and tongue will retain some memory of the individual sounds.

- Again, ask all those playing Volpone to separate out into their own group and all those playing Celia to do the same. Provide them with pens and paper and ask them to write down a list of some of the individual words that their character uses which have drawn them into the scene so far. They can either do this with the entire text or you could allocate a smaller section for them to focus on more minutely. Rather than them simply reading the text in their heads and then writing down words, encourage a few members of the group to speak the text aloud whilst the rest make notes. Make sure multiple copies are made. The finished work will be a word poem, which might read something like this:

VOLPONE (lines 185-199)	VOLPONE (lines 213-220)	CELIA (lines 240-259)	
Droops	Wisdom	Ears	Marrow
Celia	Baths	Pierced	Disfavour
Base	Juice	Eyes	Save
Husband	July-flowers	Opened	Honour
Worthy	Spirit	Heart	Kneel
Lover	Roses	Touched	Pray
Fortune	Violets	Holy	Pay
Secrecy	Milk	Saints	Thousand
Pleasure	Unicorns	Heaven	Hourly
See	Panthers	Grace	Vows
Behold	Breath	'Scape	Health
Queen	Cretan	Bountiful	Report
Expectation	Wines	Kill	Virtuous
Feed	Gold	Creature	
Possessed	Amber	Betrayed	
Crowned	Whirl	Shame	
See	Vertigo	Deign	
Rope	Dwarf	Feed	
Pearl	Dance	Wrath	
Orient	Eunuch	Lust	
Brave	Sing	Vice	
Egyptian	Fool	Manliness	
Queen	Antic	Punish	
Caroused		Unhappy	
Dissolve		Crime	
Drink		Nature	
See		Miscall	
Carbuncle		Beauty	
Eyes		Flay	
St Mark		Face	
Diamond		Poison	
Star-light		Ointments	
Jewels		Seducing	
Spoils		Blood	
Take		Rebellion	
Wear		Rub	
Lose		Hands	
Ear-ring		Eating	
Purchase		Leprosy	
State		Bones	

- Ask your actors to return to their Volpone/Celia pairs, face each other and centre their weight. They must read out their list in turn, breathing in the thought of each word to their belly before releasing it out with their objective. Encourage them to explore the essential differences between each word.

- Now get them to swap lists and repeat the exercise with each other's words, which means they might have to reject them vocally in order to play their objective. This should provide them with new insights into the words the playwright has chosen to use.

- Ask them to return to their inner and outer circles and get them to read the text of their particular character from punctuation mark to punctuation mark (only reading as far as a punctuation mark before the next Volpone/Celia takes over). The way in which the lines have been structured through the punctuation will help them to feel the rhythm and metre. Repeat the exercise but encourage them to feel/listen to the way in which the lines flow and mentally mark any abrupt changes to the rhythm.

- Finally, ask them to return to their Volpone/Celia pairs, face each other and centre themselves and try the text again. They should now allow their breath rhythm to fall into the patterns of the punctuation, line structure, rhythm and metre.

- Now engage your actors in a group discussion of the text, using the following questions as a starting point.

  - Did you discover any combinations or patterns of vowel and consonant sounds which helped you to reinforce the characters' primary objective?

  - Which words within the text helped you to pinpoint the characters' primary objective most accurately?

  - What does the rhythmic flow of the words tell you about the characters?

  - Where are the most obvious rhythmical/metrical changes within the text? What do they tell you about the characters in those particular moments of time?

   – What does the exchange or change of rhythm between characters tell you about them in those particular moments of time?

- Give your actors an opportunity to repeat the final exercise in pairs so that the outcome of the discussion can inform their performance.

- Allow some time for a group de-briefing session. Use the following questions as a starting point for the discussion:

   – What changed for you in the final performance?

   – What practical knowledge will you take away from this workshop (ie what did you learn)?

CHAPTER 15

RELISHING REVENGE

Revenge tragedies were a particular genre of dramatic writing during the late sixteenth and early seventeenth centuries. Although content varied they all focused on the notion of 'revenge', where a character, or series of characters, sought vengeance for some previous wrong that had been committed. Their quest would usually lead to violence and/ or violent death, where humanity would be portrayed in a less than flattering light. Consequently they also became known as 'the tragedy of blood'.

These plays reflected the mood of the moment. Economic depression, social unrest, religious and political conflict led to a widespread obsession with issues of justice, morality and honour. The court of James I (between 1603 and 1625) was particularly corrupt, where titles were sold to ambitious courtiers. As a result, both men and women spent their time plotting to improve their status in life, creating a constant atmosphere of distrust and suspicion.

James I was particularly sensitive about potential assassination attempts: he had been born and raised in Scotland, a place that the English mistrusted. His paranoia was understandable, given that both his parents had experienced bloody deaths: Elizabeth I had beheaded his mother, Mary Queen of Scots, and, his father, Henry Stuart (Lord Darnley) had been murdered by Scottish lords. He had been crowned King James VI of Scotland at the tender age of thirteen months and became the focus of many Scottish plots, including a kidnapping when he was only sixteen years old. As King of England, James' fears weren't unfounded when the Gunpowder Plot came to light. Although he seemed tolerant of religious faith, he continued to maintain anti-Catholic laws in England and, as a consequence, Catholic recusants attempted to blow up both him and parliament.

The Gunpowder Plot helped maintain anti-Catholic feeling and most people believed that the Catholic courts of Italy and Spain were full of treachery and intrigue, fuelled by greed and lust. Consequently many revenge tragedies were set in these countries, although this was usually a veneer for thinly masking the truth about the English Jacobean court.

No wonder then that intense, dark and violent language was used in revenge tragedies: their imagery constantly focuses on death, decay, disease, passion and sexual corruption. Actors need to be courageous in order to deal with such confronting imagery, vocally releasing it out into the space freely and easily. Pulling back on the language will only weaken the intensity of the unfolding drama. However, there's a fine line between strongly releasing the imagery and pushing it vocally. Pushing will dull the power of the play just as much as pulling back on sound. Let's take a look at how you can help your actors achieve a free vocal release and really relish revenge.

Text Sample: Relishing Revenge

The following text has been taken from Act Three, Scene Four of Thomas Middleton's and William Rowley's *The Changeling*, edited by Gamini Salgado and published by Penguin. First performed in 1622, it is commonly believed that Rowley wrote the first and last scenes and the sub-plot in the asylum, whilst Middleton focused on the main plot (described below).

The story so far (main plot only):
Beatrice Joanna is the daughter of the Governor of Alicante in Spain and has fallen in love with Alsemero, a traveller to the region. Unfortunately her father is already arranging her wedding to Alonzo de Piracquo, a wealthy courtier.

Despite Beatrice Joanna's hatred of De Flores, her father's ugly servant, she persuades him to murder Alonzo so that she can be with Alsemero. De Flores agrees as he's in love with Beatrice Joanna.

He takes Alonzo on a tour of the castle, kills him and cuts off his finger as proof. When he presents the finger to Beatrice Joanna she finds that he will not accept gold or jewels as payment for the deed but, instead, wants to sleep with her. Beatrice Joanna, a virgin, is horrified, because she was saving herself for marriage with Alsemero. She pleads her case but De Flores is unmoved and links their fortunes together through the act of Alonzo's murder. Beatrice Joanna has no choice but to submit, otherwise De Flores will reveal her to all as a murderer.

In folklore, 'changelings' were thought to be the children of fairies, trolls or elves, who had been secretly left in place of human children. Those who were ugly, crafty or unintelligent were often referred to as 'changelings' by their parents, who found it difficult to believe that the child was their own. The Jacobeans also referred to fickle women as 'changelings', however it is not only Beatrice Joanna who 'changes' across the journey of the play. De Flores is another 'changeling', starting off as an honest servant, moving into the role of murderer and blackmailer to become the lover and beloved of Beatrice Joanna.

Christopher Ricks in an essay entitled *The Moral and Poetical Structure of The Changeling*, noted that the words 'blood', 'will', 'act', 'deed' and 'service' are constantly repeated throughout the play (42). Of course their meaning changes with the context in which they're placed, however they're often given a sly sexual double-meaning as well. De Flores is particularly adept at this, despite Beatrice's lack of initial comprehension: 'Justice invites your blood to understand me'.

The scene starts at line 21 when De Flores reveals he's murdered Alonzo and presents Beatrice Joanna with the bloody finger. It's worthwhile exploring the text from this point, if you have time, however for the sake of space, I've started the exchange a little later.

BEATRICE: For my fear's sake,
          I prithee make away with all speed possible.
          And if thou be'st so modest not to name
          The sum that will content thee, paper blushes not;
          Send thy demand in writing, it shall follow
                                                  thee, – 80
          But prithee take thy flight.

DE FLORES: You must fly too, then.

BEATRICE: I?

DE FLORES: I'll not stir a foot else.

BEATRICE: What's your meaning?

DE FLORES: Why are not you as guilty, in, I'm sure,
          As deep as I? And we should stick together.
          Come, your fears counsel you but ill, my absence
          Would draw suspect upon you instantly;
          There were no rescue for you.

BEATRICE: (*Aside.*)   He speaks home.

DE FLORES: Nor is it fit we two, engaged so jointly,
          Should part and live asunder.

          (*Tries to kiss her.*)

BEATRICE: How now, sir?   90
          This shows not well.

DE FLORES: What makes your lip so strange?
This must not be betwixt us.

BEATRICE: (*Aside.*)   The man talks wildly.

DE FLORES: Come, kiss me with a zeal now.

BEATRICE: (*Aside.*)   Heaven! I doubt him.

DE FLORES: I will not stand so long to beg 'em shortly.

BEATRICE: Take heed, De Flores, of forgetfulness,
'Twill soon betray us.

DE FLORES: Take you heed first;
Faith, y'are grown much forgetful, y'are to blame
                                              in't.

BEATRICE: (*Aside.*) He's bold, and I'm blamed for't!

DE FLORES: I have eased you
Of your trouble, – think on't, – I'm in pain,
And must be eased of you; 'tis a charity;   100
Justice invites your blood to understand me.

BEATRICE: I dare not.

DE FLORES: Quickly!

BEATRICE: Oh I never shall!
Speak it yet further off, that I may lose
What has been spoken, and no sound remain on't.
I would not hear so much offence again
For such another deed.

DE FLORES: Soft, lady, soft, –
The last is not yet paid for. Oh, this act
Has put me into spirit, I was as greedy on't
As the parched earth of moisture, when the clouds
                                              weep.
Did you not mark, I wrought myself into't,   110

Nay, sued and kneeled for't: why was all that pains

took?

You see I have thrown contempt upon your gold,

Not that I want it (not), for I do piteously;

In order I will come unto't, and make use on't,

But 'twas not held so precious to begin with;

For I place wealth after the heels of pleasure,

And were I not resolved in my belief

That thy virginity were perfect in thee,

I should but take my recompense with grudging,

As if I had but half my hopes I agreed for.   120

BEATRICE: Why, 'tis impossible thou canst be so wicked,

Or shelter such a cunning cruelty,

To make his death the murderer of my honour?

Thy language is so bold and vicious,

I cannot see which way I can forgive it

With any modesty.

DE FLORES: Push, you forget yourself!

A woman dipped in blood, and talk of modesty?

BEATRICE: Oh misery of sin! Would I had been bound

Perpetually unto my living hate

In that Piracquo, than to hear these words.   130

Think but upon the distance that creation

Set 'twixt thy blood and mine, and keep thee

there.

DE FLORES: Look but into your conscience, read me there,

'Tis a true book, you'll find me there your equal:

Push, fly not to your birth, but settle you

In what the act has made you; y'are no more now.

You must forget your parentage to me:

Y'are the deed's creature; by that name

You lost your first condition; and I challenge you,

As peace and innocency has turned you out,   140
And made you one with me.

BEATRICE: With thee, foul villain?

DE FLORES: Yes, my fair murd'ress; do you urge me?
Though thou writ'st maid, thou whore in thy
                                        affection!
'Twas changed from thy first love, and that's a
                                        kind
Of whoredom in thy heart; and he's changed now,
To bring thy second on, thy Alsemero,
Whom – by all sweets that ever darkness tasted –
If I enjoy thee not, thou ne'er enjoy'st;
I'll blast the hope and joys of marriage,
I'll confess all, – my life I rate at nothing.   150

BEATRICE: De Flores!

DE FLORES: I shall rest from all lovers' plagues then;
I live in pain now: that shooting eye
Will burn my heart to cinders.

BEATRICE: Oh sir, hear me!

DE FLORES: She that in life and love refuses me,
In death and shame my partner she shall be.

BEATRICE: Stay, hear me once for all; (*Kneeling.*) I make thee
                                        master
Of all the wealth I have in gold and jewels:
Let me go poor unto my bed with honour,
And I am rich in all things.

DE FLORES: Let this silence thee: 160
The wealth of all Valencia shall not buy
My pleasure from me;
Can you weep fate from its determined purpose?
So soon may you weep me.

BEATRICE: Vengeance begins;
          Murder I see is followed by more sins.
          Was my creation in the womb so cursed,
          It must engender with a viper first?

DE FLORES: Come, rise and shroud your blushes in my
                                                   bosom;

(*Raises her.*)

          Silence is one of pleasure's best receipts.
          Thy peace is wrought for ever in this
                                        yielding.   170
          'Las, how the turtle pants! Thou'lt love anon
          What thou so fear'st and faint'st to venture on.

(*Exeunt.*)

Line 137 – *to* – in favour of.
Line 177 – *turtle* – turtle-dove.

The Changeling by Thomas Middleton and William Rowley, edited by Gamini Salgado (including notes) and published by Penguin.   (43)

Workshop Plan: Relishing Revenge

OBJECTIVES

- To release and relish the words, freely and easily, within a Jacobean revenge tragedy

MATERIALS

You will need separate copies of *The Changeling* excerpt (as provided in the previous 'Sample Text' box) for each member of the workshop group. Include the footnotes.

WARM UP

Structure a warm up from the information listed in Chapter 1; however, make sure that exercises which focus on awakening the lower breathing muscles and forward resonance are given priority so that the workshop participants can deal with the emotional power within the language.

ACTIVITIES AND EXERCISES

- Separate the group into pairs to work as De Flores and Beatrice Joanna. Ask them to face one another (eye to eye) and place the palms of their hands together (palm to palm). They should be leaning slightly towards each other, which will help them contact their lower breathing muscles, and breathing in and out through their lips (swallowing and moistening the mouth whenever it gets dry). Now ask them to imagine an open tube running from their belly to their lips, where an unobstructed breath runs up and down, freely, easily and silently. Their connection to each other through their eyes and palms should affect their breathing patterns so that their breath starts to release in sync. Give them the time and space to consolidate this before asking them to release an elongated fffff sound, followed by an elongated sssss sound, followed by an elongated vvvvv sound and then an elongated zzzzz sound.

- Now ask them to release the following words (taken from *The Changeling*) into the space: 'blood', 'will', 'act', 'deed' and 'service'. Encourage them to speak one word to one breath, still connecting to the open tube running from their bellies through to their lips, and using their lips and tongue on the release to really relish the sounds within the words. Allow them time and space to explore each word a number of times so that they can find a myriad of different meanings before you feed in the next one. They may choose to release each word together, given their syncopated breathing, or one at a time. The latter may create a mini-dialogue, depending on the meanings they choose to draw from the words. The possibilities are endless, particularly if they don't know anything about the text excerpt yet.

- Now feed in the phrase 'vengeance begins', which Beatrice Joanna utters in the second half of line 164 from the excerpt. Keep coaching them to breathe down to their lower breathing muscles so they can find the fire in their bellies for the emotional weight and power of the phrase. Also, they need to really use their lips and tongue on the release to relish the sounds within the phrase. Once again they may choose to speak together or separately.

- Allow them a short break from each other to look over *The Changeling* excerpt and mouth the words silently to themselves. They may need to shake their hands and arms out to ensure they haven't picked up any unnecessary tension, whilst palm to palm with their partner.

- Generate a whole group discussion on what the text is about but let your actors come up with the answers. Do provide them with some background information at the end of the discussion though so that the excerpt is placed within its context.

- Team each pair up with another pair to make a group of four people. For ease of reference I'm going to call them Pair A and Pair B. Ask Pair A to place their texts to one side and return to their original position, eye to eye, palm to palm. Coach them into open tube breathing again. Ask each person in Pair B to stand slightly behind one of the Pair A people. Each Pair B person now needs to feed the words, line by line, to their Pair A person, very quietly in their ear. Each person in Pair A must then repeat the words they hear from their Pair B speaker to their partner. In this way they will be freed from the text on the page and can concentrate on simply releasing the words freely and easily to their partner, from their belly. Repeat the exercise but with arms dropped. It's difficult to imagine Beatrice Joanna wanting any physical contact with De Flores, given her horror of him: being palm to palm was simply a useful way to discover the lower breathing muscles and find a free and easy emotional response to the words in the text. See if your actors can maintain this response without the hand pressure. When they're finished, swap the pairs over so that Pair B has a go at speaking the text, whilst Pair A feeds the lines to them.

- Now ask Pair A and Pair B to separate out from each other. Each person needs to find a space against a wall, preferably on the opposite side of the room from their original partner. You may choose to have everybody in the group working at once but, given that it will be difficult for De Flores and Beatrice Joanna to hear each other whilst speaking from opposite sides of the room, it may be better to try this out pair by pair (if you have the time). Ask them to press one hand against the wall so they can feel their breath supported from low in their body again. The other hand will need to be free to hold the text. Each time they speak a line they must push themselves from the wall with their hand, turning and flinging themselves into the space, making eye contact with their partner. This means that the final part of their line will be released into the middle of the space.

- Ask your actors to return to their partners, eye to eye, drop their breath down to their bellies on an elongated fffff sound and repeat the text through to the end. They should remain connected to the free release of sound and relish they found in the previous exercises and allow the rhythm of the text to fall into its natural speech beat (particularly with the many shared/split lines).

- Allow some time for a group de-briefing session. Use the following questions as a starting point for the discussion:

  - What discoveries did you make about the text and the nature of revenge in the final performance with your partner?

  - What practical knowledge will you take away from this workshop (ie what did you learn)?

NOTES

1. E M W Tillyard, *The Elizabethan World Picture* (Penguin Books, 1990); p. 73-74

2. Martin White, *Renaissance Drama in Action* (Routledge, 1998); p. 6

3. David Crystal, *'Think on My Words': Exploring Shakespeare's Language* (Cambridge University Press, 2008); p. 9

4. Thomas Heywood, *An Apology for Actors* (Elibron Classics, 2005); p. 52

5. William Shakespeare, *Hamlet* (Arden Shakespeare, 2006); Act III, Scene ii, Lines 1-4, 17-19

6. Thomas Heywood, *An Apology for Actors* (Elibron Classics, 2005); p. 29

7. G Blakemore Evans, *Elizabethan – Jacobean Drama: The Theatre in Its Time* (New Amsterdam Books, 1990); p. 99

8. Martin White, *Renaissance Drama in Action* (Routledge, 1998); p. 59

9. William Shakespeare, *Coriolanus* (Arden Shakespeare, 2006); Act IV, Scene vii, Lines 33-35

10. Thomas Middleton and William Rowley, *The Changeling* (Penguin Books, 1982); Act V, Scene iii, Lines 72-73

11. William Shakespeare, edited by John Kerrigan, *The Sonnets and A Lover's Complaint* (Penguin Books); 'Sonnet 12', p. 82

12. William Shakespeare, edited by John Kerrigan, *The Sonnets and A Lover's Complaint* (Penguin Books, 2005); 'Sonnet 20', p. 86

13. *Ibid,* 'Sonnet 144', p. 148

14. *Ibid,* 'Sonnet 130', p. 141

15. Christopher Marlowe, edited by John Barry Steane, *Edward the Second* (Penguin Books, 1983); Act Five, Scene One, Lines 51-83

16. *Ibid.* Act Five, Scene One, Lines 51-55

17. *Ibid.* Act Five, Scene One, Lines 51-57

18. *Ibid.* Act Five, Scene One, Lines 58-74

19. *Ibid.* Act Five, Scene One, Lines 75-83

20. *Ibid.* Act Five, Scene One, Line 51

21. *Ibid.* Act Five, Scene One, Line 57

22. *Ibid.* Act Five, Scene One, Line 74

23.   *Ibid.* Act Five, Scene One, Line 75

24.   Ben Jonson, edited by Michael Jamieson, *Volpone* (Penguin Books, 1983); Act Three, Scene Two, Lines 184-266

25.   *Ibid.* Act Three, Scene Two, Lines 240-242

26.   *Ibid.* Act Three, Scene Two, Lines 258-259

27.   *Ibid.* Act Three, Scene Two, Lines 186-187

28.   *Ibid.* Act Three, Scene Two, Lines 187-194

29.   *Ibid.* Act Three, Scene Two, Lines 203-205

30.   *Ibid.* Act Three, Scene Two, Lines 213-216

31.   *Ibid.* Act Three, Scene Two, Lines 252-256

32.   *Ibid.* Act Three, Scene Two, Line 195

33.   *Ibid.* Act Three, Scene Two, Line 213

34.   *Ibid.* Act Three, Scene Two, Line 214

35.   *Ibid.* Act Three, Scene Two, Lines 227-228

36.   *Ibid.* Act Three, Scene Two, Lines 236-239

37.   *Ibid.* Act Three, Scene Two, Lines 256-260

38.   *Ibid.* Act Three, Scene Two, Lines 214-216

39.   *Ibid.* Act Three, Scene Two, Lines 206-208

40.   *Ibid.* Act Three, Scene Two, Lines 245-247

41.   *Ibid.* Act Three, Scene Two, Lines 187-190

42.   Christopher Ricks, *The Moral and Poetical Structure of The Changeling,* published in *Essays in Criticism;* 1960

43.   Thomas Middleton, and William Rowley, edited by G Salgado, *The Changeling* (Penguin Books, 1982); Act Three, Scene Four, Lines 76-172

BIBLIOGRAPHY

General

Cicely Berry, *The Actor and the Text* (Virgin Books, 2000)

Cicely Berry, *From Word to Play* (Oberon Books, 2008)

G Blakemore Evans, *Elizabethan – Jacobean Drama: The Theatre in Its Time* (New Amsterdam Books, 1990)

Bill Bryson, *Shakespeare* (HarperPress, 2007)

Chris Coles, *How to Study a Renaissance Play* (Macmillan, 1988)

David Crystal, *'Think on My Words': Exploring Shakespeare's Language* (Cambridge University Press, 2008)

Antonia Fraser, *The Gunpowder Plot: Terror and Faith in 1605* (Phoenix, 2002)

Rex Gibson, *Contexts in Literature: Shakespearean and Jacobean Tragedy* (Cambridge University Press, 2007)

Kristin Linklater, *Freeing Shakespeare's Voice* (Theatre Communications Group, 1992)

Patsy Rodenburg, *Speaking Shakespeare* (Methuen, 2002)

Patsy Rodenburg, *The Need for Words* (Methuen, 1993)

Caroline Spurgeon, *Shakespeare's Imagery and what it tells us* (Cambridge University Press, 1988)

E M W Tillyard, *The Elizabethan World Picture* (Penguin Books, 1990)

Simon Trussler, *The Faber Pocket Guide to Elizabethan and Jacobean Drama* (Faber and Faber, 2006)

Stanley Wells, *Shakespeare and Co.: Christopher Marlowe, Thomas Dekker, Ben Jonson, Thomas Middleton, John Fletcher and the Other Players in His Story* (Penguin Books, 2007)

Martin White, *Renaissance Drama in Action* (Routledge, 1998)

Plays, Prose and Poetry

Thomas Heywood, *An Apology for Actors* (Elibron Classics, 2005)

William Shakespeare, (edited by Stanley Wells, edited and introduced by John Kerrigan), *The Sonnets and A Lover's Complaint* (Penguin Books, 2005)

Ben Jonson, *Three Comedies* (Penguin Books, 1983)

Christopher Marlowe, *The Complete Plays* (Penguin Books, 1983)

Cyril Tourneur, John Webster, Thomas Middleton, *Three Jacobean Tragedies* (Penguin Books, 1982)

PART FOUR:
RESTORATION COMEDY

CHAPTER 16

DEMANDS AND CHALLENGES

The Context

When the monarchy was restored to England in 1660, after eleven years of Puritan rule, so was the theatre. Theatrical exhibitions had been outlawed by the Puritan parliament, theatres had been demolished and actors declared rogues and vagabonds. King Charles II, after ascending to the throne, lost no time in granting exclusive play-staging rights to two competing companies. Much of his exile had been spent in decadent European courts, including France, where he'd been exposed to dazzling and flamboyant theatrical entertainments. It was only natural that he looked forward to more of the same on his return to England. Stylish and pleasure-seeking, Charles encouraged the court to follow his lead. Aristocrats, released from the bore of Puritan austerity, enjoyed life to the full, following the conduct of their hedonistic king. Playwriting not only became respectable but was actively encouraged and the King's preference for the witty and the bawdy led to the development of a new genre: The Comedy of Manners.

Charles was not only instrumental in reinstating the theatre but also for allowing women to appear on the stage. There had been a whole industry set up to train young boys for female roles in Elizabethan and Jacobean England but their training had ceased during Puritan rule, creating a problem when the new companies were formed at the outset of the Restoration. So in 1662 the King issued a royal patent granting women the right to take to the stage. He'd been entertained by actresses on the continent during his exile and hadn't found anything wrong or unnatural about their presence. In order to convince his detractors, Charles publicly reasoned that he thought it immoral for men to dress and present themselves as women, thereby creating a form of social acceptability for actresses at the outset. However, in reality, within the confines of the new witty comedies, their presence sexualised theatre in a fresh and deliciously entertaining way.

The Playwrights

Incredibly, there were over 400 plays written between 1660 and 1700 by around 180 playwrights (1). Many of them were aristocrats by birth who led decadent lives with personal experience of Charles and his court. However, there were also those who were accepted into the court because of their talents: the wittier a playwright the more likely they were allowed access to the inner circle of the King. Therefore, writing plays was no longer considered a lowly profession and playwrights had an opportunity to advance their status based on their ability to theatrically mirror upper class society and create a witty turn of phrase.

John Dryden (the poet laureate), William Congreve, Sir George Etheredge, George Farquhar, Thomas Otway, Edward Ravenscroft, Thomas Shadwell, William Wycherley and Sir John Vanbrugh are just a few of the men who contributed to this amazing period of theatrical re-birth and growth. However, it was also a period of growth for female playwrights. The acceptance of actresses onto the English stage and the development of leading female parts paved the way for women to formulate their own works and present them to court and playhouse.

Katherine Philips was the first with *Pompey,* a translation of a French text by Corneille. Aphra Behn was the most prolific female playwright of the period, writing eighteen plays, as well as novels and poems. She was also the first professional female writer in England, living from her earnings in order to survive after spending time in a debtor's prison. These two excerpts from the epilogue in her play *Sir Patient Fancy* (based on Moliere's *Le Malade Imaginaire*) defend female playwrights.

> I here and there o'erheard a coxcomb cry,
> Ah, rot it, 'tis a woman's comedy,
> One, who because she lately chanced to please us,
> With her damned stuff will never cease to tease us.
> What has poor woman done that she must be
> Debarred from sense and sacred poetry?

...
To all the men of wit we will subscribe
But for your half-wits, you unthinking tribe,
We'll let you see, whate'er besides we do,
How artfully we copy some of you:
And if you're drawn to th'life, pray tell me then,
Why women should not write as well as men.   (2)

Other female playwrights of the period included: Elizabeth Polwheele, Anne Finch, Frances Boothby, Delarivier Manley, Catherine Trotter, Mary Pix and Susannah Centlivre. However, female writers gravitated towards the new novel format in the eighteenth century, leaving the stage (primarily) to the men.

The Themes

The pursuit of pleasure and profit lay at the heart of court life (in reaction to the previous Puritan rule) and, because playwrights were only really interested in reflecting aristocratic experience, these pursuits became the driving forces behind the new comedies (3). However, they were presented within the boundaries of a complex code of manners that dominated aristocratic behaviour and court society.

In 1700, the satirist Thomas Brown commented on how aristocratic manners and behaviour were reflected on the stage in his publication *Amusements Serious and Comical*. However, he also noted how some members of the audience were keen to mimic these manners in order to be seen as more courtly, aristocratic and, therefore, fashionable.

> Here Lords come to Laugh, and to be Laugh'd at for being there, and seeing their Qualities ridicul'd by every Triobolary Poet. Knights come hither to learn the Amorous Smirk, the A la mode Grin, the Antick Bow, the Newest-Fashion'd Cringe, and how to adjust his Phiz, to make himself as Ridiculous by Art, as he is by Nature.   (4)

In 1698 John Dennis published *The Usefulness of the Stage* in order to defend theatre against Jeremy Collier, who had published *A Short View of the Immorality and Profaneness of the English Stage*. Dennis argued that the behaviour and manners presented on stage merely mirrored the times.

> The corruption of manners upon the Restoration appeared with all the fury of libertinism even before the playhouse was re-established... And that which gave it so licentious a vent was not only the permission but the example of the court, which, for the most part, was just arrived from abroad with the king, where it had endeavoured by foreign corruption to sweeten, or at least to soften, adversity, and having sojourned for a considerable time both at Paris and in the Low Countries, united the spirit of the French whoring to the fury of the Dutch drinking. So that poets who wrote immediately after the Restoration were obliged to humour the depraved tastes of their audience...if the poets of these times had written in a manner purely instructive, without any mixture of lewdness, the appetites of the audience were so far debauched that they would have judged the entertainment insipid; so that the spirit of libertinism which came in with the court and for which the people were so well prepared by the sham reformation of manners caused the lewdness of their plays, and not the lewdness of the plays the spirit of libertinism.   (5)

The characters in Restoration comedies spend a vast amount of time chasing love, sex and/or advantageous marriage (and relishing that chase). More often than not, this leads to intrigues, seductions, cuck-oldry and, of course, gossip. Witty conversation was highly prized and at the heart of all exchanges: those characters successful in their pursuit of pleasure and profit are often the wittiest. For this reason, wit became a comedic theme all of its own.

The Characters
Similar types of characters are portrayed within Restoration comedy with easily recognisable masks that help to drive the plot and humour forward. Helpfully, their names tend to sum up their driving or domi-nant characteristic, for example: Mr Horner, Mr Pinchwife, Sir Fopling Flutter, Mrs Squeamish. However, it's also important to recognise that there are types of characters, who speak in markedly different ways,

such as *The Wit* and *The Fop*, creating distinct vocal demands for the actor working with text from this period.

The central character or hero is often referred to as *The Wit*: someone who embodies the sophistication and elegance of the age. This means that he is physically and vocally at ease with himself and able to present a socially acceptable mask whilst at the same time pursuing his goals related to the attainment of pleasure and profit. Of course he is extremely articulate and able to manipulate language to secure his own ends in as witty a manner as possible. We are drawn to his stylish charm.

The Fop is just as skilled in his manners as *The Wit* but tends to take everything a couple of steps too far. A slave to fashion, his dress, deportment and speech exceeds the requirements of the age, making him appear foolish and silly. His speech in particular is highly mannered and will often reveal his ignorance or ineptitude. For example, Sir Fopling Flutter, in George Etheredge's *The Man of Mode*, litters his speech with French words and phrases to show off his cultural intelligence; however, he mispronounces many of them and uses others in the wrong context, which actually creates the opposite impression. Lord Foppington, in John Vanbrugh's *The Relapse*, changes some of his vowel sounds (usually 'o' for 'a') in the mistaken belief that it is more aristocratic. Although *The Fop* may appear effeminate to our modern eyes, he is still involved in the active pursuit of women, usually unsuccessfully, given his self-absorption, vanity and unfailing belief in himself. For this reason *The Wit* often has a great deal of fun at his expense.

The Original Vocal Demands
The vocal demands within Restoration comedy primarily revolve around the language the characters use and the way in which it needs to be delivered. Language was very much a reflection of the social codes, manners and behaviour of the aristocrats of the period and the primary goal was to use language as wittily as possible. This meant delivering clever combinations of words in an amusing way. It was intellectual comedy requiring a sharpness of mind, a quickness of thought and

dextrous delivery. Not everyone was capable of creating or delivering wit but all aspired to it.

A witty verbal exchange between characters might involve *vocal flaunting, verbal agility, verbal fencing, verbal dissembling* and *verbal wordplay.*

Vocal flaunting

Restoration aristocrats had a clear sense of their own superiority in the world, revealed through their physical and vocal expression. There was an ease about them, an owning of the space. Vocally this meant they would have possessed a rich, vibratory forward resonance that filled the world in which they inhabited, and, sound and word would have been relished and flaunted. A Wit would make it seem effortless, whilst a Fop would always take it too far.

Verbal agility

The plays are wordy: many characters are quick-witted but express themselves through long complex thoughts, requiring a lively and agile delivery. So there is a need for precise and delicate articulation of consonant sounds, particularly on the plosives (/ p /, / b /, / t /, / d /, / k /, / g / – see Chapter 2 for more information) without sacrificing the flow, rhythm and energy of a character's thoughts. Sometimes the text feels quite fast and speedy but it's a mistake to pick up the pace without dealing with the individual sounds first, otherwise the sense (and the audience) will be lost.

Verbal Fencing

Verbal fencing, or verbal repartee, is a series of quick, witty exchanges between characters, where words, often razor-sharp, were used like weapons (intended to wound, win an argument, assert some superiority or simply succeed at a playful game). I've also heard it referred to as verbal tennis, where the words are tossed back and forth like a ball in a tennis match. This means there's a shared vocal energy between characters, which must be held 'in the air' until the game is won. There's usually a sense of verbal topping throughout the exchange, where each character tries to outwit or outdo the other with their use of witty language in order to score points. Sometimes one character will pick up on puns or metaphors used by the other character and run with them in a different direction in order to make their point or win the game.

John Dryden (playwright and poet laureate) thought verbal fencing, or repartee, essential to the execution of a comedy. He comments on it in his *Essay of Dramatic Poesy*:

> As for comedy, repartee is one of its chiefest graces. The greatest pleasure of the audience is a chase of wit, kept up on both sides, and swiftly managed. (6)

Verbal fencing requires:

— An easy vocal energy, where the language can't be pushed or forced out. Winning depends on topping, undercutting or shooting down opponents with an elegant, effortless vocal ease.

— Secure breath support, breath energy and breath rhythm in line with the rhythm and pace of the text.

— A flexible pitch range so that the comic timing can be built appropriately, and, particular words can be 'pointed' or delicately thrust at an opponent.

— Verbal agility married to the flow, rhythm and timing of the dialogue as a whole.

Verbal Dissembling

Characters in Restoration comedy spend a great deal of their time dissembling: disguising their true opinions or feelings and playing the opposite of what they think or want. Sincerity was avoided because revelation could make one appear vulnerable, giving somebody else an advantage in the game. Feigned indifference about love, particularly in women, could help draw a declaration from a potential lover, or, appearing complimentary about someone when one meant the opposite could be used to score points. In all these cases we need to hear, ever so slightly, that the verbal opposite is true. For example, if a character is speaking about not wanting to get married when she clearly does, then perhaps she may be speaking just a little bit too loudly about it and using a slightly wider intonation range than usual, giving us a tiny glimpse into her insincerity. Vocal subtlety is the key.

Verbal Wordplay

Puns, double entendres, similes, metaphors and epigrams are just some of the devices that characters in Restoration comedies use when playing their verbal games.

• Puns and Double Entendres

Puns are created by confusing two different meanings in a word and, in Restoration comedy, this is usually sexually suggestive. The term *double entendre* more accurately describes this type of innuendo. According to Styan in *Restoration Comedy in Performance* double entendre first entered the English language during the Restoration period and became a major feature of plays of the period (7). Some characters deliver double entendres with a knowing slyness whilst others use them in all innocence, unaware of any innuendo, much to the amusement of the other characters (and audience). In the following example, from Wycherley's *The Country Wife*, we find both types. Sir Jasper sends his wife off with Horner, whom he mistakenly believes to be a eunuch and therefore a safe and chaste companion for her. However, Lady Fidget and Horner intend to take full advantage of Sir Jasper's absence to engage in some physical pleasure of their own. Innocent Sir Jasper says:

> ...get you gone to your business together; go, go, to your business, I say, pleasure, whilst I go to my pleasure, business.

Lady Fidget knowingly comments:

> Who for his business from his wife will run,
> Takes the best care to have her business done!   (8)

If double entendres are knowingly used by a character they need to be lightly drawn out of their seemingly innocent context with a small lift in pitch, a tiny lengthening in sound, a dash of extra breath force and the hint of sexual suggestion. This will let the other characters, or audience, know that there may be more to this than they originally thought.

- Similes

Restoration comedies are littered with similes (where one thing is likened to another, as described in Chapter 3) although they're often referred to as *similitudes* within the play texts themselves. Similes provide an opportunity for witty characters to show-off their linguistic accomplishments: Fops think they're using them in the same way although the comparisons are often so silly or the similes themselves are so over-used that it has the opposite effect. Witwoud, in William Congreve's *The Way of the World*, is particularly partial to 'similitudes' and tortures Millamant with, what he believes, is his skilful and superior use of language.

MIRABELL: You seem to be unattended, madam. You used to have the *beau monde* throng after you, and a flock of gay fine perukes hovering around you.

WITWOUD: Like moths about a candle. I had like to have lost my comparison for want of breath!

MILLAMANT: Oh I have denied myself airs today. I have walked as fast through the crowd –

WITWOUD: As a favourite in disgrace; and with as few followers.

MILLAMANT: Dear Mr Witwoud, truce with your similitudes; for I am as sick of 'em –

WITWOUD: As a physician of a good air – I cannot help it madam, though 'tis against myself.

MILLAMANT: Yet again! Mincing, stand between me and his wit.

WITWOUD: Do Mrs. Mincing, like a screen before a great fire. I confess I do blaze today, I am too bright.   (9)

The delivery of Restoration similes really depends on who is speaking them, a character of wit or a character who believes themselves to be witty but falls short of the mark. The images within the simile or 'similitude' still need to be thought through, engaged with and released into the space by both types of characters, so that the full effect of the comparison can be conveyed; however a Fop would tend to flaunt this more than a Wit.

- Metaphors

The use of metaphors is also common in Restoration comedies. Within witty exchanges, characters pick up on each other's metaphors and run with them, trying to out do one another. In this exchange from George Etherege's *The Man of Mode*, Dorimant and Harriet use illness as a metaphor for love and become so carried away that they build it into a death metaphor.

DORIMANT:	(*Aside.*) I love her and dare not let her know it. I fear sh'as an ascendant o'er me and may revenge the wrongs I have done her sex. (*To her.*) Think of making a party, madam; love will engage.
HARRIET:	You make me start. I did not think to have heard of love from you.
DORIMANT:	I never knew what 'twas to have a settled ague yet, but now and then have had irregular fits.
HARRIET:	Take heed; sickness after long health is commonly more violent and dangerous.
DORIMANT:	(*Aside.*) I have took the infection from her and feel the disease now spreading in me. (*To her.*) Is the name of love so frightful that you dare not stand it?
HARRIET:	'Twill do little execution out of your mouth on me, I am sure.
DORIMANT:	It has been fatal –
HARRIET:	To some easy women, but we are not all born to one destiny. I was informed you used to laugh at love, and not make it. (10)

The words directly related to the metaphor of illness and death will need lifting out lightly with stress and pitch to link them to each other and build their importance within the scene.

- Epigrams

Epigrams, in Restoration comedies, are witty and pointed statements in the style of a proverb or saying. Characters use them to sum up a moment, make a judgement on a situation or offer a contradictory perspective to the matter in hand. Consequently epigrams often use paradox, antithesis and irony to make their point. They give the impression of superiority: the characters who speak epigrammatically seem to think they are above and beyond ordinary, everyday matters and therefore amuse themselves by turning reality on its head (verbally at least).

In *The Country Wife*, the wits Harcourt, Horner and Dorilant often speak epigrammatically.

HORNER: Well, a pox on love and wenching! Women serve but to keep a man from better company. Though I can't enjoy them I shall you the more. Good fellowship and friendship are lasting, rational, and manly pleasures.

HARCOURT: For all that, give me some of those pleasures you call effeminate too. They help to relish one another.

HORNER: They disturb one another.

HARCOURT: No, mistresses are like books – if you pore upon them too much they doze you and make you unfit for company, but if used discreetly you are the fitter for conversation by 'em.

DORILANT: A mistress should be like a little country retreat near the town – not to dwell in constantly, but only for a night and away, to taste the town the better when a man returns. (11)

In order for epigrams to work, the speaker must draw them out vocally from the drama (almost like a little announcement) without disrupting the flow or rhythm of the scene. Any puns, ironies, paradoxes or antithesis must be delicately lifted out and explored vocally as well in order to point the wit.

The Original Delivery

Restoration comedies were performed in small and intimate indoor theatres, which strengthened the relationship between actors and their audiences. Auditoriums were fully lit, crowded and noisy, with some members of the audience seated on stage: no wonder there was heckling on both sides of the divide. Playwrights wrote with this in mind, creating prologues, epilogues and asides that spoke directly to the audience.

Asides communicated the inner thoughts of the character to the audience away from the ears of other characters. Jacobean playwrights used asides extensively but Restoration playwrights developed them further, which created humour in a deliciously witty and satirical way. Of course some asides were written in simply to further the plot but comedic asides were the most effective. Audiences enjoyed being in on a joke or a barbed criticism, denied to the characters they were directed towards.

Actors didn't step out of character in their delivery of an aside (after all they were still speaking the character's inner thoughts) but they did have to step out of the action, momentarily, to deliver them. This was done vocally more than physically as any major movement away from the scene could disrupt its rhythm and flow and leave the other characters hanging around in the space without much to do. Therefore, they were usually marked by some sort of vocal change, primarily to do with pitch and pace, which required a great deal of vocal agility and flexibility on the part of the actor.

Of course, the sheer rowdiness within the playhouse must have required actors to be secure in their projection of sound and word. They had to drive their words through a barrage of noise and disruption, without pushing their voices. Any direct communication with the audience provided by the playwright was helpful as they were then able to focus their voices much more acutely.

Here, Mr Sparkish, a fop from *The Country Wife*, explains why he makes so much noise when visiting the playhouse.

> Gad, I go to a play as to a country treat. I carry my own wine
> to one, and my own wit to t'other, or else I'm sure I should not
> be merry at either. And the reason why we are so often louder
> than the players is because we think we speak more wit, and so
> become the poet's rivals in his audience. For to tell you the truth,
> we hate the silly rogues; nay, so much that we find fault even
> with their bawdy upon the stage, whilst we talk nothing else in
> the pit as loud.   (12)

Audience laughter was another disruption, particularly to the rhythm, pace, flow and energy of verbal repartee. What to do when the audience was laughing so hard that they couldn't hear the next line? Actors had to become adept in vocal timing, incorporating laughs rhythmically into the scene when they occurred.

Sir Colley Cibber was an actor and playwright of variable success who wrote his memoirs in 1740. He included some thoughts on the most prolific actors of the late seventeenth century (when the cult of celebrity was born and audiences were drawn to the theatre by particular performances), giving us an insight into the vocal and textual delivery of the period. Here, he describes the importance of technique for Restoration actors:

> The voice of a singer is not more strictly ty'd to time and tune,
> than that of an actor in theatrical elocution: the least syllable
> too long, or too slightly dwelt upon in a period, depreciates it
> to nothing; which very syllable, if rightly touch'd, shall, like the
> heightening stroke of light from a master's pencil, give life and
> spirit to the whole.   (13)

He praised the actor, William Monfort, describing his voice as 'clear, full and melodious' (14) and appreciating his skills in delivering verbal wit.

> He had a particular talent, in giving life to *bon mots* and *repar-*
> *tees*: the wit of the poet seem'd always to come from him *extem-*

pore, and sharpen'd into more wit, from his brilliant manner of delivering it; he had himself a good share of it, or what is equal to it, so lively a pleasantness of humour, that when either of these fell into his hands upon the stage, he wantoned with them, to the highest delight of his auditors.   (15)

However, he also recognised Monfort's skill in playing fops.

He had besides all this, a variety in his genius which few capital actors have shewn, or perhaps have thought it any addition to their merit to arrive at; he could entirely change himself; could at once throw off the man of sense, for the brisk, vain, rude, and lively coxcomb, the false, flashy pretender to wit, and the dupe of his own sufficiency. Of this he gave a delightful instance in the character of Sparkish in Wycherly's *Country Wife*. In that of Sir Courtly Nice his excellence was still greater. There his whole man, voice, mien, and gesture, was no longer Monfort, but another person. There the insipid, soft civility, the elegant, and formal mien; the drawling delicacy of voice, the stately flatness of his address, and the empty eminence of his attitudes were so nicely observ'd and guarded by him, that had he not been an intire master of nature, had he not kept his judgment, as it were, a centinel of himself, not to admit the least likeness of what he us'd to be to enter into any part of his performance, he could not possibly have so completely finish'd it.   (16)

So Montfort not only delivered wit brilliantly but was also capable of making significant changes to his voice in order to create character (particularly fops).

Past to Present
So what does all this mean for an actor working with Restoration texts today?

Coping with the Words and Thoughts
Restoration comedy uses a lot of words often in long complex phrases so it's very easy for contemporary actors to lose the thread of what they're saying. Combine this with the intellectual and insincere nature

of the content and the problems increase. Actors need to think through each thought carefully as they speak it in order to make sense of the whole, despite having to work lightly and quickly. There needs to be a careful balance between staying in the moment of what they're speaking whilst always knowing what's about to come next. This will require serious practice time so that the words and thoughts sit comfortably in the mouth and become an essential part of the character.

Dealing with the Variety of Vocal Demands

Each one of the original verbal demands (vocal flaunting, verbal agility, verbal fencing, verbal dissembling and verbal wordplay) is technically demanding in its own right. Each one requires a specific delivery depending on the type of character who is using it and its placement within the text as a whole. However, it isn't uncommon for all of these features to be present within the one scene or, indeed, the one verbal exchange between characters. So actors need to be clear about the individual technical requirements without losing sight of the whole picture. Contemporary actors, particularly those who have trained or worked extensively on modern naturalistic and realistic texts, may have difficulties working with such technically demanding material. Instinctually they may want to approach the text organically but this can lead to sloppy and generalised humour and the wit will lose its edge. The audience may find only the physical aspects of the characters funny without truly understanding the verbal elements. Therefore, it's important that actors take the time to explore the vocal techniques within these features, however superficial that may seem to them, before placing them back into the organic whole of character and story.

Deciding on Accent

Contemporary English productions of Restoration comedies tend to rely on Received Pronunciation to depict aristocratic class and create a more agile delivery. However, Received Pronunciation is a relative newcomer in the accent world, having developed into its current form and status within the nineteenth century. The only problem with not using it in contemporary productions is that modern audiences tend to equate aristocrats with the use of RP and could find the use of other accents confusing. In other regions of the English speaking world, posh versions of local accents are often used successfully to re-create the characters' verbal precision. Any choices you make regarding accent must reflect the true nature of the character and his/her status in society and be flexible enough to deliver verbal wit appropriately.

Marrying Voice and Movement

The physical demands within Restoration comedies are just as specific and detailed as the vocal demands, again reflecting the social codes, manners and behaviour of aristocrats from the period.

For men, there were particular ways of standing, sitting, gesturing, bowing, taking snuff, strolling and using a hat, which were all designed to show off their physical attributes, their clothes and, ultimately, their grace and culture. So physical relish and display helped men maintain their social standing just as much as vocal relish and display, as long as it appeared elegant, natural and effortless. Playwrights did tend to mock men who went too far, though: Sir Fopling Flutter's obsession with his physical appearance is a constant source of humour in *The Man of Mode*.

For women, there were specific ways of moving as well, particularly to do with standing, sitting, strolling, gesturing and curtsying. Most of these movements were defined by the restrictions within their costume. Corsets kept their spines straight, pinched their waists smaller and pushed up their breasts into advantageous display. Of course they had difficulties breathing and, ultimately, speaking because of this restriction. Their fan was an important means of non-verbal communication and was often manipulated to convey or emphasise a point. For example, a closed fan held to the lips usually instructed somebody within the room to keep quiet, whereas fluttering an open fan might indicate passion.

The challenge for the contemporary actor is to meet the specific technical requirements of the physical and vocal demands and integrate them successfully. Voice and movement need to support each other: both were drawn from an aristocratic sense of superiority, where there was an owning of the space and, therefore, an easy, effortless communication. Although it's useful to separate them out in workshops and rehearsals to master them technically, they do need to be practised together in order to feed off one another.

Also, given the restrictive nature of the clothing and the specific physical requirements that may require characters to hold particular positions, it's important to ensure that breath isn't restricted at the same time. Actors need to spend time on breathing exercises in costume and in any physically restricting movements or positions. This is the only way in which their voices can remain released and easy within their performances.

Creating character rather than caricature
It may seem as if many of the characters are one-dimensional, given their flippant preoccupations and superficial vocal and physical characteristics. For this reason, contemporary actors often find themselves portraying sketchy caricatures, which may generate a few laughs initially but soon become tedious because they fail to engage the audience in the character's journey through the plot. It's important to remember that characters within Restoration comedies are still fully rounded human beings and there is usually serious intent behind their games and façades. This means that their external characteristics need to be drawn from their inner needs and drives. For example, there are reasons why characters flaunt themselves vocally: perhaps they're trying to showoff their verbal skills in order to increase their status in society, or, perhaps they're using their voice as a mask to hide their true feelings from the world around them so that their vulnerabilities aren't exposed to ridicule. There will always be a reason behind a particular vocal characteristic that needs to be fully explored in the rehearsal process.

Given the specific techniques and demands required by Restoration comedy I've divided the workshops into:
- Fencing and Dissembling
- Playing with Words
- Marrying Voice with Movement
- Flaunting the Fop

CHAPTER 17

FENCING AND DISSEMBLING

Verbal fencing (or repartee) between the sexes in Restoration Comedy of Manners, often involves some form of dissembling, where characters disguise their true feelings in order to secure what they want as part of the game of love. So a quick, lively exchange of wit can be insincere. More often than not it is the woman who dissembles in order to draw the man into her web. The more she shows herself uninterested, the more the man wants to conquer her ('treat him mean, keep him keen'). Revealing her inner thoughts and emotions would weaken her position in the game.

The combination of verbal fencing (repartee) and dissembling requires the actor to focus on producing:

- Secure breath support and strong forward resonance to provide an effortless and easy vocal energy. This will help give the impression that the characters don't really care about winning the game (when, of course, the opposite is true).

- Agile articulation to cope with the flow, rhythm and pace of the dialogue, as well as make complex thoughts clear so that individual points can be driven home precisely.

- Flexible pitch (on individual notes within a phrase) so particular words can be lifted out ('pointed') and delicately thrust towards the other character.

- Flexible intonation (on a pattern of notes across a phrase) so there is a subtle indication that the character is not quite revealing the truth about his/her inner thoughts and feelings.

- A combination of flexible pace and intonation so that the timing of the overall exchange can be built appropriately.
- Flexible breath rhythm in line with the rhythm and pace of the text.

The game of love is expertly played by Dorimant and Harriet in George Etherege's *The Man of Mode*, and by Mirabell and Millamant in William Congreve's *The Way of the World*. There is a battle of wits between both couples although the men tend to play their hands more openly whilst the women dissemble in order to draw in their suitors. The difference between Text Sample 1 (*The Man of Mode*) and Text Sample 2 (*The Way of the World*) is that Dorimant and Harriet are still in the initial stages of their acquaintance, circling around each other like wary animals, whilst Mirabell and Millamant know each other very well already so the game is an old one. This means that Dorimant and Harriet are very serious about the game, whilst Mirabell and Millamant are much more playful, given that their relationship has grown and developed over time. The game has almost been won by Millamant but she continues to play it right to the final stages of the comedy.

Text Sample 1: Fencing and Dissembling

The following text has been taken from Act IV Scene i of George Etherege's *The Man of Mode*, edited by Scott McMillin (reproduced by permission of A&C Black). First performed in 1676 at Dorset Garden and published in the same year.

The story so far:
Dorimant is already involved with Mrs Loveit (whom he is tired of) and Belinda (whom he is trying to bed) before he meets Harriet.
Harriet is supposed to marry Young Bellair, an arrangement brokered by his father, Old Bellair, and her mother, Lady Woodvill. However, Harriet and Young Bellair privately agree not to marry so that he can pursue Emilia (despite his father wanting Emilia for himself) and so that Harriet can pursue her own agenda with Dorimant.

Meanwhile, Sir Fopling Flutter, *The Man of Mode* of the play's title, returns from Paris in order to flaunt his new manners and clothes around town. He is encouraged by Dorimant to pursue Mrs Loveit so that she is out of the way of his liaison with Belinda. However, Dorimant is soon drawn in by Harriet's wit, charm and beauty.

About the characters:

Dorimant's character is supposedly based on the libertine and rake, John Wilmot, the 2nd Earl of Rochester (1647-1680). He lived at the heart of the Restoration court and wrote some extremely witty and bawdy poetry. Like Rochester, Dorimant is self-absorbed, self-serving and lives for pleasure. Despite this we are drawn to his magnetic charm.

Harriet is witty and charming as well and it is clear from the start of their first meeting that these two are destined to be together. Dorimant has met his match. She has a streak of independence, refusing to settle for the man whom her mother wishes her to marry and so falls into playing a battle of wits with Dorimant, hiding her true feelings in order to subdue him into becoming a dutiful suitor. On first meeting him, she speaks in an aside, 'I feel as great a change within, but he shall never know it' (17).

DORIMANT: (*He bows to HARRIET; she curtsies.*) That demure curtsy is not amiss in jest, but do not think in earnest it becomes you.

HARRIET: Affectation is catching, I find. From your grave bow I got it.

DORIMANT: Where had you all that scorn and coldness in your look?

HARRIET: From nature, sir; pardon my want of art. I have not learnt those softnesses and languishings which now in faces are so much in fashion.

DORIMANT: You need 'em not. You have a sweetness of your own, if you would but calm your frowns and let it settle.

HARRIET: My eyes are wild and wand'ring like my passions, and cannot yet be tied to rules of charming.

DORIMANT: Women, indeed, have commonly a method of managing those messengers of love. Now they will look as if they would kill, and anon they will look as if they were dying. They point and rebate (1) their glances, the better to invite us.

HARRIET: I like this variety well enough, but hate the set face that always looks as it would say, 'Come love me' – a woman who at plays makes the *doux yeux* (2) to a whole audience and at home cannot forbear 'em to her monkey.

DORIMANT: Put on a gentle smile and let me see how well it will become you.

HARRIET: I am sorry my face does not please you as it is; but I shall not be complacent and change it.

DORIMANT: Though you are obstinate, I know 'tis capable of improvement, and shall do you justice, madam, if I chance to be at court when the critics of the circle pass their judgement; for thither you must come.

HARRIET: And expect to be taken in pieces, have all my features examined, every motion censured, and on the whole be condemned to be but pretty – or a beauty of the lowest rate. What think you?

DORIMANT: The women – nay, the very lovers who belong to the drawing room – will maliciously allow you more than that. They always grant what is apparent, that they may the better be believed when they name concealed faults they cannot easily be disproved in.

HARRIET: Beauty runs as great a risk exposed at court as wit does on the stage, where the ugly and the foolish all are free to censure.

DORIMANT: (*Aside.*) I love her and dare not let her know it. I fear sh'as an ascendant o'er me and may revenge the wrongs I have done her sex. (*To her.*) Think of making a party, madam; love will engage.

HARRIET: You make me start. I did not think to have heard of love from you.

DORIMANT: I never knew what 'twas to have a settled ague yet, but now and then have had irregular fits.

HARRIET: Take heed; sickness after long health is commonly more violent and dangerous.

DORIMANT: (*Aside.*) I have took the infection from her and feel the disease now spreading in me. (*To her.*) Is the name of love so frightful that you dare not stand it?

HARRIET: 'Twill do little execution out of your mouth on me, I am sure.

DORIMANT: It has been fatal –

HARRIET: To some easy women, but we are not all born to one destiny. I was informed you used to laugh at love, and not make it.

DORIMANT: The time has been, but now I must speak.

HARRIET: If it be on that idle subject, I will put on my serious look, turn my head carelessly from you, drop my lip, let my eyelids fall and hang half o'er my eyes – thus, while you buzz a speech of an hour long in my ear and I answer never a word. Why do you not begin?

DORIMANT: That the company may take notice how passionately I made advances of love and how disdainfully you receive 'em.

HARRIET: When your love's grown strong enough to make you bear being laughed at, I'll give you leave to trouble me with it. Till when, pray forbear, sir.

1. Blunt.
2. Make eyes at.

The Man of Mode by George Etherege, edited by Scott McMillin (including notes) and published by Norton. (18)

Text Sample 2: Fencing and Dissembling

The following text has been taken from Act II Scene i of William Congreve's *The Way of the World*, edited by Brian Gibbons and published by New Mermaids. First performed in 1700 at Lincoln's Inn Fields and published in the same year.

The story so far:
Mirabell is in love with Millamant but needs the blessing of Lady Wishfort, Millamant's aunt, if he is to secure her significant dowry on marriage. Unfortunately, Lady Wishfort hates Mirabell because he tried to make love to her in order to hide his true agenda with Millamant. She wants her own nephew, Sir Wilful, to marry Millamant. Mrs Marwood, who is bitter after having her advances towards Mirabell rejected, revealed the deception to Lady Wishfort. So Mirabell organises for his servant, Waitwell, to marry Lady Wishfort's maid, Foible, and disguises Waitwell as his uncle, Sir Rowland in order to trick Lady Wishfort into a false marriage. The plan is that when Waitwell's identity is revealed and Lady Wishfort is desperate to escape such a degrading situation, Mirabell will offer help if Lady Wishfort consents to his marriage with Millamant. He will then produce Waitwell's and Foible's marriage certificate.

Millamant knows about the plan but still keeps Mirabell at arms length, despite her feelings for him. She spends time with Witwoud and Petulant, fops who think themselves wits, which enrages Mirabell.

About the characters:
Mirabell and Millamant are the most witty, charming, beautiful and successful people in their world (like Dorimant and Harriet in *The Man of Mode*). Despite scheming for his own profit and pleasure, Mirabell wins the hearts of all the women in the play, even his cast-off mistress, Mrs Fainall. Millamant lives at the centre of a circle of wits and fops, drawing people around her (according to Witwoud 'like moths about a candle' (19). Their relationship may seem flippant because of their continual repartee but they do feel genuine love towards each other. Mirabell is frustrated by Millamant's dissembling, however, and when he accuses her of cruelty which isn't in her nature, she reveals 'one's cruelty is one's power, and when one parts with one's cruelty one parts with one's power; and when one has parted with that, I fancy one's old and ugly' (20). Mirabell's comment 'I say that a man may as soon make a friend by his wit, or a fortune by his honesty, as win a woman with plain dealing and sincerity' (21) is probably justified.

MIRABELL: You had the tyranny to deny me last night, though you knew I came to impart a secret to you that concerned my love.

MILLAMANT: You saw I was engaged.

MIRABELL: Unkind. You had the leisure to entertain a herd of fools – things who visit you from their excessive idleness, bestowing on your easiness that time which is the incumbrance of their lives. How can you find delight in such society? It is impossible they should admire you, they are not capable; or if they were, it should be to you as a mortification: so sure to please a fool is some degree of folly.

MILLAMANT: I please myself; besides, sometimes to converse
with fools is for my health.

MIRABELL: Your health! Is there a worse disease than the
conversation of fools?

MILLAMANT: Yes, the vapours; fools are physic for it next to
assafoetida.   (1)

MIRABELL: You are not in a course of fools?   (2)

MILLAMANT: Mirabell, if you persist in this offensive freedom,
you'll displease me. I think I must resolve after all
not to have you – we shan't agree.

MIRABELL: Not in our physic, it may be.

MILLAMANT: And yet our distemper in all likelihood will be the
same; for we shall be sick of one another. I shan't
endure to be reprimanded nor instructed; 'tis so
dull to act always by advice, and so tedious to be
told of one's faults: I can't bear it. Well, I won't
have you, Mirabell. I'm resolved – I think – you
may go. Ha, ha, ha! What would you give, that
you could help loving me?

MIRABELL: I would give something that you did not know I
could not help it.

MILLAMANT: Come, don't look grave then. Well, what do you
say to me?

MIRABELL: I say that a man may as soon make a friend by his
wit, or a fortune by his honesty, as win a woman
with plain dealing and sincerity.

MILLAMANT: Sententious Mirabell! Prithee don't look with that
violent and inflexible wise face, like Solomon
at the dividing of the child in an old tapestry
hanging.   (3)

MIRABELL: You are merry, madam, but I would persuade you for one moment to be serious.

MILLAMANT: What, with that face? No, if you keep your countenance, 'tis impossible I should hold mine. Well, after all, there is something very moving in a love-sick face – ha, ha, ha! – well I won't laugh; don't be peevish. Heigh-ho! Now I'll be melancholy, as melancholy as a watch-light (4). Well, Mirabell, if ever you will win me, woo me now. Nay, if you are so tedious, fare you well.

1. *assafoetida* – a resinous gum with a strong alliaceous odour, procured in Central Asia; used as an antispasmodic (OED)
2. *course of fools* – the company of fools is supposedly medicinal
3. *Solomon* – the episode of I Kings 3
4. *watch-light* – night-light

The Way of the World by William Congreve, edited by Brian Gibbons (including notes) and published by New Mermaids.   (22)

Workshop Plan: Fencing and Dissembling

OBJECTIVES

- To explore the vocal demands of verbal fencing (repartee), including secure breath support, strong forward resonance, agile articulation and flexible pitch/intonation.

- To experiment with the pace, timing and overall delivery of repartee, without sacrificing vocal technique.

- To find an appropriate vocal level for the feigned indifference of dissembling.

- To explore the long complex thoughts within Restoration comedy in order to clarify meaning for an audience.

ATERIALS

You will need:
- Separate copies of *The Man of Mode* and *The Way of the World* excerpts (as provided in the previous 'Sample Text' boxes) for each member of the workshop group. Include the footnotes.
- Rolled up newspapers.

TIMING

Given the amount of exercises in this plan you may need to break the work down into two different sessions to allow your actors time to absorb and explore it appropriately.

WARM UP

Structure a warm up from the information listed in Chapter 1. Breathing and resonance exercises are important, however, articulation exercises should be given extra emphasis.

ACTIVITIES AND EXERCISES

General exercises for verbal fencing (repartee)

- Ask your actors to do some facial mirroring, as described in Chapter 1. They should work in the pairs you intend them to work in on the text, later in this workshop. Facing each other, one person starts by pulling various faces and the other person follows their actions: the lead can change at any time. Encourage them to work with the facial muscles, lips and tongue. After a few minutes, ask them to experiment with trying to create a reaction in their partner through the various 'faces' they may pull during the course of the exercise. Not only will this warm up the muscles required for agile articulation but it will also help your actors to play with each other, albeit non-verbally.

- Now ask your actors to extend this 'playing' into sound. They need to remain in their pairs and use only the six plosive sounds (/ p /, / b /, / t /, / d /, / k /, / g / – see Chapter 2 for more information). Maintaining the bite within each sound (but playfully, rather than aggressively) they must verbally volley them back and forth between each other. Using imaginary tennis racquets can be helpful. Encourage them to swap around between the sounds.

- Take away the imaginary tennis racquets and ask your actors to have a gossipy conversation with their partners, using only the six plosive sounds. This will help loosen up their pitch range whilst at the same time maintaining agile articulation.

- Now hand out copies of the sample texts, varying the two different excerpts around the room. Ask them to read the text in their heads and then try it out aloud with each other a few times so their mouths are familiar with the movements they need to make.

- Open up a short discussion so they can share their initial thoughts on what's happening in each of the texts. Provide some background information about the plot and characters, if necessary, at this point. Make sure you focus on 'what the characters want' and 'how they try to achieve it' at some point in the discussion.

- Get them to try the text in a number of different ways:
  1. Slowly – biting into any plosive sounds, relishing the vowel sounds and enjoying the sound of their own voices.
  2. Slowly – thinking their way carefully through each thought so they're absolutely clear about what they're saying
  3. Slowly – exploring their character's breath rhythm ie where their character might breathe through the long complex phrases, without breaking into the middle of any thoughts
  4. Speedily and lightly, without losing the relish, the clarity or the arc of each thought.

  Ask them to repeat all three versions to ensure that sound and thought aren't lost in the quick rendition. Speeding things up without working (painstakingly) through a process will only create very fast words which are usually unintelligible to an audience. If necessary, ask them to repeat this exercise again at the end of the workshop.

- Bring back the imaginary tennis racquets and ask them to speak the text volleying the lines between each other. They should focus on finding out the exact point in a line when they need to hit the ball, where they need to top each other (playing forehand) and where they need to undercut each other (playing backhand). Their pitch and intonation patterns will automatically and organically follow this process. Take away the imaginary tennis racquets and ask them to speak the text again. They should still work to score points against each other, albeit only verbally.

- Hand out rolled-up newspapers and ask them to speak the text again. This time they will need to gently poke or slap their partner with the newspaper (like a sword) every time they find a word that pins down the point they're trying to make. Encourage them to choose carefully, finding the puns, metaphors and similes (eg Dorimant and Harriet use words of illness and death to describe love, topping each other with every new metaphor). Once again their pitch will automatically and organically follow this process. Take away the newspapers and ask them to speak the text again. They should still 'fence' with the same words, only this time just verbally, whilst trying to score points against each other.

General exercises for dissembling

- Keep your actors in the same pairs and ask them to find a topic that they disagree about. They need to argue it out as pleasantly as possible whilst still working to win. The more they try to win, the more pleasant they are, like silk or velvet. It's important that they don't show how much they care. This time their tone colour, pitch and intonation will automatically and organically follow this process.

- Now ask them to apply this exercise to the text, without losing any of the verbal fencing (repartee) gained from the previous exercises. Of course this will be more relevant to the women (Harriet and Millamant) than the men.

Putting it all together

- Now get each pair to perform their scene for the rest of the group. Ask for feedback from the audience regarding the clarity of the text, the verbal fencing and the dissembling. There should be two different types of feedback – from those who have been working on the same scene, and, from those who have been working on a different scene (and will be listening to the text for the very first time). If necessary, ask each group to repeat the text again so that these comments can inform their performances.

- Allow some time for a group de-briefing session. Use the following questions as a starting point for the discussion:

  - Can you articulate/describe the vocal techniques required for verbal fencing (repartee)?

  - Can you articulate/describe the vocal techniques required for dissembling?

  - What practical knowledge will you take away from this workshop (ie what did you learn)?

CHAPTER 18

PLAYING WITH WORDS

Chapter Seventeen touched on word play in the workshop plan for 'Fencing and Dissembling' as it's an essential part of witty repartee. However, it was only approached organically as part of the newspaper exercise and in the de-briefing session (where your actors were asked to describe the vocal requirements as a whole). Chapter Eighteen will work more from the other end of the process, focusing on and rehearsing the specific techniques required to 'point' words.

'Pointing' literally means 'pointing out' individual words that require precise and explicit emphasis for the audience and/or other characters in the play. In Comedy of Manners, these words usually live in *puns*, *double entendres*, *similes*, *metaphors* and *epigrams* and create much of the wit and humour. Technically, this translates into a light lift in pitch, a tiny lengthening of sound and a dash of extra breath force on the word, as well as a mental focus on its meaning. Very occasionally a tiny pause can be added just before an ambiguous word for extra 'pointed' emphasis. However, it's important that whilst working technically, the flow and through-line of the whole thought is maintained.

William Wycherley was a master at playing with words and used them to great comic effect. His play *The Country Wife* is littered with useful examples for workshop treatment. Performed and published only fifteen years after the restoration of the monarchy, the play is a product of its time, reacting against Puritan values by exploring the ruthless pursuit of profit and pleasure by aristocratic society. Lust and sexual conquest drive most of the comedy so consequently the language is not only witty but extremely lewd (there is even a bawdy pun in the title of the play). Take a look at the following text sample, where the characters break down some sexual barriers through word play. The Puritans must have been horrified.

The following text has been taken from Act IV Scene iii of William Wycherley's *The Country Wife*, edited by John Dixon Hunt and published by A&C black. First performed in 1675 at Drury Lane and published in the same year.

The story so far:
Horner, as his name implies, is a highly-sexed rake operating in aristocratic circles. Unfortunately his reputation is well known so he circulates a false rumour about becoming impotent in order to secretly pursue seductions with aristocratic married women without arousing the suspicions of their husbands. His plan works perfectly and he is allowed into the company of women with unblemished reputations who are secretly seeking extra-marital affairs. Lady Fidget is one of them. Her husband, Sir Jasper, is content to leave his wife alone with Horner, safe in the knowledge that he is incapable of doing anything with her.

Horner is also in the process of pursuing Margery, a young, pretty but naive girl from the country, who is married to a middle-aged man (and former libertine), Pinchwife. Pinchwife keeps locking her away for safe-keeping, afraid that some rake will take advantage of Margery and cuckold him. Horner manages to do just that.

In this scene, Lady Fidget intends to submit to Horner but first asks that her honour is protected. A woman's reputation is her status and security within society so no wonder Lady Fidget wants it safeguarded. However, her longing for Horner is apparent and she finally submits to his embrace. Unfortunately her husband, Sir Jasper, enters the scene and finds her in Horner's arms. Horner and Lady Fidget convince him that their embrace is innocent whilst, at the same time, pursuing their sexual agenda under his nose. Part of this is achieved through the use of complex puns, double entendres, metaphors and epigrams, as well as a conveniently locked door.

LADY FIDGET: Well, Horner, am not I a woman of honour? You see, I'm as good as my word.

HORNER: And you shall see, madam, I'll not be behindhand with you in honour. And I'll be as good as my word too, if you please but to withdraw into the next room.

LADY FIDGET: But first, my dear sir, you must promise to have a care of my dear honour.

HORNER: If you talk a word more of your honour, you'll make me incapable to wrong it. To talk of honour in the mysteries of love is like talking of heaven or the deity in an operation of witchcraft, just when you are employing the devil; it makes the charm impotent.

LADY FIDGET: Nay, fie, let us not be smutty. But you talk of mysteries and bewitching to me – I don't understand you.

HORNER: I tell you, madam, the word 'money' in a mistress's mouth, at such a nick of time, is not a more disheartening sound to a younger brother (1) than that of honour to an eager lover like myself.

LADY FIDGET: But you can't blame a lady of my reputation to be chary.

HORNER: Chary! I have been chary of it already, by the report I have caused of myself.

LADY FIDGET: Ay, but if you should ever let other women know that dear secret, it would come out. Nay, you must have a great care of your conduct, for my acquaintance are so censorious, – oh 'tis a wicked censorious world, Mr Horner! – I say, are so censorious and detracting that perhaps they'll talk to the prejudice of my honour, though you should not let them know the dear secret.

HORNER: Nay, madam, rather than they shall prejudice your honour, I'll prejudice theirs; and to serve you, I'll lie with 'em all, make the secret their own, and then they'll keep it! I am a Machiavel in love, madam.

LADY FIDGET: Oh no, sir, not that way.

HORNER: Nay, the devil take me, if censorious women are to be silenced any other way!

LADY FIDGET: A secret is better kept, I hope, by a single person than a multitude. Therefore pray do not trust anybody else with it, dear, dear Mr Horner. (*Embracing him.*)

(*Enter SIR JASPAR FIDGET.*)

SIR JASPAR: How now!

LADY FIDGET: (*Aside.*) O my husband!…prevented!…and what's almost as bad, found with my arms about another man…that will appear too much…what shall I say? – Sir Jaspar, come hither. I am trying if Mr Horner were ticklish, and he's as ticklish as can be. I love to torment the confounded toad. Let you and I tickle him.

SIR JASPAR: No, your ladyship will tickle him better without me, I suppose. But is this your buying china? I thought you had been at the china house? (2)

HORNER: (*Aside.*) China house! That's my cue, I must take it. – A pox! Can't you keep your impertinent wives at home? Some men are troubled with the husbands, but I with the wives. But I'd have you to know, since I cannot be your journeyman (3) by night, I will not be your drudge (4) by day, to squire your wife about and be your man of straw, or scarecrow, only to pies and jays (5) that would be nibbling at your forbidden fruit. I shall shortly be the hackney (6) gentleman-usher of the town.

SIR JASPAR: (*Aside.*) He, he, he! Poor fellow, he's in the right on't, faith! To squire women about for other folks is as ungrateful (7) an employment as to tell (8) money for other folks. He, he, he! – Ben't angry, Horner.

LADY FIDGET: No, 'tis I have more reason to be angry, who am left by you to go abroad indecently alone; or, what is more indecent, to pin myself upon such ill-bred people of your acquaintance as this is.

SIR JASPAR: Nay, prithee, what has he done?

LADY FIDGET: Nay, he has done nothing.

SIR JASPAR: But what d'ye take ill, if he has done nothing?

LADY FIDGET: Ha, ha, ha! Faith, I can't but laugh, however. Why, d'ye think the unmannerly toad would not come down to me to the coach? I was fain to come up to fetch him, or go without him, which I was resolved not to do; for he knows china very well, and has himself very good, but will not let me see it lest I should beg some. But I will find it out, and have what I came for yet.

(*Exit LADY FIDGET and locks the door, followed by HORNER to the door.*)

HORNER: (*Apart to LADY FIDGET.*) Lock the door, madam. – So, she has got into my chamber and locked me out. Oh, the impertinency of womankind! Well, Sir Jaspar, plain dealing is a jewel. If ever you suffer your wife to trouble me again here, she shall carry you home a pair of horns, by my Lord Mayor she shall! Though I cannot furnish you myself, you are sure, yet I'll find a way.

SIR JASPAR: (*Aside.*) Ha, ha, he! At my first coming and finding her arms about him, tickling him it seems, I was half jealous, but now I see my folly. – He, he, he! Poor Horner.

HORNER:	(*Aside.*) Nay, though you laugh now, 'twill be my turn ere long. – Oh, women, more impertinent, more cunning and more mischievous than their monkeys (9), and to me almost as ugly.... Now is she throwing my things about, and rifling all I have...but I'll get into her the back way, and so rifle her for it.
SIR JASPAR:	Ha, ha, ha! Poor angry Horner.
HORNER:	Stay here a little, I'll ferret her out to you presently, I warrant.
	(*Exit HORNER at t'other door*)
SIR JASPAR:	Wife! My Lady Fidget! Wife! He is coming into you the back way!
	(*SIR JASPAR calls through the door to his wife: she answers from within.*)
LADY FIDGET:	Let him come, and welcome, which way he will.
SIR JASPAR:	He'll catch you, and use you roughly, and be too strong for you.
LADY FIDGET:	Don't you trouble yourself, let him if he can.

1. *younger brother* – traditionally impecunious, since elder brothers inherited
2. *china house* – house where china was exhibited, often place of assignation
3. *journeyman* – hireling who works for another
4. *drudge* – slave, hack, hard toiler
5. *pies and jays* – fops
6. *hackney* – hired
7. *ungrateful* – thankless
8. *tell* – count
9. *monkeys* – kept as pets

The Country Wife by William Wycherley, edited by John Dixon Hunt (including notes) and reproduced by permission of A&C Black. (23)

Puns and *double entendres* are in abundance throughout this scene. Horner and Lady Fidget use them as foreplay, creating a secret sexual language for themselves, which builds to the act itself. Of course, Sir Jasper doesn't pick up on their bawdy word play, misconstruing their sense and taking their meaning at face value. He even contributes to the innuendo himself, using double entendres in all innocence ('Wife! My Lady Fidget! Wife! He is coming into you the back way!'), which Horner and Lady Fidget pick up on and exploit. Basically, everything that has a hint of bawdiness or lewdness should be drawn out of the text in delivery to make the most of the comedy.

The double entendres of Horner and Lady Fidget should carry a mere whiff or hint of sexual suggestion in addition to the slight techni- cal changes in pitch, length and breath force. This will help the audi- ence understand their sexual word play. Overplaying it will not only kill the humour but also reveal too much information to Sir Jasper (so the scene will not be believable).

Wycherley's characters often use a seemingly innocent word in place of a bawdy one in order to disguise their true meaning. Horner and Lady Fidget make use of the word 'china' as a replacement for the sexual act itself, placing it half-way between a metaphor and a double-en- tendre. Shopping becomes a metaphor for sex (a bought commodity) whilst 'china' becomes a metaphor for various aspects of the sexual act and/or sexual anatomy (something valuable, breakable and hard). 'China', therefore, needs to be dealt with technically in much the same way as a pun or double entendre (albeit with a different intention).

The 'china' joke is exploited even further, later on the scene, after Lady Squeamish discovers Horner and Lady Fidget behind the locked door. Of course, she wants some china too.

LADY FIDGET: And I have been toiling and moiling for the prettiest piece of china, my dear.

HORNER: Nay, she has been too hard for me, do what I could.

SQUEAMISH: O lord, I'll have some china too. Good Mr Horner, don't you think to give other people china, and me none. Come in with me too.

HORNER: Upon my honour, I have none left now.

SQUEAMISH: Nay, nay, I have known you deny your china before
                now, but you shan't put me off so. Come.

HORNER: This lady had the last there.

LADY FIDGET: Yes indeed, madam, to my certain knowledge he has
                no more left.

SQUEAMISH: Oh, but it may be he may have some you could not
                find.

LADY FIDGET: What, d'y think if he had had any left, I would not
                have had it too. For we women of quality never think
                we have china enough.   (24)

Horner is quite accomplished in his use of witty and amusing *epigrams*, particularly when securing a seduction. He tells Lady Fidget about how talking of her honour could destroy the moment, likening the sexual act to a religious experience, albeit an inverted, paradoxical one.

> If you talk a word more of your honour, you'll make me incapable to wrong it. To talk of honour in the mysteries of love is like talking of heaven or the deity in an operation of witchcraft, just when you are employing the devil; it makes the charm impotent.

The key here is for the actor to 'point' or draw out the language related to honour, love, religion, spirituality and sex (in order to explore the antithesis and paradox at its heart) whilst at the same time driving through to the key word, *impotent*.

Workshop Plan: Playing with Words

OBJECTIVES

- To play with the language within Restoration Comedy in order to realise the humour.

- To explore the delivery of puns, double entendres, metaphors and epigrams through the technique of 'pointing'.

MATERIALS

You will need:
- Separate copies of *The Country Wife* excerpt (as provided in the previous 'Sample Text' box) for each member of the workshop group. Include the footnotes.
- Pages ripped out of an old telephone directory (advertising directories are best).

WARM UP

Structure a warm up from the information listed in Chapter 1. Breathing and resonance exercises are important, however, articulation exercises should be given extra emphasis.

ACTIVITIES AND EXERCISES

General exercises for 'pointing' metaphors, puns and double entendres.

- Hand out pages from an old telephone book (advertising directories are best). Ask your actors to work in groups of three (the grouping you intend them to work in for the text, later in this workshop). Now ask them to have a witty conversation with each other, using only the words from the page. Make sure they're clear about the topic of conversation before they start – it might be gossip or about someone they fancy. Encourage them to really play with the sounds within the words they're speaking (even if it's only an advertisement for plumbers) and ask them to enjoy the sound of their own voices in the process.

- Ask them to repeat the exercise but this time they need to 'point' particular words as though they're metaphors, puns or double entendres with a bawdy subtext ('pointing' may require a specific explanation).

- Now get them to repeat the exercise but this time ask two of them to use the metaphors, puns and double entendres to flirt with each other, whilst trying to maintain an innocent (still gossipy) conversation with the third person (a little like the text of *The Country Wife*). This should help them to maintain subtlety.

- Hand out copies of the sample text and ask them to read it through in their heads so they're clear about the sense. Now ask them to try it aloud in their group a few times so their mouths are familiar with the movements they need to make. If necessary, spend some time getting them to exaggerate the consonant sounds, followed by the vowel sounds (just as an exercise) to find the bite and relish.

- Open up a short discussion so they can share their initial thoughts on what's happening in the text. Provide some background information about the plot and characters, if necessary, at this point. Make sure you focus on 'what the characters want' and 'how they try to achieve it' at some point in the discussion.

- Now ask them to apply what they've learnt about 'pointing' puns and double entendres in their delivery of the text. They should try it aloud a number of times through. Each reading should reveal more about the bawdy subtext. It might also be useful to try the famous 'china' scene with Horner, Lady Fidget and Lady Squeamish, at this point.

- Get the group to make a list of all the words in the text that have some sort of sexual innuendo or bawdy subtext attached to them. They should appoint a note taker who can report back to the whole group in discussion. Make sure you talk about any differences between the group lists.

- Ask each group to repeat the text so they can enjoy relishing anything they might have missed prior to the discussion.

General exercises for 'pointing' epigrams

- Ask each group to find the epigrams in the text and discuss their meaning, including any ironies and paradoxes.

- Now ask them to return to the phone book exercise but every so often, 'announce' a saying in as witty a manner as possible (again, even if the words are some mundane advertisement). Make sure they understand that they must drive their point home to the final word. Ask them to experiment with the rhythm, pace and overall timing of each of their imaginary epigrams.

- Even though it is primarily Horner who uses epigrams in the sample text, ask all of your actors to try them out as a witty announcement, 'pointing' the words and driving through to the final word. Again, ask them to experiment with the rhythm, pace and overall timing.

- Now place them back into their context by asking each group to repeat the sample text. Performance in front of the rest of the group may help them to play with the words a little more.

- Allow some time for a group de-briefing session. Use the following questions as a starting point for the discussion:
  - Can you articulate/describe the vocal techniques required for 'pointing' metaphors, puns, double entendres and epigrams?
  - What practical knowledge will you take away from this workshop (ie what did you learn)?

CHAPTER 19

MARRYING VOICE WITH MOVEMENT

This chapter provides a starting point for integrating voice and movement within Restoration comedies. Your actors need to be able to breathe and speak freely through the physical restrictions of the period as well as use non-verbal movements to punctuate and emphasise the verbal wit.

Aristocrats were judged just as much by the way in which they physically conducted themselves as by the way in which they verbally handled wit. Grace, elegance, poise and self-assurance were cultivated, with a focus on physical relish and display. The driving forces behind aristocratic physicality were:

1. Wearing fashionable clothing (that not only reflected their status in society but also restricted their bodies and limited the way in which they moved).

2. Following social codes of behaviour (that required them to conform to set rules of physical conduct, such as curtsying, bowing, using a fan or taking snuff).

3. Pursuing profit and pleasure (that entailed adorning themselves like peacocks and flaunting their sexuality).

If successfully managed, these elements combined to reinforce their social status (Wits). If taken a step too far, they became the butt of jokes (Fops).

Given that fashionable clothing dictated so much of Restoration movement, it's important that actors spend some time focusing on pictures and paintings from the period to build an awareness of the style as well as wearing rehearsal costumes once they start working practically with the text. Here are some suggestions:

- Men: shoes with a heel, breeches or trousers with the legs rolled or pushed up to just below the knee, a large shirt with flamboyant cuffs, a coat with tails, a handkerchief and a hat.
- Women: closed in shoes with a heel, a corset, a floor-length skirt, a fan.

Professional companies usually have these items available for rehearsal, however, student actors are quite good at sourcing them, primarily because they don't need to be from the period (hats don't have to be plumed; an old straw hat can work just as well, for example). The only item that you might have to provide for rehearsal purposes with students are the corsets.

Once your actors have studied costumes from the period and have their rehearsal clothing, they will need to focus on *Posture and Stance, Sitting, Walking, Gesturing* and *Gesturing with Props*.

Posture and Stance (Men)

Restoration men had upright postures, which flaunted their elegance, showed-off their clothes and reinforced their status (allowing them to look down on people). Their spines were aligned and lengthened, aided by a waistcoat and long tail coat (although thwarted by the weight of heavy wigs). It's important that actors don't pull themselves up too far as their abdominal muscles will tighten, making it difficult to breathe and vocalise sound freely.

The feet were turned out, which showed off the legs. This was the least clothed part of men and so was flaunted sexually. One leg was further forward than the other (with about a foot's width between the two) and the weight tended to be on the back foot.

At rest, the arms were often held a little bit away from the body in readiness for gesturing and flourishing. A favourite position seemed to be with one hand on a hip and the other bent at the elbow showing off cuffs or a lace handkerchief.

Posture and Stance (Women)

Women's spines were also upright and long: it was impossible to slump with a corset on. However, this length extended up through the neck to the base of the skull. It's important that your actors are laced into their corsets whilst extending their ribcages (as on an in-breath) which should give them a little room to breathe. However, lacing it up too loose may mean their breasts fall out so a balance needs to be found. Again, like the men, their abdominal muscles need to remain released.

The feet were often placed in first position (for ballet) and the arms were held away from the body because of bulky skirts. However, it was unusual for women to lower their arms because their hands would have been engaged with a fan or a mask. When the fan wasn't being used, it was held closed in the right hand at the base of the corset, resting in the palm of the left hand.

Sitting (Men)

Sitting for men was dictated by their clothing: only the edge of the chair was used, to prevent too much strain on the breeches. One leg would be forward, the other leg would bend and the bottom would be eased onto the edge of the chair. At the same time the coat tails were flipped out to ensure they weren't sat on and the sword was placed at the side of the chair out of harm's way. Once seated, the forward leg would turn out to display the calf.

Sitting (Women)

Sitting for women was also dictated by clothing and, again, only the edge of the chair was used, primarily because of the lack of manoeuvrability in a stiff corset and the amount of fabric in the skirt. There might also have been a train to kick out of the way prior to lowering the body. Spinal length was kept throughout the movement and once seated a toe might have peeped out from under the skirt.

Walking (Men)

Maintaining length in the spine was just as important when walking as when standing still. There was probably a slight extension of the leg before placing it on the ground (with possibly a toe to heel action) and the feet were partially turned out to display the calves. The stride wouldn't have been particularly wide, otherwise the body would have bounced along.

Walking (Women)
The spine remained erect because of the corset and only small steps were taken to minimise the sway of the skirt. The feet were turned out slightly and were probably needed to kick (surreptitiously) some of the fabric out of the way. The effect was one of gracefulness and elegance.

Gesturing (Men)
Gesturing was accompanied by a turn out of the wrist and delicate finger work, usually designed to show off various parts of clothing, such as lace cuffs. However, tossing the curls of the wig was also a useful way of drawing attention to oneself physically.

Gesturing (Women)
Female gesturing was often part of a flirtatious game, for example, fluttering the eyelashes or lifting and dropping the shoulders to show off the décolletage. In Etherege's *The Man of Mode*, Medley pours scorn on a new book that outlines some of these gestures.

> Then there is *The Art of Affectation*, written by a late beauty of quality, teaching you how to draw up your breasts, stretch up your neck, to thrust out your breech, to play with your head, to toss up your nose, to bite your lips, to turn up your eyes, to speak in a silly soft tone of a voice, and use all the foolish French words that will infallibly make your person and conversation charming...   (25)

Gesturing with Props (Men)
Men carried a number of objects about their person that were gracefully employed as flourishes in their own right or as emphasis to a verbal point (for example, at the climax of an epigram). These might include waving a handkerchief, playing with long cuffs, toying with a cane, looking at a watch drawn from a waistcoat pocket, holding onto

a sword hilt and taking snuff. The fingers and hands were always used delicately and elegantly.

Snuff was a powdered tobacco, sometimes flavoured and/or scented, that was inhaled through the nose. It became fashionable for Restoration men to carry a small, ornate box for their snuff that could be concealed easily in their clothing. The box was held between the thumb and forefinger of one hand, gently tapped by the other hand (to release any snuff stuck on the inside of the lid) and the lid spring released by the holding thumb. The snuff was pinched between the thumb and third finger of the free hand, lifted to the nostrils and sniffed. Finally, the hands and clothes were elegantly dusted off with a handkerchief.

Gesturing with Props (Women)

Women usually had a range of accessories at their disposal, such as a fan, a mask, a drawstring purse, a pomander, a parasol and a muff. However, it was the fan and mask that were the most important in terms of gestural meaning.

Masks gave women the opportunity to disguise their identity, particularly at court and in the playhouse. They were often referred to as vizard masks – vizard meaning 'a disguise'. There were a number of ways in which one could be worn; held to the face, pinned to the hair or even gripped from behind by the teeth (with a small holder for that purpose). As time progressed, vizard masks became popular with prostitutes at the playhouse, which gave aristocratic women an opportunity to secure sexual favours incognito.

A fan made of silk, satin or lace was an indispensable prop for any lady of the period. It was used as a communication device, sending out signals and conveying inner thoughts and feelings that would be too risky to verbalise. Lyn Oxenford in *Playing Period Plays* states

> The fan can almost be classed as a weapon; it was used for skirmishes, pitched battles and absolute surrender. (26)

It conveyed a myriad of meanings and emotions, open, closed or fluttered. Restoration women were very clear about its purpose and never waved one about without reason. Examples of different fan positions can be researched from portraits of the period, deportment books and, of course, play texts. However, there is no reason why an actor can't come up with their own fan language. It's a good idea to start with the fan at rest (one hand resting the closed fan in the palm of the other hand at the bottom edge of the corset) and work from there. Here are some ideas:

- To indicate 'be quiet', touch the lips with a closed fan
- To indicate 'don't say anything', touch an ear with a closed fan
- To indicate 'I love you', touch the heart with a closed fan
- To indicate (flirtatiously) 'I'm interested in you', peer over the top of an open fan
- To indicate that you're overcome with passion, flutter an open fan.

Once your actors have experimented and become physically comfortable with all these movements they will need to focus on integrating the voice and the verbal demands of the text, including:

- Breathing and speaking through any costume restrictions
- Breathing and speaking through the physical line of the character
- Breathing and speaking through any complex movements, tasks or gestures
- Choreographing any complex movements, tasks or gestures with the words of the text.

Of course all this needs significant amounts of rehearsal so that it appears a natural, effortless extension of the character. Any choreographed movements, such as using a fan or taking snuff, need special attention so they become a seamless and organic part of the performance.

The following sample text from Etherege's *The Man of Mode* is a useful starting point for not only learning about the physical life of Restoration characters but also for practising the integration of voice and movement. Clear physical directions are given by the characters themselves.

Text Sample: Marrying Voice and Movement

The following text has been taken from Act III Scene i of George Etherege's *The Man of Mode*, edited by Scott McMillin (reproduced by permission of A&C Black). First performed in 1676 at Dorset Garden and published in the same year.

The story so far:

Harriet is supposed to marry Young Bellair, an arrangement brokered by his father, Old Bellair, and her mother, Lady Woodvill. However, Harriet and Young Bellair privately agree not to marry so that he can pursue Emilia (despite his father wanting Emilia for himself) and Harriet can pursue her own agenda with Dorimant, a witty and charming libertine. In this scene, they try to fool their (watching) parents that they're interested in each other so they will be left alone to follow their true desires. They give each other direction on how to physically dissemble; in other words, provide non-verbal clues to make it seem as though they're flirting with each other. The scene can be played as a duologue by deleting the text of Old Bellair and Lady Woodvill.

YOUNG BELLAIR: What generous resolution are you making, madam?

HARRIET: Only to be disobedient, sir.

YOUNG BELLAIR: Let me join hands with you in that.

HARRIET: With all my heart. I never thought I should have given mine so willingly. Here.

(*They join hands.*)

I, Harriet –

YOUNG BELLAIR: And I, Harry –

HARRIET: Do solemnly protest –

YOUNG BELLAIR: And vow –

HARRIET: That I with you –

YOUNG BELLAIR: And I with you –

HARRIET/YOUNG BELLAIR: Will never marry.

HARRIET: A match!

YOUNG BELLAIR: And no match! How do you like this indifference now?

HARRIET: You expect I should take it ill, I see.

YOUNG BELLAIR:'Tis not unnatural for you women to be a little angry, you miss a conquest – though you would slight the poor man were he in your power.

HARRIET: There are some, it may be, have an eye like Bart'lomew, big enough for the whole fair; (1) but I am not of the number, and you may keep your gingerbread.(2) 'Twill be more acceptable to the lady whose dear image it wears.

YOUNG BELLAIR: I must confess, madam, you came a day after the fair.

HARRIET: And own then you are in love?

YOUNG BELLAIR: I do.

HARRIET: The confidence is generous, and in return I could almost find in my heart to let you know my inclinations.

YOUNG BELLAIR: Are you in love?

HARRIET: Yes – with this dear town, to that degree I can scarce endure the country in landscapes and in hangings.

YOUNG BELLAIR: What a dreadful thing 'twould be to be hurried back to Hampshire!

HARRIET: Ah, name it not.

YOUNG BELLAIR: As for us, I find we shall agree well enough. Would we could do something to deceive the grave people!

HARRIET: Could we delay their quick proceeding, 'twere well. A reprieve is a good step towards the getting of a pardon.

YOUNG BELLAIR: If we give over the game, we are undone. What think you of playing it on booty? (3)

HARRIET: What do you mean?

YOUNG BELLAIR: Pretend to be in love with one another. 'Twill make some dilatory excuses we may feign pass the better.

HARRIET: Let us do't, if it be but for the dear pleasure of dissembling.

YOUNG BELLAIR: Can you play your part?

HARRIET: I know not what it is to love, but I have made pretty remarks by being now and then where lovers meet. Where did you leave their gravities?

YOUNG BELLAIR: I' th' next room. Your mother was censuring our modern gallant.

(*Enter OLD BELLAIR and LADY WOODVILL.*)

HARRIET: Peace, here they come. I will lean against this wall and look bashfully down upon my fan while you, like an amorous spark, modishly entertain me.

LADY WOODVILL: (*To OLD BELLAIR.*) Never go about to excuse 'em. Come, come it was not so when I was a young woman.

OLD BELLAIR: Adod, they're something disrespectful –

LADY WOODVILL: Quality was then considered and not rallied by every fleering fellow.

OLD BELLAIR: Youth will have its jest, adod it will.

LADY WOODVILL: 'Tis good breeding now to be civil to none but players and Exchange women (4). They are treated by 'em as much above their condition as others are below theirs.

OLD BELLAIR: Out, a pize on 'em. Talk no more: the rogues ha' got an ill habit of preferring beauty, no matter where they find it.

LADY WOODVILL: See your son and my daughter. They have improved their acquaintance since they were within.

OLD BELLAIR: Adod, methinks they have! Let's keep back and observe.

YOUNG BELLAIR: (*To HARRIET.*) Now for a look and gestures that may persuade 'em I am saying all the passionate things imaginable.

HARRIET: Your head a little more on one side. Ease yourself on your left leg and play with your right hand.

YOUNG BELLAIR: Thus, is it not?

HARRIET: Now set your right leg firm on the ground, adjust your belt, then look about you.

YOUNG BELLAIR: A little exercising will make me perfect.

HARRIET: Smile, and turn to me again very sparkish.

YOUNG BELLAIR: Will you take your turn and be instructed?

HARRIET: With all my heart.

YOUNG BELLAIR: At one motion play your fan, roll your eyes, and then settle a kind look upon me.

HARRIET: So.

YOUNG BELLAIR: Now spread your fan, look down upon it, and tell the sticks with a finger.

HARRIET: Very modish.

YOUNG BELLAIR: Clap your hand upon your bosom, hold down your gown. Shrug a little, draw up your breasts and let 'em fall again, gently, with a sigh or two, *etc.*

HARRIET: By the good instructions you give, I suspect you for one of those malicious observers who watch people's eyes, and from innocent looks make scandalous conclusions.

YOUNG BELLAIR: I know some, indeed, who out of mere love to mischief are as vigilant as jealousy itself, and will give you an account of every glance that passes at a play and i' th' Circle.   (5)

HARRIET: 'Twill not be amiss now to seem a little pleasant.

YOUNG BELLAIR: Clap your fan then in both your hands, snatch it to your mouth, smile, and with a lively motion fling your body a little forwards. So! Now spread it, fall back on the sudden, cover your face with it, and break out into a loud laughter. – Take up! Look grave and fall a-fanning to yourself. Admirably well acted!

HARRIET: I think I am pretty apt at these matters.

OLD BELLAIR: (*To LADY WOODVILL.*) Adod, I like this well.

LADY WOODVILL: This promises something.

1. An allusion to Bartholomew Cokes in Jonson's *Bartholomew Fair*, who wants to buy everything in sight. The fair was held annually in August.
2. A popular item at the fair.
3. Conspiring against the others.

4. Shopkeepers at the New Exchange.
5. Circular path in Hyde Park.

The Man of Mode by George Etherege, edited by Scott McMillin (including notes) and published by Norton.　　(27)

Workshop Plan: Marrying Voice and Movement

OBJECTIVES

- To experiment with different physical states of Restoration characters, whilst maintaining breath release and support for speaking.

- To explore breathing and speaking through any complex movements, tasks or gestures.

- To marry the physical and vocal life of Restoration characters through a piece of period text.

MATERIALS

You will need:
  - Rehearsal clothing (Men – shoes with a heel, breeches or trousers with the legs rolled or pushed up to just below the knee, a large shirt with flamboyant cuffs and a coat with tails: Women – closed in shoes with a heel, a corset and a floor-length skirt)
  - Rehearsal props (large handkerchiefs, small boxes for taking snuff, fans)
  - Separate copies of *The Man of Mode* excerpt (as provided in the previous 'Sample Text' box) for each member of the workshop group. Include the footnotes.

TIMING

Given the amount of exercises in this plan you may need to break the work down into a few different sessions to allow your actors time to absorb and explore it appropriately.

NINETEEN: MARRYING VOICE WITH MOVEMENT

WARM UP

Structure a warm up from the information listed in Chapter 1. Release exercises should be given priority, particularly work on Grounding, Centring and Aligning. These should be followed by work on breath, resonance and articulation.

ACTIVITIES AND EXERCISES

- Ask your actors to start in a physically neutral position, ie grounded, centred and aligned (see Chapter 1 for details) in their rehearsal clothes. Maintaining centre will be a little more difficult in heels as their weight will be pitched forward. Allow them time to play around with finding a firm connection to the ground. If you do want the women to work with corsets then they will need to practise lacing themselves in first whilst extending their rib cage on an in-breath, giving them some room for manoeuvrability with the breathing muscles.

- Give your actors directions on how to adjust their *posture and stance* for Restoration men and women as outlined at the beginning of this chapter. Explore some breathing exercises with them whilst they remain in these positions. Simply feeling the in-breath drop down to the belly and releasing out a long fffff sound is useful (followed by sssss, vvvvv and zzzzz). This is particularly important for female actors wearing corsets. Because they won't have much intercostal or rib cage movement they must focus the breath down to the abdominal muscles.

- Ask them to remain in this *posture and stance*, breathe down to the belly and release out some Restoration oaths and curses (most are usually verbalised by men in Restoration texts but this is still a useful exercise for women). The satirist Thomas Brown mentioned some in his publication *Amusements Serious and Comical* in 1700 (see top of page 260). Otherwise, you could research other curses and oaths from play texts of the period or ask your actors to devise some of their own to work with. Keep ensuring that they retain their breath support as they work.

A Huge great Muff, and a Gaudy Ribbon hanging at a Bully's Backside, is an Excellent Jest; and New Invented Curses, as Stap my Vitals, Damn my Diaphragm, Slit my Wind-Pipe.   (28)

- Give your actors directions on *walking* for Restoration men and women as outlined at the beginning of this chapter. Ask them to focus on walking and breathing, again trying out some long sounds (fffff, sssss, vvvvv and zzzzz) as they move through the space. You may like to feed in some different paces and tempos as well. Finally, ask them to try out the curses and oaths from the previous exercise, as they move.

- Give your actors directions on *sitting* for Restoration men and women as outlined at the beginning of this chapter. Ask them to practise this a few times through so they can perform the movements comfortably and fluently. Now ask them to focus on breathing at specific points in the process. Here are some ideas:

  Sitting down – Breathe in as you pivot close to the chair in preparation for sitting, breathe-out as you move your coat tails (men) or your dress fabric (women) out of the way and lower your body to the edge of the chair.

  Standing up – Breathe in as you slide the forward foot back to the other and slightly incline the torso, breathe out as you lift up from the chair.

- In preparation for *gesturing*, ask your actors to return to the *posture and stance* or *sitting* position for Restoration men and women. The following exercises loosen up arms, hands and fingers in preparation for gestural work. Keep feeding the word 'graceful' into your directions. Ask them to breathe in as their arms float up by the elbows (as if they're puppets and strings are attached to their elbows with a puppet master on the ceiling pulling them upwards) and breathe out as their elbows float back down. Keeping their arms bent, the women will need to gently rest one hand in the other, whilst men can leave their hands in mid-air, palms facing outwards, with some of their fingers extended (showing off their lace cuffs). In addition, ask the men to draw some imaginary figure of eights in the air with their fingers, hands and wrists. Make sure they keep breathing.

- Now ask them to do some *gesturing with props*. Separate the group into two: men and women. Ask the men to practise taking snuff (as outlined at the beginning of this chapter) until the movements are comfortable and fluent. Encourage them to work with the breath, first silently and then with sound (fffff, sssss, vvvvv and zzzzz) so that they don't hold their breath in tension whilst they're working. Finally, ask them to try an epigram whilst they carry out the movements. Ask them to find out at which point in the text each movement might best be performed without disrupting word flow, pace and rhythm. Certain movements, for example the actual pinching of the snuff, might help them to punctuate witty points within the epigram. The following epigrams from Wycherley's *The Country Wife* can be useful for this work and provide an opportunity for the men to work in pairs.

HARCOURT: Mistresses are like books – if you pore upon them too much they doze you and make you unfit for company, but if used discreetly you are the fitter for conversation by 'em.

DORILANT: A mistress should be like a little country retreat near the town – not to dwell in constantly, but only for a night and away, to taste the town the better when a man returns (29).

- Whilst the men are practising taking snuff, the women need to devise their very own fan 'language'. Ask them to come up with a series of different fan positions that convey specific meanings, such as, 'I fancy you' or 'keep this a secret'. Once they've had time to make these movements clear, comfortable and fluent, encourage them to work with the breath silently (make sure they're not holding their breath in tension whilst they're working). They will have an opportunity of marrying this work with text later in the workshop.

- Now ask the two groups to watch each other's work. You might like to ask a selection from each group to show their work individually, or, if there is time, ask them all to have a go. The women should note whether the men's epigrams are clear and witty: the men should try and guess the meanings the women are trying to convey. If anything remains unclear, uncomfortable or disjointed then send the groups away to re-rehearse.

- Divide the group in two rows, facing each other. Leave enough space for a fashion parade runway down the middle of these two rows. Now ask them, one by one, to spend time showing off their clothes and physicality down the catwalk. If you're not working in rehearsal clothing then they can show off their contemporary clothing in a flamboyant way, or, show off imaginary Restoration clothing. Make sure they breathe as they move.

- Once everybody has had a go, repeat the exercise but, this time, call out a name from a Restoration comedy that indicates a particular type of character (e g Horner, Squeamish, Fidget, Mincing or Bellair). The person on the catwalk will then need to adjust their character physicality and movement to meet the character's name. This will help them to vary the centre of their movement as well as their pace and rhythm from the set Restoration movements they've already worked on.

- Now ask them to repeat the exercise again and speak an epigram as they move through the space as the character. One of Millamant's epigrams from Congreve's *The Way of the World* is useful for this work.

  'Tis a lamentable thing I'll swear that one has not the liberty of choosing one's acquaintance as one does one's clothes.   (30)

- Finally, hand out copies of the sample text excerpt from George Etherege's *The Man of Mode* and ask them to read it through in their heads so they're clear about the sense. Now ask them to try it aloud in pairs a few times so their mouths are familiar with the movements they need to make.

- Open up a short discussion so they can share their initial thoughts on what's happening in the text. Provide some background information about the plot and characters, if necessary, at this point. Make sure you focus on 'what the characters want' and 'how they try to achieve it' at some point in the discussion.

- Now ask them to apply what they've learnt about Restoration movement in their delivery of the text, following Young Bellair's and Harriet's instructions. They should try it a number of times through so that the movement is clear, effortless and integrated successfully with the verbal dialogue.

- Performing the text to each other will help them clarify this work further. It's also interesting to see how the movements and gestures between each group differ, despite having the same instructions.

- Allow some time for a group de-briefing session. Use the following questions as a starting point for the discussion:

  - What did you find the most challenging about integrating the voice with movement in Restoration text?

  - What practical knowledge will you take away from this workshop (ie what did you learn)?

CHAPTER 20

FLAUNTING THE FOP

Chapters 17, 18 and 19 focused on wits as an ideal image of *aristocratic, urbane English masculinity* (31). Whatever we think about their morals we are still attracted by their charm, polish and witty sophistication. The presence of fops (effeminate, affected and witless fools, often obsessed with French style and fashion) helps elevate the status of wits even further. In comparison, the wits appear even more attractive. Of course, the fops believe themselves to be cultured, stylish and witty but betray themselves vocally and physically every time they appear on stage and end up only promoting their own foppishness and foolishness.

Fops also operate as a sexual threat to wits. Sometimes, the company of fops is appealing to female characters: they love to gossip, are interested in fashion and like playing cards. They're usually involved in the active pursuit of a female character, particularly one who can provide them with money. Of course they don't succeed but only after the wits have outsmarted them and made them appear even more foolish.

So fops are an important part of the comic plot in Restoration plays and not just humorous in their own right. However, there was another reason for their inclusion: many of these characters were based on real men in English society at the time and playwrights had a great deal of fun satirising and ridiculing their foppery. Sparkish in *The Country Wife* verbalises his fears about being represented on stage, particularly since his songs have already been mocked there.

> Damn the poets! They turned 'em into burlesque, as they call it.
> That burlesque is a hocus-pocus trick they have got, which by
> the virtue of hictius doctius, topsy-turvy, they make a wise and

witty man in the world a fool upon the stage, you know not how.
– And 'tis therefore I hate 'em too, for I know not but it may
be my own case; for they'll put a man into a play for looking
asquint. Their predecessors were contented to make serving-men
only their stage-fools, but these rogues must have gentlemen,
with a pox to 'em, nay knights. And, indeed, you shall hardly see
a fool upon the stage but he's a knight. And to tell you the truth,
they have kept me these six years from being a knight in earnest,
for fear of being knighted in a play, and dubbed a fool.   (32)

It's customary for a group of wits to talk disparagingly about fops in
Restoration plays, exposing their follies and affectations before the
audience has even met them. This sets them up as an object of ridicule
the moment they step on stage. It also helps to juxtapose the differences between wits and fops even further. The following are examples
taken from the plays we've worked on in the previous three chapters:
The Country Wife, The Man of Mode and *The Way of the World*.

In *The Country Wife*, the wits, Horner, Harcourt and Dorilant, reveal
their thoughts about the fop, Sparkish.

BOY: Mr Sparkish is below, sir.

HARCOURT: What, my dear friend! A rogue that is fond of me
                only, I think, for abusing him.

DORILANT: No, he can no more think the men laugh at him
                than that women jilt him, his opinion of himself is so
                good.

HORNER: Well, there's another pleasure by drinking I thought
                not of – I shall lose his acquaintance, because he
                cannot drink. And you know 'tis a very hard thing to
                be rid of him for he's one of those nauseous offerers at
                wit, who, like the worst fiddlers, run themselves into
                all companies.

HARCOURT: One that by being in the company of men of sense would pass for one.

HORNER: And may so to the short-sighted world, as a false jewel amongst true ones is not discerned at a distance. His company is as troublesome to us as a cuckold's when you have a mind to his wife's. (33)

In *The Man of Mode*, the wits, Dorimant, Medley and Bellair expose the affectations of the fop, Sir Fopling Flutter (the man of mode in the play's title).

YOUNG BELLAIR: He thinks himself the pattern of modern gallantry.

DORIMANT: He is indeed the pattern of modern foppery.

MEDLEY: He was yesterday at the play, with a pair of gloves up to his elbows and a periwig more exactly curled than a lady's head newly dressed for a ball.

YOUNG BELLAIR: What a pretty lisp he has!

DORIMANT: Ho, that he affects in imitation of the people of quality of France.

MEDLEY: His head stands for the most part on one side, and his looks are more languishing than a lady's when she lolls at stretch in her coach or leans her head carelessly against the side of a box 'i the playhouse.

DORIMANT: He is a person indeed of great acquired follies. (34)

In *The Way of the World*, Mirabell and Fainall discuss the foppishness of Sir Wilfull Witwoud and his half-brother, Witwoud. Here, Mirabell describes the 'wit' of Witwoud.

MIRABELL: He is a fool with a good memory and a few scraps of other folks' wit. He is one whose conversation can never be approved, yet it is now and then to be endured. He has indeed one good quality, he is not

exceptious*; for he so passionately affects the reputation of understanding raillery, that he will construe an
affront into a jest, and call downright rudeness and ill
language satire and fire.   (35)

Fops have many of the same vocal and physical characteristics as wits
but while a wit would make it all seem effortless, a fop would always
over-step the mark. This means that it's very easy for actors to create
one-dimensional caricatures rather than embody a fully rounded character. Fops *are* extreme in their vocal and physical behaviour but they
still have wants and needs. Therefore, it's important to ensure that
actors are clear about the internal mechanism of the character, ie what
drives him and what he's trying to achieve.

Vocally, a fop can be recognised by extreme vocal flaunting,
over-relish of sound and word, inappropriate word-play, and, some
form of vocal affectation.

Vocal flaunting
Fops enjoy the sound of their own voice and, therefore, flaunt it around
the space. Technically, actors need to have secure breath support,
strong forward resonance and agile articulation to over-relish sound
and word.

Verbal word-play
Fops enjoy playing with words, thinking they're being witty and
urbane. However, the puns, double entendres, similes or metaphors they choose to use are very silly or over-used or over-the-top.
Technically, actors need flexible pitch and intonation to over-point the
words. At the same time they need to communicate the belief that
they're delivering something witty.

Vocal affectation
Often fops have some type of vocal affectation, ie a feature in their
voice that they believe makes them seem cultured and stylish but, in
fact, reveals their silliness and pretentiousness. In the previous extract
from *The Man of Mode*, Young Bellair laughs about Sir Fopling Flutter's

---

*   *exceptious* – disposed to make objections

'pretty lisp', which Dorimant reveals 'he affects in imitation of the people of quality of France'. Indeed, Sir Fopling Flutter is obsessed with all things French and uses many a French word or phrase to flaunt his supposed sophistication. However, he mispronounces many of them and uses others in the wrong context, creating the opposite impression. Lord Foppington, in John Vanbrugh's *The Relapse*, changes some of his vowel sounds (usually 'o' for 'a') in the mistaken belief that it's more aristocratic. Then there's Sir Feeble Fainwould's nauseating baby talk to Leticia in Aphra Behn's *The Lucky Chance*.

Knowing what we do from the previous extracts about Sparkish in *The Country Wife*, Sir Fopling Flutter in *The Man of Mode* and Witwoud in *The Way of the World*, here are some short extracts where each of these characters speak, offering up opportunities for actors to experiment with their vocal features.

Text Sample 1: Flaunting the Fop

The following text has been taken from Act II Scene i of William Wycherley's *The Country Wife*, edited by John Dixon Hunt (reproduced by permission of A&C Black). Here, Sparkish (a fop) has introduced Harcourt (a wit) to his betrothed, Alithea. He refuses to believe Alithea that Harcourt has been making love to her and only takes offence when she reveals Harcourt has called him an idiot and disparaged his wit.

ALITHEA: Mr Sparkish, do you bring people to rail at you?

HARCOURT: Madam…

SPARKISH: How! No, but if he does rail at me, 'tis but in jest, I warrant – what we wits do for one another and never take any notice of it.

ALITHEA: He spoke so scurrilously of you, I had no patience to hear him; besides, he has been making love to me.

HARCOURT: (*Aside.*) True, damned, telltale woman.

SPARKISH: Pshaw! to show his parts – we wits rail and make love often but to show our parts; as we have no affections, so we have no malice; we...

ALITHEA: He said you were a wretch, below an injury.

SPARKISH: Pshaw!

HARCOURT: (*Aside.*) Damned, senseless, impudent, virtuous jade! Well, since she won't let me have her, she'll do as good, she'll make me hate her.

ALITHEA: A common bubble.   (1)

SPARKISH: Pshaw!

ALITHEA: A coward.

SPARKISH: Pshaw, pshaw!

ALITHEA: A senseless, drivelling idiot.

SPARKISH: How! Did he disparage my parts? Nay, then my honour's concerned; I can't put up that, sir, by the world. Brother, help me to kill him. (*Aside.*) I may draw now, since we have the odds of him! 'Tis a good occasion, too, before my mistress...

1. *bubble* – fool (easily deflated, like a bubble)   (36)

The following text has been taken from Act IV Scene ii of George Etherege's *The Man of Mode*, edited by Scott McMillin (reproduced by permission of A&C Black). Here, Medley, Young Bellair and Sir Fopling visit Dorimant (interrupting his assignation with Belinda). They have been out drinking and Sir Fopling is nonplussed to find there isn't a mirror to see himself dancing, revealing his obsession with appearance.

SIR FOPLING: Prithee, Dorimant, why hast not thou a glass hung up here? A room is the dullest thing without one.

YOUNG BELLAIR: Here is company to entertain you.

SIR FOPLING: But I mean in case of being alone. In a glass a
                 man may entertain himself –

DORIMANT: The shadow of himself, indeed.

SIR FOPLING: – Correct the errors of his motions and his
                 dress.

MEDLEY: I find, Sir Fopling, in your solitude you
                 remember the saying of the wise man, and
                 study yourself.

SIR FOPLING: 'Tis the best diversion in our retirements.
                 Dorimant, thou art a pretty fellow and wear'st
                 thy clothes well, but I never saw thee have
                 a handsome cravat. Were they made up like
                 mine, they'd give another air to thy face.
                 Prithee, let me send my man to dress thee but
                 one day. By heav'ns, an Englishman cannot tie
                 a ribbon!   (37)

The following text has been taken from Act III Scene i of William
Congreve's *The Way of the World*, edited by Brian Gibbons (reproduced with permission of A&C Black). Here, the fops Witwoud
and Petulant explain their supposed animosity towards each other.

WITWOUD: We hit off a little wit now and then, but no
                 animosity; the falling out of wits is like the falling
                 out of lovers – we agree in the main like treble
                 and bass. Ha, Petulant?

PETULANT: Ay, in the main, but when I have a humour to
                 contradict.

WITWOUD: Ay, when he has a humour to contradict, then I
                 contradict too. What, I know my cue. Then we
                 contradict one another like two battledores (1): for
                 contradictions beget one another.

PETULANT: If he says black's black – if I have a humour to say
            'tis blue – let that pass; all's one for that. If I have
            a humour to prove it, it must be granted.

WITWOUD: Not positively must – but it may – it may.

PETULANT: Yes it positive'y must, upon proof positive.

WITWOUD: Ay, upon proof positive it must; but upon proof
            presumptive it only may. That's a logical distinc-
            tion now, madam.

MRS MARWOOD: I perceive your debates are of importance and
            very learnedly handled.

1. *battledores* – players striking a shuttlecock to and from each other, as
in badminton   (38)

Aphra Behn's *The Lucky Chance* offers up a longer and more detailed focus on the differences between fops and wits.

Text Sample 2: Flaunting the Fop

The following text has been taken from Act IV Scene i of Aphra Behn's *The Lucky Chance*, edited by Jane Spencer (reproduced by permission of Oxford University Press). It was first performed in 1686 at Drury Lane.

The story so far:
The merchants, Sir Feeble Fainwould and Sir Cautious Fulbank have bought themselves young brides, Leticia and Julia. Sir Feeble tricked Leticia into believing that Belmour, the man she truly loves, is dead. Julia's marriage to Sir Cautious was more of a conscious decision on her part, despite her feelings for Gayman. Belmour and Gayman plot to manipulate Leticia and Julia away from their foolish old husbands.

Meanwhile, it seems as if Diana, Sir Feeble's daughter, is to become the next victim, having been promised in marriage to Mr Bearjest (the foppish nephew of Sir Cautious). Bearjest is not only obsessed with status, money and appearance but also looks down on those who have not travelled the world. In an earlier scene he reveals Ireland as the extent of his travels ('Why, that's the end of the world; and sure a man can no further.' (39)).

Of course, Diana isn't interested in Bearjest at all: her affections lie with Bredwell, Leticia's brother. In this scene, Bearjest foolishly allows Bredwell to woo Diana on his behalf, not realising that he is actually listening to Bredwell's and Diana's true feelings for each other.

BEARJEST: Look, Ned, you had a mind to have a full view of my mistress, sir, and here she is.

(*BREDWELL stands gazing at DIANA.*)

Go, salute her. (*Aside.*) Look how he stands now: what a sneaking thing is a fellow who has never travelled and seen the world! (*To DIANA.*) Madam, this is a very honest friend of mine, for all he looks so simply. (1)

DIANA: (*To BREDWELL.*) Come, he speaks for you, sir.

BEARJEST: He, madam! Though he be but a banker's 'prentice, madam, he's as pretty a fellow of his inches as any i'th' city (2). He has made love in dancing schools and to ladies of quality in the middle gallery, (3) and shall joke ye, and repartee with any foreman within the walls (4). (*To BREDWELL.*) Prithee to her, and commend me; I'll give thee a new point cravat (5).

DIANA: He looks as if he could not speak to me.

BEARJEST: Not speak to you? Yes, Gad, madam, and do anything to you too.

DIANA:	(*To BEARJEST, in scorn.*) Are you his advocate, sir?
BEARJEST:	For want of a better.
	(*BEARJEST stands behind BREDWELL, pushing him on.*)
BREDWELL:	An advocate for love I am, And bring you such a message from a heart –
BEARJEST:	Meaning mine, dear madam.
BREDWELL:	– That when you hear it, you will pity it.
BEARJEST:	(*Aside.*) Or the devil's in her.
DIANA:	Sir, I have many reasons to believe It is my fortune you pursue, not person.
BEARJEST:	(*Behind him.*) There's something in that, I must confess. But say what you will, Ned.
BREDWELL:	May all the mischiefs of despairing love Fall on me if it be.
BEARJEST:	That's well enough.
BREDWELL:	No: were you born an humble village maid That fed a flock upon the neighbouring plain, With all that shining virtue in your soul, By heaven, I would adore you, love you, wed you, Though the gay world were lost by such a nuptial.
	(*BEARJEST looks on him.*)
	(*Recollecting.*) This – I would do, were I my friend the squire.
BEARJEST:	(*Aside.*) Aye, if you were me, you might do what you pleased; but I'm of another mind.
DIANA:	Should I consent, my father is a man whom interest sways, not honour, and whatsoever promises he's made you, he means to break 'em all, and I am destined to another.

BEARJEST:	How, another? His name, his name, madam. Here's Ned and I fear ne'er a single man i'th' nation. What is he? What is he?
DIANA:	A fop, a fool, a beaten ass; a blockhead.
BEARJEST:	What a damned shame's this, that women should be sacrificed to fools, and fops must run away with heiresses; whilst we men of wit and parts dress and dance, and cock and travel, for nothing but to be tame keepers.
DIANA:	But I, by heaven, will never be that victim: But where my soul is vowed, 'tis fixed for ever.
BREDWELL:	Are you resolved, are you confirmed in this? Oh, my Diana, speak it o'er again:
	(*BREDWELL runs to DIANA and embraces her.*)
BEARJEST:	Hold, hold, dear Ned: that's my part, I take it.
BREDWELL:	Your pardon, sir, I had forgot myself.

1. *looks so simply* – looks so foolishly.
2. *as pretty…inches* – 'tall of his inches' meant a tall fellow, while 'pretty' (sometimes used of a man at this period) implied both attractive and small: hence a joke about Bredwell's height, perhaps exploiting a height difference between the original Bredwell, John Boman, and Bearjest, played by the thin and probably tall, Thomas Jevon.
3. *ladies…gallery* – a joke, as prostitutes were known to sit in the middle gallery at the theatre.
4. *any foreman within the walls* – the foreman of any jury in the city.
5. *point cravat* – a cravat made from needle-point lace.

The Lucky Chance by Aphra Behn, edited by Jane Spencer (including notes) and published by Oxford University Press. (40)

Workshop Plan: Flaunting the Fop

OBJECTIVES

- To experiment with vocal flaunt, relish and affectation with foppish characters in Restoration texts.

- To maintain vocal truth and believability whilst working with vocal flaunt, relish and affectation.

MATERIALS

You will need:
- Separate copies of Sample Text 1 (*The Country Wife, The Man of Mode* and *The Way of the World* excerpts) for each member of the workshop group (include the footnotes)
- Separate copies of Sample Text 2 (*The Lucky Chance* excerpt) for each member of the workshop group (include the footnotes)
- Flip-chart, white board or large sheets of paper for brainstorming ideas
- Rehearsal clothing and rehearsal props as described in Chapter 19 (optional).

Although the fops in these texts are male, for the purposes of experimentation within a workshop context, they are appropriate for work with a mixed gender group of actors.

ACTOR PREPARATION

Ask your actors to come prepared for this workshop with a joke they like telling or enjoyed hearing. It must have a punchline. They should practise it aloud prior to the workshop, focusing on timing, delivery and pointing of the humour.

WARM UP

Structure a warm up from the information listed in Chapter 1. Breathing and resonance exercises are important, however, exercises for articulation and stretching the pitch range should be given extra emphasis.

ACTIVITIES AND EXERCISES

- Ask your actors to start in a physically neutral position ie grounded, centred and aligned (see Chapter 1 for details). Then get them to experiment with posture and stance for Restoration men (see Chapter 19 for details) but ask them to take it to the extreme. They should imagine they're a still photo snapshot of a Restoration man who loves his appearance. Make sure they're still breathing within the physical restrictions they've created. If necessary add in some breathing exercises at this point.

- Within this physicality they should practice verbalising the joke they've already rehearsed at home. They need to focus on relishing the telling – enjoying, admiring and flaunting the sound of their own voice in the space (using the individual sounds). Get them to share this work with the rest of the group: vocal flaunting usually requires an audience.

- Now ask them to tell it again but adjust it so that it's no longer funny (perhaps they could change a word or mix up the words in the punchline so they no longer make sense). It's important that they don't apologise for doing this, maintaining the idea that it's still funny. Again, get them to share their work with the rest of the group.

- Repeat the fashion parade exercise from Chapter 19 on. Divide the group in two rows, facing each other. Leave enough space for a fashion parade runway down the middle of these two rows. Now ask your actors, one by one, to spend time showing off their clothes and physicality down the catwalk. This time, however, they should flaunt and relish their physical appearance and clothing more than they did previously. If they're not working in rehearsal clothing they can show off their contemporary clothing in a flamboyant way, or, show off imaginary Restoration clothing. Make sure they breathe as they move.

- Once everybody has had a go, repeat the exercise but, this time, call out foppish names from Restoration comedies (eg Sparkish, Sir Fopling Flutter, Witwoud, Petulant, Sir Feeble Fainwould, Sir Cautious Fulbank or Bearjest) as they move along the catwalk. Each actor will need to adjust their foppish physicality and movement to meet the name of the character allocated to them.

- Now ask them to repeat the exercise again and re-tell their joke as they move through the space embodying aspects of their allocated name. Their voice should now adjust to meet this physical foppishness.

- Hand out copies of the Sample Text 1 excerpts (from *The Country Wife*, *The Man of Mode* and *The Way of the World*). You might also like to provide them with the text excerpts provided earlier in this chapter, where the fops from these plays are discussed by the wits. Ask them to read through all the texts in their heads so they're clear about the sense. They might also like to try them aloud in small groups for further clarification.

- Start a discussion, based on the information provided about the fops in both sets of texts. It's a good idea to have a flip-chart or white board or large pieces of paper that you can pin up around the room later in order to list some of the ideas that come out of the discussion. Here are some starting points:

  — How would you describe a fop (in comparison to a wit)?

  — What drives his behaviour (what might he want)?

  — Describe some vocal affectations that a fop might use (eg a particular way of pronouncing a sound, a word or a set of words).

  — Is there any justification for these affectations within the texts?

- Now ask your actors to choose some isolated lines of a fop from one of the excerpts. They should return to their foppish physicality and try these lines aloud, flaunting and relishing the sound as they did with their joke. However, because of the discussion, they will be clearer about *why* their character speaks in this way.

- Ask them to try it again but experiment with adding in one or two of the vocal affectations that were brainstormed in the discussion. This may require a little rehearsal time so that it remains rooted in the character (applying vocal affectation without a reason will only create a superficial caricature). Allow them time to try out their work on the rest of the group. Fops always need an audience.

- Hand out copies of the Sample Text 2 excerpt from Aphra Behn's *The Lucky Chance* and ask them to read it through in their heads so they're clear about the sense. Now ask them to try it aloud in groups of three a few times so their mouths are familiar with the movements they need to make.

- Open up a short discussion so they can share their initial thoughts on what's happening in the text. Provide some background information about the plot and characters, if necessary, at this point. Make sure you focus on 'what the characters want' and 'how they try to achieve it' at some point in the discussion.

- Now ask them to apply what they've learnt about Restoration text so far in their delivery (ie the actors playing Bearjest can use some of their experiences from this workshop, whilst the actors playing Diana and Bredwell can draw from experiences in previous workshops). They should try it a number of times through so that the vocal and physical delivery is on its way to becoming effortless. Performing the text to each other will help them clarify this work further.

- Allow some time for a group de-briefing session. Use the following questions as a starting point for the discussion:
  - How would you describe the technical requirements of vocal flaunting?
  - What practical knowledge will you take away from this workshop (ie what did you learn)?

NOTES

1. J L Styan, *Restoration Comedy in Performance* (Cambridge University Press, 1998); p. 5

2. Aphra Behn, *Sir Patient Fancy* Epilogue

3. Simon Callow, *Acting in Restoration Comedy* (Applause, 1991); p. 9, and, Thomas Brown, *Amusements Serious and Comical* (Kessinger Publishing, 2004); p. 10

4. Thomas Brown, *Amusements Serious and Comical* (Kessinger Publishing, 2004); p. 20

5. John Dennis, *The Usefulness of the Stage*; (first published in 1698). Currently published in *Restoration and Eighteenth-Century Comedy*, edited by Scott McMillin (A Norton Critical Edition, 1997); p. 509-510

6. John Dryden, *Essay of Dramatic Poesy* (first published in 1668, and revised in 1684). Currently published in *John Dryden The Major Works* (Oxford University Press, 2003); p. 105

7. J L Styan, *Restoration Comedy in Performance* (Cambridge University Press, 1998); p. 201

8. William Wycherley, *The Country Wife* (New Mermaids 1989); Act II, Scene i. Reproduced by permission of A&C Black

9. William Congreve, *The Way of the World* (New Mermaids, 1979); Act II. Reproduced by permission of A&C Black

10. George Etherege, *The Man of Mode* (Norton Critical Editions, 1997); Act IV, Scene i. Reproduced by permission of A&C Black

11. William Wycherley, *The Country Wife* (New Mermaids 1989); Act I, Scene i. Reproduced by permission of A&C Black

12. *Ibid.* Act III, Scene ii

13. Coley Cibber, *An Apology For His Life* (Kessinger Publishing, 2007); p. 62

14. *Ibid.* p. 70

15. *Ibid.* p. 71

16. *Ibid.* p. 71

17. George Etherege, *The Man of Mode* (Norton Critical Editions, 1997); Act III, Scene iii. Reproduced by permission of A&C Black

18. *Ibid.* Act IV, Scene i

19. William Congreve, *The Way of the World* (New Mermaids, 1979); Act II, Scene i. Reproduced by permission of A&C Black

20. *Ibid.*

21. *Ibid.*

22. *Ibid.*

23. William Wycherley, *The Country Wife* (New Mermaids 1989); Act IV, Scene iii. Reproduced by permission of A&C Black

24. *Ibid.*

25. George Etherege, *The Man of Mode* (Norton Critical Editions, 1997); Act II, Scene i. Reproduced by permission of A&C Black

26. Lyn Oxenford, *Playing Period Plays* (J. Garnet Miller, 1984); p.185

27. George Etherege, *The Man of Mode* (Norton Critical Editions, 1997); Act III, Scene i

28. Thomas Brown, *Amusements Serious and Comical* (Kessinger Publishing, 2004); p. 22

29. William Wycherley, *The Country Wife* (New Mermaids 1989); Act I, Scene i. Reproduced by permission of A&C Black

30. William Congreve, *The Way of the World* (New Mermaids, 1979); Act III, Scene i. Reproduced by permission of A&C Black

31. Pat Gill, *Gender, Sexuality and Marriage* in *The Cambridge Companion to English Restoration Theatre*, edited by Deborah Payne Fisk (Cambridge University Press, 2007); p. 202

32. William Wycherley, *The Country Wife* (New Mermaids 1989); Act III, Scene ii. Reproduced by permission of A&C Black

33. *Ibid.* Act I Scene i

34. George Etherege, *The Man of Mode* (Norton Critical Editions, 1997); Act I, Scene i. Reproduced by permission of A&C Black

35. William Congreve, *The Way of the World* (New Mermaids, 1979); Act I, Scene i. Reproduced by permission of A&C Black

36. William Wycherley, *The Country Wife* (New Mermaids 1989); Act II Scene i. Reproduced by permission of A&C Black

37. George Etherege, *The Man of Mode* (Norton Critical Editions, 1997); Act IV Scene ii. Reproduced by permission of A&C Black

38. William Congreve, *The Way of the World* (New Mermaids, 1979); Act III Scene i. Reproduced by permission of A&C Black

39. Aphra Behn, *The Lucky Chance* (Oxford University Press, 1995); Act I, Scene iii

40. *Ibid.* Act IV, Scene i

BIBLIOGRAPHY

General

Simon Callow, *Acting in Restoration Comedy* (Applause, 1991)

John Harrop, & Sabin Epstein, *Acting with Style* (Prentice Hall, 1990)

Fidelis Morgan, *The Female Wits: Women Playwrights of the Restoration* (Virago, 1989)

Scott McMillan (ed.), *Restoration and Eighteenth-Century Comedy* (Norton Critical Edition, 1997)

Lyn Oxenford, *Playing Period Plays* (J. Garnet Miller, 1984)

Deborah Payne Fisk (ed.), *The Cambridge Companion to English Restoration Theatre* (Cambridge University Press, 2007)

Suzanne Ramczyk, *Delicious Dissembling: A Compleat Guide to Performing Restoration Comedy* (Heinemann, 2002)

J L Styan, *Restoration Comedy in Performance* (Cambridge University Press, 1998)

Plays, Prose and Poetry

Aphra Behn (edited by Jane Spencer), *The Rover and Other Plays* (Oxford University Press, 1995)

Thomas Brown, *Amusements Serious and Comical* (Kessinger Publishing, 2004)

Coley Cibber, *An Apology For His Life* (Kessinger Publishing, 2007)

William Congreve (edited by Brian Gibbons), *The Way of the World* (New Mermaids, 1979)

John Dryden, *The Major Works* (Oxford University Press, 2003)

George Etherege (edited by Scott McMillan), *The Man of Mode* (Norton Critical Editions, 1997)

William Wycherley (edited by John Dixon Hunt), *The Country Wife* (New Mermaids, 1989)